T0366117

Application of Quantitative Techniques for the Prediction of Bank Acquisition Targets

Series on Computers and Operations Research

Series Editor: P. M. Pardalos *(University of Florida)*

Series on Computers and Operations Research | Vol. 5

Application of Quantitative Techniques for the Prediction of Bank Acquisition Targets

Fotios Pasiouras
Coventry University, UK & Technical University of Crete, Greece

Sailesh Tanna
Coventry University, UK

Constantin Zopounidis
Technical University of Crete, Greece

World Scientific

NEW JERSEY · LONDON · SINGAPORE · BEIJING · SHANGHAI · HONG KONG · TAIPEI · CHENNAI

Published by

World Scientific Publishing Co. Pte. Ltd.

5 Toh Tuck Link, Singapore 596224

USA office: 27 Warren Street, Suite 401-402, Hackensack, NJ 07601

UK office: 57 Shelton Street, Covent Garden, London WC2H 9HE

British Library Cataloguing-in-Publication Data
A catalogue record for this book is available from the British Library.

APPLICATION OF QUANTITATIVE TECHNIQUES FOR THE PREDICTION OF BANK ACQUISITION TARGETS
Series on Computers and Operations Research — Vol. 5

ISBN-13 978-981-256-518-1
ISBN-10 981-256-518-3

Printed in Singapore

Dedications

To my parents, Kleanthis and Katerina, and my sister Eleftheria
F. Pasiouras

To my wife Jayshree, and my children Nishil and Riya
S. Tanna

To my wife Kalia, and my children Dimitris and Helene
C. Zopounidis

Preface

This book is concerned with the application of quantitative classification methods for the prediction of acquisition targets. We use publicly available data for a sample of EU banks to develop and compare a range of prediction models that distinguish the acquired banks from the non-acquired. As is presumed in the corporate finance literature, a model's ability to predict acquisitions is of major value to investors who could then decide on holding the target's portfolio of stocks in the expectation of high returns. Indeed, the empirical evidence is quite strong that shareholders of acquired firms earn abnormal returns around the announcement date of acquisition. From a managerial perspective, prediction models could be useful (to managers of acquirers) in examining cases of acquired firms that are close to the typical profile of the target firm. In a similar manner, managers could also determine whether their own firm is a potential target, allowing them to take appropriate steps to avoid a hostile takeover attempt.

From a purely academic perspective, researchers have employed a number of classification methods to develop prediction models for identifying takeover targets. Our survey of the literature (in Chapter 2) reveals that, over the last thirty years, about 30 studies have examined the prediction of takeover targets using financial or non-financial data, but all of these have focused on samples of firms drawn from the non-financial sectors (i.e. manufacturing, retail, hospitality, etc.) and excluded banks from their analysis. The present book distinguishes itself in being concerned with the development of prediction models specifically for the banking industry, and we utilize and evaluate a variety of classification methods on a common sample of banks covering

15 European Union countries (the former EU15). One reason for the exclusion of banks in previous studies on acquisition targets is the unusual structure of banks' financial statements suggesting that certain bank specific characteristics distinguish them from non-financial firms, and so most of the variables we have considered for developing prediction models are unique to the banking industry. We focus on the EU banking industry for three reasons. First, the recent trends of banks' M&As have not only significantly transformed the European banking industry but also provided an opportunity for collecting a broad-based sample with an adequate number of acquired banks, thus making an appropriate empirical basis for our study. Second, most of the previous studies relating to M&As in banking have focused on the US and, consequently, similar studies on EU banks are limited in number, these being more recent and focused on examining other aspect of banks M&As, such as the operating performance of banks (Vander Vennet, 1996; Huizinga et al., 2001; Diaz et al., 2004), the impact of M&A announcement on the share prices of the merged banks (Tourani Rad and Van Beek, 1999; Cybo-Ottone and Murgia, 2000; Lepetit et al., 2004), and the takeover premium paid (Dunis and Klein, 2005). Finally, we also find that studies on the prediction of takeover targets have focused on individual countries, with the majority of them investigating the US and the UK. We have therefore sought to apply prediction techniques to the EU banking sector as a whole, given the emerging trends and the current academic interest on the subject. Indeed, our study fills a gap in the literature in attempting to develop prediction models for M&As in the banking sector, using a sample of banks for the EU countries.

The structure of this book has been designed to fulfill three main objectives. The first is to present an overview of the M&A trends in the EU banking industry and to survey the literature on the reasons and motives for M&As in banking, as well as the wider literature on the development of prediction models applied to M&As, with the intention of identifying the nature of underlying factors, financial as well as non-financial, influencing takeovers. Consequently, Chapter 1 begins with a discussion of recent M&As trends in the EU banking industry and goes on to review the evidence, referring to acquisition theories such as synergy, hubris and agency along with practitioners' views as outlined in the reports of the European Central Bank (2000) and the Group of Ten (2001). We also review recent studies that deal with other aspects of banks' M&As as noted above. This is followed in Chapter 2 by an extensive study-by-study review of the literature on acquisition targets prediction, where we group studies according to three classification approaches (statistical, econometric, and various others including recently developed non-parametric multi-criteria and machine learning methods). The broader remit of these two chapters is intended to inform the reader to the wider range of issues making up the two strands of the literature we cover, one dealing with M&As specifically in the banking sector and the other with the empirical evidence on the predictions of M&As at large, although both these chapters provide the essential theoretical and empirical background to our study.

The second purpose for this book is to provide a methodological review of the classification procedures extant in the literature with an eye on presenting a proper evaluative basis for our empirical approach. Thus, in Chapter 3 we discuss the appropriate framework for the development and evaluation of prediction models, dealing extensively with issues such as sampling, variables selection techniques, available quantitative techniques used for classification problems and measures of evaluating models' performance in this respect. Although this chapter focuses mainly on the prediction of acquisition targets, the issues discussed are also relevant to other classification problems in finance and accounting, such as bankruptcy prediction, credit risk assessment and auditing. Our empirical analysis begins with Chapter 4, providing an account of the data sources and issues relating to sample selection and the choice of variables for model development. Here we explain, for example, how we construct a base sample of commercial banks covering 15 EU countries, and select financial variables measuring capital strength, profit and cost efficiency, liquidity, growth, size and market power, with data obtained in both raw and country-adjusted form (i.e. raw variables adjusted relative to the industry average for the corresponding country). In order to allow a proper comparative evaluation of models, we select common subsets of the base sample and input variables with high discriminatory power, dividing the sample period (1998-2002) into training sub-samples for model development (1998-2000) and holdout samples for model evaluation (2001-2002).

While the methodology for prediction rests on identifying past cases of acquired firms and combining these with a sample of non-acquired firms, the predictive performance of the model depends on how accurately it classifies the proportions of the two groups of firms in a holdout sample (i.e. firms not used for model development). This leads to our third objective, dealt with in Chapters 5 and 6, which has been to conduct extensive empirical analysis involving a comparison of the prediction accuracies of various classification methods. In Chapter 5, seven different classification methods are employed (including two not previously applied to acquisition targets) to develop prediction models with raw and country-adjusted financial ratios, and these are evaluated on common holdout samples to provide a proper basis for comparison. Chapter 6 extends the analysis further to a comparison of two integrated methods of combining prediction models (i.e. multi-classifiers) in an attempt to investigate their predictive performance relative to the individual classification methods considered in Chapter 5. Integrated prediction models offer the advantage of counterbalancing relatively poor performance of some classification methods with good performance of others, but in doing so may not out-perform the individual classification methods. In general, our results tend to support the findings of most studies on non-financial firms, highlighting the difficulties in predicting acquisition targets, although the prediction models we develop show classification accuracies generally higher than chance assignment based on prior probabilities.

Although we limit our empirical study to commercial bank acquisitions in the EU, an important feature of the book is the methodological contribution we provide for a comparative evaluation of seven different classification methods, almost double in number compared to most previous studies.[1] Consequently, we believe that this book will serve as a basic reference for researchers and graduate students

---

[1] Of the 30 studies we review in Chapter 2, there are only eight that offer a comparison of various methods, of which four compare just two methods while the remaining four compare either 3 or 4 methods.

in the field of M&As and corporate takeovers, and indeed it could serve as a useful textbook for a specialist graduate course dealing with the application of classification methods in decision sciences. Furthermore, in the concluding chapter, while summarizing our main findings and suggesting possible extensions for further research, we seek to explain why prediction results differ with the use of different algorithms in solving classification problems.

F. Pasiouras
S. Tanna
C. Zopounidis

Contents

Chapter 1

Bank M&As: Motives and Evidence

1.1 Overview

Over the last two decades, a number of significant changes occurred in the banking industry, such as deregulation, globalisation, financial innovations, improvements in communication and computing technology, increased competition from within the sector and from non-bank financial intermediaries, to name a few. In response to these changes, banks have attempted to adopt strategies to improve efficiency, increase output and expand the range of services offered (Goddard *et al.*, 2001). The trend towards M&As can be interpreted as the outcome of moves to achieve these goals (Berger *et al.*, 1999; Beitel and Schiereck, 2001).

M&As of financial institutions as a trend began in the United States in the 1980s and quickly increased worldwide in the 1990s, becoming a global phenomenon. Data provided by Amel *et al.* (2004) indicate that most of the M&A activity in the financial sector between 1990 and 2001 involved banking firms, accounting for nearly 53% of all mergers in the financial sector (with 8,144 bank acquisitions among a total of 15,502 financial mergers), representing a value of $1,835 billion, approximately 68% of the total value of financial M&As[1] ($2,693.9 billion). Thus, it is not surprising, as Sobek (2000) claims that during the second half of the

---

[1] The data were obtained from Thomson Financial and SDC Platinum and refer to majority interests.

1990s the most frequent words used in reports on banking were "merger" and "acquisition".

The last decade has also shown an increase in the number and value of large M&A deals, including "megamergers" (i.e. M&As between institutions with assets over 1$ billion). As Rhoades (2000) points out, in the US far more banks with assets greater than 1$ billion were acquired in the 1990s than over the 1980s. The report of the Group of Ten (2001) also indicates that over the 1990s this trend was more evident towards the end of the decade. Of the 246 mega-deals that took place over the period 1990-1999, 197 (over 80%) occurred during the second half of this period (1995-1999). In Europe, a number of mega-deals occurred between 1999 and 2002 that resulted in the creation of five of the largest European banking groups (BNP Paribas in France, IntesaBsci in Italy, Banco Santander Central Hispano and Banco Bilbao Vizcaya Argentaria in Spain, and Natwest-Royal Bank of Scotland in the UK). Some M&As also reached the scale of "supermegamergers" (i.e. M&As between institutions with assets over $100 billion each). Based on market values, nine of the ten largest M&As in the US history took place in 1998 and four of these (Citicorp-Travelers, BankAmerica-NationsBank, Bank One – First Chicago and Norwest-Wells Fargo) occurred in banking (Moore and Siems, 1998).

Given the scale of such activity, numerous empirical studies have been conducted to address different aspects of bank M&As. In this chapter, we begin by outlining recent M&As trends in the EU banking industry and then review the theoretical and the empirical literature, as well as practitioners' views as outlined in the reports of the European Central Bank (2000) and the Group of Ten (2001). As explained earlier, this chapter has the broader aim of informing the reader to other aspects of work that relates to the EU banking sector, but we also seek to understand the nature of the underlying factors, whether internal or external to the industry, leading to M&As in banking.

1.2 M&As Trends in the European Union

Mergers and acquisitions within the European financial sector have significantly transformed the European banking market in the last decade. For example, the number of European banking institutions fell from 12,378 in 1990 to 8,395 in 1999 (European Central Bank - ECB, 2000) while 18 of the 30 largest European banks emerged as a result of recent M&As (Belaisch *et al.*, 2001). Over the period 1995 to the first half of 2000, ECB (2000) records 2,153 M&As of credit institutions in the EU. Data from Table 1.1 provide a clear picture of the types of these M&As.

Table 1.1 Number of Total bank M&As (domestic and international) in the EU

	1995	1996	1997	1998	1999	First half 2000	Total
Total bank M&As	326	343	319	434	497	234	2153
- of which domestic	275	293	270	383	414	172	1807
- of which within EEA	20	7	12	18	27	23	107
- of which with third country	31	43	37	33	56	39	239

Source: ECB (2000)

Out of the total of 2,153 M&As, 84% were between banks from the same country, 5% occurred within European Economic Area (EEA) and 11% with banks from a third country. Over the above period domestic M&As were far more common than cross-border ones. Nevertheless, cross-border M&As of acquiring European banks, and in particular of large ones, have increased significantly since 2000. Beitel and Schiereck (2001) report that the share of cross-border M&A transactions in 2000 reached 50% and approximately 70% in terms of number and volume respectively. Another interesting observation is that M&As with institutions located in third countries have outnumbered M&As within the EEA during all years, and more than doubled on an aggregate basis for the entire period. Most European banks have chosen to expand into Latin America (e.g. banks from Netherlands, Spain, Portugal and Italy), South-East Asia (e.g. banks from Netherlands) and Central and Eastern Europe (e.g. banks from Netherlands and Ireland) probably in search for markets offering higher margins or due to historical connections (ECB, 2000). Nevertheless, in some cases they have also expanded into developed markets such as the US (e.g. banks from Germany). Table 1.2 presents the geographical distribution of these M&As. It is interesting to note that around 80% of total M&As have involved credit institutions from Germany, Italy, France and Austria.

Table 1.2 Total number of M&As of credit institutions (domestic and cross-border) in the EU

	1995	1996	1997	1998	1999	1st half 2000	Average 1995-99
Austria	14	24	29	37	24	8	26
Belgium	6	9	9	7	11	3	8
Germany	122	134	118	202	269	101	169
Denmark	2	2	2	1	2	2	2
Spain	13	11	19	15	17	29	15
Finland	9	6	5	7	2	5	6
France	61	61	47	53	55	25	55
Greece	0	1	3	9	8	1	4
Ireland	3	4	3	3	2	0	3
Italy	73	59	45	55	66	30	60
Luxembourg	3	2	3	12	10	8	6
Netherlands	7	11	8	3	3	5	6
Portugal	6	6	2	5	2	9	4
Sweden	1	2	5	1	7	2	3
UK	6	11	21	24	19	6	16
Total	326	343	319	434	497	234	

Source: ECB (2000)

Focusing on domestic bank M&As, 1999 was a peak year with 414 deals, a 50.55% increase from the 275 deals that occurred in 1995. With respect to the size of M&As (distinguishing between small and large M&As - the latter implying that at least one of the involved institutions had assets above 1 billion euros) Figure 1.1 shows that domestic M&As have occurred mainly between smaller institutions. An obvious explanation is that the smaller institutions operating in the EU are by far much greater in number than the larger institutions. Nevertheless, since 1996, there has also been some increase in larger M&As. The number of large domestic M&As as a percentage of total domestic M&As reached 22.09% in the first half of 2000 compared to 9.56% in 1995.

Turning to the value of M&As (Tables 1.3, 1.4 and 1.5), two general conclusions can be drawn. First, more domestic M&As tended to be involved during the period 1995-1998, and this trend continued in France and Spain beyond 1998. Second, large differences occurred among EU countries, both at the level of banking assets involved in M&As and in the trends either upwards or downwards.

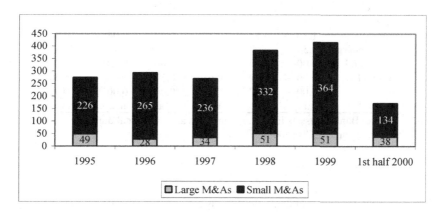

Figure 1.1 Breakdown of domestic M&As in the EU by size (Source: ECB, 2000)

For example, increases in the values have been observed in Austria, Belgium, Germany, France, Italy and Luxembourg with assets ranging from less than 5% of banking assets involved in Germany to more than 50% in France in 1999, while decreases in relation to values (and numbers) have occurred in Portugal and Sweden. Furthermore, according to data from the Securities Data Company (SDC Merger and Acquisition Database, produced by Thomson Financial Securities Services), the total value of European financial M&As increased from $22,769.6 million in 1990 to $147,025.6 in 1999. Over the same period, the average target value in Europe ($467.7 millions) was higher than in the US ($334 millions) and the main industrial countries (G10 countries plus Australia and Spain) on an aggregate basis ($383.2 millions).

Table 1.3 Value of domestic mergers of credit institutions[1]

	1995	1996	1997	1998	1999	1st half 2000
Austria	5.42	3.01	13.37	13.68	1.16	0.31
Belgium	8.49	14.71	12.48	20.09	0.12	0.00
Germany	0.34	0.78	0.39	4.57	2.40	4.00
Denmark	0.40	7.70	0.10	15.50	0.00	0.10
Spain	0.50	7.70	0.00	1.40	20.12	18.44
Finland	45.59	3.36	0.21	29.43	0.00	3.18
France	2.90	12.10	19.00	10.80	57.50	10.28
Greece	0.00	0.00	9.94	32.78	9.01	0.00
Ireland	n.a.	n.a.	n.a.	1.40	0.00	0.00
Italy	1.30	0.17	0.10	1.07	0.04	0.00
Luxembourg	1.54	0.00	2.59	12.22	7.40	4.45
Netherlands	0.00	0.00	n.a.	0.00	0.00	0.17
Portugal	0.00	0.00	0.00	0.10	0.00	5.40
Sweden	0.00	0.07	18.00	0.00	0.00	0.00
UK	n.a.	n.a.	n.a.	n.a.	n.a.	n.a.

[1]Value: Banking assets involved in mergers as a % of total domestic banking assets, Source: ECB (2000)

Table 1.4 Value of domestic majority acquisitions of credit institutions [1]

	1995	1996	1997	1998	1999	1st half 2000
Austria	n.a.	0	0	0.16	0.15	0
Belgium	0	0	0	0	0.11	0
Germany	0.07	0.01	0.07	0	0	0
Denmark	n.a.	n.a.	n.a.	n.a.	n.a.	n.a.
Spain	4.64	0.28	0	0.11	0	0
Finland	0	0	0	0	0	0
France	19.4	38	16.7	12	43.89	0.17
Greece	0	0	0	3.67	4.36	0
Ireland	n.a.	n.a.	n.a.	n.a.	n.a.	n.a.
Italy	4.57	1.08	3.42	9.54	14.35	2.27
Luxembourg	0	0	0	0	0	0
Netherlands	0	n.a.	n.a.	0	0	0
Portugal	11.5	5.9	0.3	0	0	0.01
Sweden	0	0	0	0	0	0
UK	n.a.	n.a.	n.a.	n.a.	n.a.	n.a.

[1]Value: Banking assets involved in mergers as a % of total domestic banking assets, Source: ECB (2000)

Table 1.5 Value of domestic full acquisitions of credit institutions [1]

	1995	1996	1997	1998	1999	1st half 2000
Austria	0	0	34.84	2.38	0	0.06
Belgium	0.39	1.03	2.81	0.18	0.23	0
Germany	0.77	0.46	0.09	0.01	0.02	1.5
Denmark	n.a.	n.a.	n.a.	n.a.	n.a.	n.a.
Spain	0	0.01	0	0.11	0.24	0
Finland	0.77	0	0.03	0	0	0
France	n.a.	n.a.	n.a.	n.a.	n.a.	n.a.
Greece	0	0	0.21	0.12	0.9	0
Ireland	0.13	0.2	n.a.	0.1	0.1	0
Italy	0.34	0.3	0.71	1.33	0.35	0.06
Luxembourg	0	0.21	0	1.82	0.05	0
Netherlands	n.a.	n.a.	n.a.	0	0.01	0.02
Portugal	13.3	1.9	0	0	0	5.29
Sweden	0.2	11.2	23	0.3	0.5	0
UK	n.a.	n.a.	n.a.	n.a.	n.a.	n.a.

[1]Value: Banking assets involved in acquisitions as a % of total domestic banking assets, Source: ECB (2000)

Table 1.6 Values of M&As in European countries 1990-1999[1]

Deal Type	Value ($ millions)	1990-1999
Within- Border	Total Value	414,421.9
	Average Value	520.6
Cross-Border	Total Value	89,893.4
	Average Value	343.1
Within- Industry	Total Value	408,651.1
	Average Value	562.1
Cross-Industry	Total Value	95,664.2
	Average Value	289.0
Banking	Total Value	326,079.9
	Average Value	630.7
Insurance	Total Value	126,565.8
	Average Value	629.7
Securities/other	Total Value	51,669.8
	Average Value	152.0

[1]Deals classified by country and sector of target firm
Source: Group of Ten (2001)

Table 1.6 shows that in Europe, over the 1990s the average target value in within-industry deals ($562.1 millions) was almost double than in cross-industry ones ($289.0 millions). Furthermore, during the same period both total and average value of domestic mergers was by far higher than those of cross-border deals.   Finally, with respect to the market segments, the average value of targets in banking ($630.7 millions) and insurance industry ($ 629.7 millions) was much higher than the average target value of security and other financial firms ($152.0 millions).

1.3 Reasons and Motives for Banks M&As

Often there is not one single reason but a number of reasons that lead management to the decision to merge with or acquire another firm. This section considers two issues. The first points to the main firm level motives and external factors for banks M&As. The second focuses on practitioner's views on reasons for banks M&As, as discussed in the reports of the European Central Bank (2000) and the Group of Ten (2001).

1.3.1 Firm level motives and external factors of M&As

In the neoclassical perspective, all firm decisions including acquisitions are made with the objective of maximizing the wealth of the shareholders of the firm. Nevertheless, agency conflicts between shareholders and managers could also lead to M&As that are motivated by managers' self interest. Such firm level motives could also be influenced by external factors (i.e regulations & laws, globalisation, technological progress, economic conditions, *etc.*), as shown in Figure 1.2. In line with Berkovitch and Narayanan (1993) and Ali-Yrkko (2002) among others, the analysis that follows here classifies the firm level motives into: synergy (or economic) motives, agency (or managerial) motives and hubris motives. With respect of the value maximization and non-value maximization distinction, the first set of motives that refers to synergy, are considered as value maximization, while the other two (i.e agency and hubris) are non-value maximization motives.

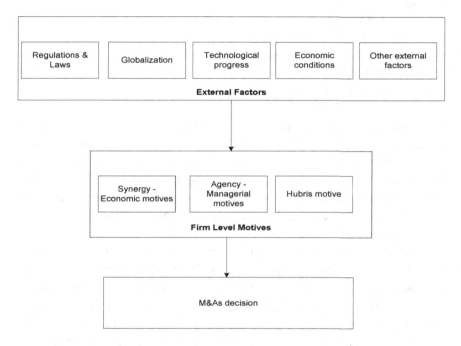

Figure 1.2   Motives and factors for M&As

1.3.1.1 Firm level motives

Synergy

Synergy, which is the name given to the concept that the combined entity will have a value greater than the sum of its parts, is one of the most often cited motives for M&As. The expected existence of synergistic benefits allows firms to incur the expenses of the acquisition process and still be able to afford to give target shareholders a premium for their shares. Synergy may allow the combined firm to appear to have a positive net present value:

$$NAV = V_{AB} - [V_A + V_B] - P - E = [V_{AB} - (V_A + V_B)] - (P+E)$$

Where,

V_{AB} = the combined value of the two firms

V_A = Firm's measure of its own value

V_B = the market value of the shares of firm B

P = premium paid for B

E = expenses of the acquisition process

The synergistic effect, which is the term in square brackets, must be greater than the sum of Expenses (E) and premium (P) to justify going forward with the acquisition or merger. Otherwise (i.e. the case where the bracketed term is not greater than the sum of P+E), the bidding firm will have overpaid for the target. Often synergy is expressed in the form 1+1 =3. The above equation for present value simply express the intuitive approach in slightly more scientific terms.

According to Lawrence (2001) synergy can arise from three primary sources: (i) operating economies, (ii) financial economies, and (iii) increased market power. Furthermore, some researchers view synergy more broadly and include the elimination of inefficient management by installing a more capable management in the acquired firm. As Gammelgaard (1999) points out, in the classical synergy approach, the acquiring firm improves the performance of the acquired firm by transferring resources and knowledge to the new subsidiary. Most common is the transfer of managerial resources. The main approach here is the differential efficiency theory where the purpose is to improve the management in the acquired firm by bringing it up to the same level as in the acquiring firm (Weston *et al.*, 1990).

Economies of Scale

This theory assumes that economies of scale do exist in the industry and that prior to the merger, the firms are operating at levels of activity lower than those required to achieve the potential for economies of scale. The merger of two firms is thus an opportunity to produce lower average costs by spreading fixed costs across a larger volume of output. Achieving economies of scale has been suggested to be the natural goal of horizontal mergers. Many different types of economies of scale exist, such as those associated with marketing, production, distribution, finance and management sharing. The banking industry is one of the most well known examples. In the 1970s, there were many small banks in the United States. Many of them have grown by systematically buying up smaller banks and streamlining their operations. Most of the cost savings have come from closing redundant branches, consolidating systems and back offices, processing checks and credit-card transactions and payments (Brealey *et al.*, 2001).

According to Dettmer (1963), the merger or acquisition leads naturally to the access of extra and sometimes unused production facilities, and the purpose of the investment is to reduce the overhead cost per unit. For example, many businesses possess assets such as buildings, machinery or people skills, which are not used to their full limits. In the case of banks, potential for scale economies arise because neither the buildings nor the services of employees in a branch are utilised as intensively as they could be. Thus, once a merger is completed, a number of branches are closed, leaving one or two in a particular location, with consequent savings made on property and labour costs.

Early research, especially in the United States, indicated that scale economies appeared mainly in small banks rather than in large ones (Short, 1979; Miller and Noulas, 1996). According to Clark (1988) and Hunter and Timme (1989), economies of scale appear to exist in banking institutions at assets levels below $5 billion, while Hunter and Wall (1989) state that costs of production in financial institutions appear to be relatively constant for asset sizes up to $25 billion. Most recent studies, both in the US (Berger and Mester, 1997) and in Europe (Molyneux et al, 1996, Vander Vennet, 2002) find unexploited scale economies even for fairly large bank sizes due to economic development and market liberalization. Vander Vennet (1998), however, found evidence of economies of scale only for the smallest banks with assets under ECU 10 billion in the EU, with constant returns thereafter and diseconomies of scale for the largest banks exceeding ECU 100 billions. A recent study by Pasiouras and Kosmidou (2005) has found a negative relation between size and bank's performance for both domestic and foreign banks operating in the EU over the period 1995 to 2001. The authors interpret this negative coefficient in their regressions as an indication of either economies of scale (and scope) for smaller banks or diseconomies for larger financial institutions. In general, research on the existence of scale economies in retail commercial banking finds a relatively flat U-shaped average cost curve, with a minimum somewhere below $10 billion of assets, depending on the sample, country and time period analysed (Amel *et al.*, 2004). Hughes *et al.* (2001) argue that most research finds no economies of scale because it ignores differences in banks' capital structure and risk taking and demonstrate that scale economies exist but are elusive. They show that estimated scale economies depend critically on the way banks' capital structure and risk-taking are modelled. More specifically when they include equity capital, in addition to debt, in the production model and cost is computed from the value-maximizing expansion path rather than the cost-minimizing path, banks are found to have large-scale economies that increase with size.

Economies of Scope

As pointed out by Amel *et al.* (2004), exploitation of economies of scope is probably the second most quoted reason for M&As in the financial sector. Economies of scope can be cost based or revenue based. Costs based are those achieved by offering a broad range of products or services to a customer base and can originate from fixed costs incurred in gathering an information database or computer equipment. Revenue based is related to the ability of the firm to utilise one set of inputs to offer a broader range of products and services through cross selling to an existing customer base.

A common example in financial institutions M&As is the case of sharing inputs and offering a wider range of services through units such as the department of economic research. Smaller banks might not be able to afford the cost of creating these departments, while inputs such as computers systems can be shared to process a wide variety of loans and deposit accounts. Another example often quoted is the case of banking and insurance products offered from the combined entity after the merger of a bank and an insurance firm.

Increased Market Power

Another reason for M&As is the increase of market power. Gaughan (1996) argues that there are three sources of market power: product differentiation, barriers to entry and market share. Banking markets in the EU can be characterized as a system of national oligopolies (Vander Vennet, 1996). Therefore there is a potential for increased market power, defined as the ability of the firm to set and maintain price above competitive levels, and associated market gains are likely to occur as a result of the combined power of two firms within the same industry. Nevertheless, Gaughan (1996) argues that an increase in market share without product differentiation or barriers to entry could prevent a firm from raising the price above marginal cost, as this may only attract new competitors who will drive price down towards marginal cost.

Many studies have attempted to test the view that the consolidation trend in the banking industry has been motivated by a desire to gain market power and extract monopolistic profits. Vander Vennet (1994a,b) has shown for a large sample of EC credit institutions that when barriers to entry exist, the incumbent banks may be able to exploit the possibility of quasi-monopoly profits. Moore (1996) argues that bank's market share could influence the probability of being acquired through several channels. First of all, in a banking market where only banks with substantial market share can compete effectively, a bank with small share is likely to be acquired, by an in-market bank, since the assets of the small bank would become more valuable after the merger with the large bank. A problem that arises in this context, particularly applicable to horizontal mergers, is the legislative obstacle caused by the regulators concerned about the potential anticompetitive practices of the combined firms. This has the effect of reducing the probability of an in-market merger between two or more banks with a significant market share. Another reason for M&A is associated with the inefficient management hypothesis, which argues that the bank's small share could reflect a lack of success in the market, giving the potential acquirer the incentive to take over the firm in order to improve its market share and efficiency. Gilbert (1984), in a review of 45 studies employing the Structure-Conduct-Performance paradigm (SCP), according to which banks in highly concentrated markets tend to collude and therefore earn monopoly profits, found that only 27 provided evidence in support of this hypothesis, while Berger (1995) points out that the relationship between bank concentration and performance in the US depends critically on what other factors are held constant.

The Market for Bank Control - Inefficient Management Replacement

Academics have discussed the inefficient management hypothesis for many years. The inefficient management hypothesis, due to Manne (1965), argues that if the managers of a firm fail to maximize its market value, then the firm is likely to be an acquisition target and inefficient managers will be replaced. Thus, takeover targets are motivated by a belief that the acquiring firm's management can manage better the target's resources. This view is supported by two specific arguments. First, the firm might be poorly run by its current management, partly because their own objectives are at variance from those of the shareholders. In this case, the takeover threat can serve as a control mechanism limiting the degree of variance between management's pursuits for growth from shareholders desire for wealth maximization. A merger may not be the only way to improve management, but if disappointed shareholders cannot accomplish a change in management that will increase the value of their investment within the firm, either because it is too costly or too slow, then a merger may be the more simpler and practical way of achieving their desired goals. Second, the acquirer may simply have better management experience than the target. There are always firms with unexploited opportunities to cut costs and increase sales and earnings, and that makes them natural candidates for acquisition by other firms with better management (Arnold, 1998). Therefore, if the management of the acquirer is more efficient than the management of the target bank, a gain could result with a merger if the management of the target is replaced.

Grossman and Hart (1980) have challenged the view that companies not run in shareholder's interests will be taken over. The reason is that in every bid there are two groups of shareholders involved, those of the acquired and of the acquirer, with often conflicting, economic objectives. The acquirer will make an effort to offer a price that will allow realising a profit on the deal to compensate itself for the cost of making the bid, and the shareholders of the target have to be willing to sell their shares to the bidding company at that price. However, each individual shareholder, facing the option to keep or sell the shares and under the belief that the new management will succeed to improve the firm's performance, will probably hold on the shares in expectation of a rise in the price in the future. Thus, shareholders will be willing to sell their shares only if they will be offered a price that will reflect these future gains, which should therefore be higher than the one that could compensate the acquirer for the real resource cost involved in undertaking the bid. Consequently, the incentive small shareholders have to freeride, prevents the bid from occurring in the first place, and hence the market for corporate control cannot operate effectively.

The results from the existing empirical work are somewhat mixed. While some authors (e.g. Singh, 1971, 1975; Meeks, 1977; Levine and Aaronovitch, 1981; Cosh *et al.*, 1984) indeed suggest that acquired companies are more likely to be less profitable, others (e.g. Dodd and Ruback, 1977; Hannan & Rhoades, 1987) are not supportive of the inefficient management hypothesis.

Risk Diversification

Another primary reason often advanced for M&As is risk diversification. The main argument is that the integration of two firms can lower bank risk and reduce the probability of bank failure, if the firms' cash flow streams are not perfectly correlated. The two most common forms of diversification are geographic and product diversification. The former offers a reduction of risk, because the return on loans and other financial instruments issued in different locations may have relatively low or negative correlation. In a similar manner, the latter may reduce risk because the returns across different financial services industries may have relatively low or negative correlation. For example, Berger *et al.* (2000) found that correlations of bank earnings across international borders are often very low or negative, thereby supporting the possibility of diversification benefits from cross-border consolidation of banking organizations. In addition, Neely and Wheelock (1997) found that US banks' earnings are strongly influenced by economic growth of the states where they are located.

The assumption behind diversification as a motive for M&As is that firm-based diversification is more efficient than diversification purchased on the market, such as credit derivatives and loan sales (Froot and Stein, 1998). However, Winton (1999) argues that diversification may not always reduce the risk of bank failure, pointing to the benefits and costs of monitoring loans and the possibility that diversification may lead banks into new sectors in which they might have less expertise. Craig and Santos (1997) confirm the reduction of risk (as measured by the z-score statistic of default probability and by stock return volatility) and relate it to benefits from diversification. Benston *et al.* (1995) argue on the basis of pre-merger earnings volatility and target-acquirer correlation that the motivation for mergers in the first half of the 1980s must have been risk reduction through diversification, rather than the exploitation of the put option on deposit insurance funds. Akhavein *et al.* (1997) and Demsetz and Strahan (1997) find that bank mergers serve to diversify banks, allowing them to take on more investment risk for a given level of firm risk. Finally, Laderman (2000) examined the potential diversification and failure reduction benefits of bank expansion into non-banking activities, based on a sample of Bank Holding Companies (BHCs) and especially of large BHCs during the periods 1979-1986 and 1987-97. Her results showed significant (negative) effects of investment levels on the standard deviation of BHC return on assets (ROA), implying that appreciable levels of investment in life insurance underwriting, casualty insurance underwriting, and securities brokerage were optimal for reducing the probability of bankruptcy of the BHC.

Capital Strength

The importance of decisions relative to the amount of capital becomes obvious by the fact that financial regulators require commercial banks to sustain a minimum capital adequacy ratio. Although provisions and cumulative loan loss reserves provide early lines of defence against bad loans, bank's capital is the ultimate line of defence against the risk of bank's technical insolvency. This becomes apparent when considering that if the bank will face a serious asset quality problem then loan loss reserves will not be sufficient to allow all bad loans to be written off against the bank and consequently the excess will have to be written off against shareholders' equity.

Thus, since low capital to asset ratios may indicate financial weakness, an acquirer may strengthen the acquired bank's financial position. Wheelock and Wilson (2000) found that the less well capitalized a bank is, the greater the probability that it will be acquired, suggesting support for the acquisition of some banks just before they become insolvent. In addition, well-capitalized banks face lower risk of going bankrupt which increases their creditworthiness and consequently reduces the cost of funding. Therefore, in contrast to the above, banks with insufficient amounts of capital may acquire banks with relatively high capital to assets ratios. That could allow them to gain better access to financial markets and enjoy lower costs of raising capital, as the combined entity will be considered to be less risky and would probably be able to issue bonds offering a lower interest rate than before.

Agency Motives (Managerial Motives)

The agency theory extends the previous work by Manne (1965), who analysed the market for corporate control and viewed takeovers as a threat if a firm's management lacked performance either because of inefficiency or because of agency problems. Jensen and Meckling (1976) formulated the implications of agency problems, which typically arise when management owns only a small proportion of share capital. It is well known that the modern economy, is characterised by large corporations with widespread distribution of ownership that is separated from management, in which case there is a potential for managers to pursue their own objectives such as enhance their salary and prestige, diversify personal risk or secure their job through empire-building, rather than maximize profits, at the expense of shareholders. For example, although shareholders of acquired banks experience large increases in the value of their shares, top executives of acquired banks may often lose their autonomy and accept diminished job responsibilities or may even be forced to terminate their employment. Thus, during the bank merger negotiations, managers may be forced to choose between shareholders' best interest by accepting a value maximizing the takeover offer or their own best interest by maintaining their bank's independence (Hadlock *et al.*, 1999).

The wage explanation implicit in the above argument is considered to be one of the most important managerial motives for M&As. Managers may want to increase the size of their firm as in most cases their wage is a function of firm size (Mueller, 1969). Thus having responsibility for a larger firm means that the managers have to be paid a lot of remuneration. In addition, most large firms set compensation by looking at the compensation of peer group executives, and size is the main determinant of which firms are in a peer group. Murphy (1999) provides a review of the compensation literature and observes that many studies report a strong link between firm size and managerial rewards (see e.g Roberts, 1956; Ciscel and Carroll, 1980; Agarwal, 1981). Bliss and Rosen (2001) examined the relationship between bank mergers and CEO compensation during 1986-1995 and found that acquisitions significantly increased CEO compensation even after accounting for the typical announcement data stock price decline. They argue that, although the decline in existing wealth partially offsets some of the subsequent salary gains, the vast majority of mergers increase the overall wealth of CEO, often at the expense of shareholders. Nevertheless, Anderson *et al.* (2004) examined bank CEO compensation changes associated with mergers among large banks in the 1990s and found no evidence of empire-building motives on the part of banks CEOs who engage in mergers. They found that changes in CEO compensation after mergers are positively related to anticipated gains from mergers measured at that announcement date.

Ravenscraft and Scherer (1987) argue that being in charge of a larger business and receiving a higher salary also brings increased status and power, and mergers constitute a rapid way of increasing balance sheet totals that attracts media attention when rankings are published. In addition, managers may also attempt to reduce insolvency risk through M&As by diversifying banks' portfolio below the level that is in shareholders' interest in order to increase their job security.

Finally, managers may also engage in empire-building for job security reasons rather than compensation or prestige. It has been claimed by both financial analysts and researchers that, on average, acquisitions tend to occur between a large acquirer and a small target. Thus, the belief is that large banking organisations are less likely to be targets of hostile takeovers and hence it is less likely that the current management will be out of a job. Therefore firms may merge in order to become large themselves for the survival of the management team and not primarily for the benefit of the shareholders. An alternative hypothesis states that some mergers may have been motivated by managers' concerns, but by increasing the chances of becoming the target of friendly takeovers rather than hostile takeovers.

The numerous empirical event studies that found negative wealth effects for bidding banks' shareholders (e.g. Hawawini & Swary, 1990; Baradwaj *et al.*, 1992; Houston & Ryngaert, 1994; Madura & Wiant, 1994; Siems, 1996) potentially provide support to the above arguments, namely that many M&As are motivated by managers own motives rather maximisation of shareholders' value.

Hubris Motives

An interesting hypothesis, proposed by Roll (1986), suggests that managers commit errors of over-optimism in evaluating M&As opportunities due to excessive prediction or faith in their own abilities. Consequently they engage in M&As even when there is no synergy. More specifically, the pride of bidders' management allows them to believe that their own valuation of the target is correct, even if objective information shows that target's true economic value, as reflected in its market valuation, is lower. Because of this arrogance (hubris) acquirers end up overpaying target firms, virtually transferring all gains from the transaction to the target shareholders.

As Gaughan (1996) points out, Roll did not intend the hubris hypothesis to explain all takeovers, but rather to reveal that an important human element enters takeovers when individuals are interacting and negotiating the purchase of a company. Thus, although hypothetically management's acquisition of a target should be motivated purely by a desire to maximize shareholder wealth, this is not necessarily the case, and the extent to which such motives play a role will vary from one

M&A to another. Arnold (1998) suggests that hubris may also help explain why mergers tend to occur in greatest numbers when the economy and companies generally have had a few good years of growth arguing that during such periods managers are feeling rather pleased with themselves.

1.3.1.2 External factors

The Group of Ten report (2001) highlights three major external forces that are creating pressures for change in the financial services industry and may help explain the recent pace of M&As activity: deregulation; technological advances, and globalisation of the market place. In addition, shareholder pressures and the introduction of the euro are also stated as additional forces. Finally, macroeconomic conditions may have either direct or indirect effects on banks decisions to be involved in M&As. All these issues are considered in turn below.

Deregulation and Laws

Over the last twenty years or so, following changes in the legal and regulatory framework in which financial institutions operate, many barriers to consolidation have been relaxed. There are, however, five main ways through which governments can influence the restructuring process (Group of Ten, 2001). These are:

1. Through effects on market competition and entry conditions (e.g. placing limits on or prohibiting cross-border mergers or mergers between banks and other types of service providers in the interests of preserving competition).
2. Through approval / disapproval decisions for individual merger transactions.
3. Through limits on the range of permissible activities for service providers.
4. Through public ownership of institutions.
5. Through effects to minimise the social costs of failures.

The liberalisation of geographic restrictions on U.S. banking institutions beginning in the late 1970s has often been cited as one of the main reasons for the rapid consolidation of the U.S. banking industry. Berger *et al.* (1999) argue that the prior geographic restrictions on competition may have allowed some inefficient banks to survive, and the removal of these constraints allowed some previously prohibited M&As to occur, which may have forced inefficient banks to become more efficient by acquiring other institutions, by being acquired, or by improving management practices internally. In addition, removal of in-state branching restrictions also increased consolidation in the US, as Banks Holding Companies tended to merge their subsidiary banks into branching systems.

Europe has also been undergoing deregulation over the last 50 years. Dermine (2002) mentions that the actions taken by the European Commission and the Council of Ministers can be divided into five main periods: the removal of entry barriers into domestic markets (1957-1973), the harmonisation of banking regulations (1973-1983), the completion of the internal market (1987-1992), the creation of economic and monetary union leading to the single currency (1993-1999), and the financial services action plan (1999-2005). Tourani-Rad and Van Beek (1999) argue that the merger wave in the European banking industry observed in the late 1980s as well as the late 1990s appear to be largely related to the Second Banking Directive. Under this directive, issued in 1989 and implemented in 1992, all credit institutions authorised in an EU country were able to establish branches or supply cross-border financial services in other countries within the EU without further authorisation, provided the bank was already authorised to provide such services in the home state. In other words, the EU banking directive permitted competition in the European marketplace through home country authorisation of entry, although banks had to operate under host country conduct of rules. This universal banking model adopted by the EU permitted banks to undertake investment banking activities, while leaving it to national regulators to control financial conglomerates, the ownership structure of the banks and their relationship with the industry.

Regulators (both national and European) often prevent M&As if the rise in concentration is expected to result in excessive increases in market power. For example, the Competition Commission in Britain blocked Lloyds TSB's 18.2 GBP billion hostile bid for Abbey National in July 2001, because the new bank would have dominated the segment of current accounts, with a 27% market share, and would have increased to 77% the market share of the top four British banks. Also in 2001, the European Commission opened an investigation into the announcement of 7.9 billion euro merger between Skandinaviska Enskilda Banken (SEB) and Foreningsparbanken (Swedbank) which would have resulted in the largest bank in Sweden that would probably have attained a dominant position in the domestic retail-banking sector. The two banks finally called of their plans to merge, blaming the European Commission's insistence that they should make large-scale divestitures in the retail banking segment for the deal to be approved, which would have undermined the logic of the deal.

It should be noted that while regulatory authorities have served to protect the public's interest in preserving competition in the market place, the national governments have also provided financial assistance or otherwise state aid to troubled financial institutions in periods of financial crises. For instance, in the US, the Federal Deposit Insurance Corporation (FDIC) provided financial assistance to allow healthy banks to purchase over 1000 insolvent US banks between 1984 and 1991 (Berger *et al.*, 1999), while a new 1991 rule allows the FDIC to takeover a financial institution whose capital falls below 2% of its risk adjusted assets, without waiting for further depletion of its capital base (Zanakis and Walter, 1994).

Technological Developments

Technology, apart from deregulation, has been considered a catalyst for the recent wave of bank M&As. As Goddard *et al.* (2001) point out technological advances are currently having a dramatic impact on the structure, operations and economies of European banking markets. It is obvious that the same applies for banking markets around the world. Overall, banks are involved in introducing new technologies in the following four main areas: customer-facing technologies, business management technologies, core processing technologies, support and integration technologies (Goddard *et al.*, 2001).

Technological changes may affect the restructuring of financial services in three direct ways (Group of Ten, 2001). First, through increases in the feasible scale of production of certain products and services (e.g. credit cards and asset management). Second, through scaled advantages in the production of risk management such as derivative contracts and other off-balance sheet guarantees that may be more efficiently produced by larger institutions. Third, through economies of scale in the provision of services such as custody, cash management, bank office operations and research.

Goddard *et al.* (2001) review six studies that examined the impact of technological changes on bank costs in the US (Hunter and Timme, 1991; Humphrey, 1993), Japan (McKillop *et al.*, 1996), Spain (Maudos *et al.*, 1996), Germany (Lang and Welzel, 1996) and the EU in total (Altunbas *et al.*, 1999). Three conclusions are drawn from these studies: (1) Reductions in costs up to 3.6% were found; (2) The impact of technological change on costs seems to have accelerated during the 1990s; (3) Larger banks benefit more than smaller ones.

In general, technological developments, apart from deregulatory changes, have helped to alter the competitive conditions of the financial sector, at both the production and the distribution level, and have created greater incentives for new output efficiency (Group of Ten, 2001).

Globalisation

Globalisation has been characterised as a by-product of technology and deregulation. On the one hand, technological developments have decreased computing costs and telecommunications, while expanding capacity, thus making a global reach economically more feasible. On the other hand, deregulation has relaxed the restrictions in activities undertaken by foreign firms in both developed and developing countries around the world that has allowed entry into many markets (Group of Ten, 2001).

The globalisation process has also contributed to a shift from a bank-centred system to a market-based one (Group of Ten, 2001). Furthermore, the number of foreign banks has increased in every banking market leading to intensified competition and reduced profit margins in many European national banking sectors (Goddard *et al.*, 2001). It is obvious that in such a competitive environment only the most efficient institutions will be able to survive in the long term, and M&As are an inevitable consequence of this endeavour.

Shareholder Pressures

The increased importance attributed to the "shareholder value" concept, has led naturally to a focus on the return on assets and return on equity as benchmarks for performance, especially by large well-informed investors. Thus, in a sense, managers are under pressure to increase profits in an environment of intense competition, and this can only be accomplished through the creation of new sources of earnings, generation of fee income, reduction of cost-to-income ratios, optimal use of excess capital, or for some institutions, recapitalisation after a major crisis (Group of Ten, 2001). Obviously, these goals can be achieved through business gains, enhancement or more effective balance sheet management. Another way, perceived to be an easier strategy for many institutions, is through M&As.

Introduction of the Euro

The introduction of the euro is considered to have an impact on the competitive environment in which financial institutions operate and consequently on the consolidation activity especially in the European arena. The Group of Ten (2001) report emphasises a number of ways through which the introduction of euro can motivate M&As. In summary, these are: the integration of money market, the impact of the euro on the treasury activities of the corporate sector, the integration of the capital markets and the government bond markets. Opportunities for cost savings or revenue enhancement arising from these changes are therefore potential motives for bank consolidation.

Macroeconomic Conditions

Macroeconomic conditions are considered to be another factor that could directly influence the decision of firms to merge with or acquire other firms. For example, merger waves seem to coincide with economic booms (Mueller, 1989). By definition, during booms the economy enjoys a rapid growth rate and the stock market prices surge. Nelson (1959) reports that M&As are positively correlated with stock market prices. Furthermore, in some cases, macroeconomic changes lead to excess capacity and ultimately downsizing and exit (Ali-Yrkkö, 2002).

Macroeconomic conditions may also have an indirect effect on the decisions of banks to merge through their impact on banks' profitability. For example, the growth of GDP is expected to have a positive impact on banks' performance, according to the well-documented literature on the association between economic growth and financial sector performance (e.g. King and Levine, 1993; Levine, 1997, 1998; Rajan and Zingales, 1998). Inflation may also affect both the costs and revenues of any organisation including banks. Perry (1992) points out that the effect of inflation on bank performance depends on whether the inflation is anticipated or unanticipated. A number of studies (e.g. Molyneux and Thorton, 1992; Abreu and Mendes, 2001; Staikouras and Wood, 2003; Pasiouras and Kosmidou, 2005) have empirically examined the determinants of EU banks profitability and reported the existence of a significant relationship between profits and various macroeconomic factors, such as GDP, inflation, unemployment and interest rates.

1.3.2 Practitioners' views on reasons for banks M&As

At this point, apart from the reasons that have been proposed by academic scholars and researchers, using either theoretical formulations or empirical evidence, it is essential to mention the views of practitioners (i.e. bankers and financial industry professionals). We have referred at various places to the finding of two main reports, conducted by the European Central Bank (ECB) and the Group of Ten respectively, that among others have examined the issue of the causes of M&As in the financial sector. However, it makes sense to offer a more comprehensive picture of the opinions of banking professionals to appreciate the main factors involved in bank M&As.

The European Central Bank Report (2000)

In order to reveal the motives for M&As in the EU banking sector from an industry perspective, the ECB examined the views of bankers through a process of interviews and consultation of the views of bank supervisors. The report was prepared by the Banking Supervision Committee (BSC) and covered the period 1995 to 2000. The main reasons that were identified in the analysis of the rationale for M&As are presented in Table 1.7, and summarized below.

With respect to the domestic bank M&As, economies of scale was found to be the main rationale for small bank M&As, which sought to obtain critical mass to explore synergies arising from size and diversification. In addition, M&As were also intended to avoid takeovers. As for the large banks, M&As often reflected a repositioning of the institutions involved. The increase in size reflected a need to become big enough to compete in the domestic market. Larger banks aimed at increased market power and a larger capital base, with a greater focus on increasing revenue, in contrast to smaller banks, which sought to explore synergies and avoid the threat of takeover. With regard to international bank M&As, the need to be big enough for regional or global markets indicates that size is the main motive, although for international conglomerates economies of scale and scope are also important.

As for domestic conglomerates, economies of scope were also indicated as the main motive. These financial institutions aimed at achieving economies through cross-selling of different financial products to the larger customer base of the combined entity, utilizing new distribution channels to make more efficient use of the fixed costs associated with the banks' branches. Specifically, the amalgamation of banks and insurance firms occurred to achieve risk and income diversification and consequently to reduce sensitivity to economic cycles. With regard to international conglomeration, the two major reasons, as noted above, were economies of scope and size, aimed principally at increasing revenue through cross-selling and strong brands that is attractive to large international clients.

Table 1.7   Main motives and possible rationalisations for the four types of Bank M&As

	Within one country	In different countries
	Domestic bank M&As	International bank M&As
Between credit institutions	- Economies of scale linked to costs are the main motive - Cutting distribution networks and administrative functions (rationalisation), including information technology and risk management areas	- Size, i.e the need to be big enough in the market, is the main motive -Matching the size of clients and following clients - Possible rationalisation within administrative functions
Across different sectors	Domestic conglomeration - Economies of scope through cross selling is the motive - Risk and revenue diversification - Optimum usage of complementary distribution networks - Possible rationalisations within administrative functions may lead to economies of scale linked to costs	International conglomeration - Economies of scope through cross-selling together with size are the two main motives - Risk and revenue diversification - The M&A offers few rationalisations because institutions are in different countries and subject to different regulation and practices

Source: ECB (2000)

The Group of Ten Report (2001)

In a similar manner the Group of Ten conducted interviews with 45 selected financial sector participants and industry experts from the G10 countries[2]. The interviewees were asked for their opinions on the basis of a common interview guide, which listed a number of factors leading to M&A activity. Table 1.8 lists the factors that formed the basis for the interviews.

---

[2] The G10 comprises the following set of countries: Belgium, Canada, France, Germany, Italy, Japan, Netherlands, Sweden, Switzerland, United Kingdom, and United States. Note there are eleven countries in the G10. The "ten" refers to the members of the Group who constitute the members of the International Monetary Fund. Switzerland, which joined the Group in 1984, is the eleventh member. Also added in the report were surveys for Australia and Spain.

Table 1.8 The interview guide used in the Group of Ten (2001) report

List of Factors		
Motives for consolidation	Forces encouraging consolidation	Forces discouraging consolidation
Cost savings attributable to:	Technology:	Market inefficiencies
- Increased size (economies of scale)	- Information and communications	Legal and regulatory constraints
- Product diversification (economies of scope)	- Financial innovation	Cultural constraints (cross-firm and cross-segment)
Revenue enhancement due to:	- Electronic commerce	Deconstruction (breaking up of institutions into more
- Increased size (ability to serve larger customers)	Globalisation:	specialized units)
- Product diversification (ability to provide "one-stop shopping")	- expansion of domestic and international capital markets	Outsourcing
	- trade in non-financial products	Internet
Risk reduction due to product diversification	- Institutionalisation of savings	
Change in organisational focus	- creation of euro	
Increased market power	Deregulation	
Managerial empire building and retrenchment	Privatisation	
	Bailouts or financial conditions of firms	
	Climate of capital markets	

Tables 1.9 and 1.10 summarize the main findings for the US and a selection of the EU countries that were considered in the report, outlining the particular firm-level motives as well as the external factors for M&As. In general, irrespective of the county of origin, the main reasons concerning firm-level motives can be summarised as follows.

With respect to within-country, within-segment mergers, the single strongest motivation factor has been the desire to achieve economies of scale. Other important motivating factors were revenue enhancement due to increased size and increased market power. It is important to mention at this point that most interviewees interpreted market power to mean market share, rather than the ability to influence price. Risk reduction due to product diversification and change in organisational focus were considered largely irrelevant for this type of consolidation, while economies of scope, revenue enhancement due to product diversification, and managerial empire building and entrenchment were considered to be more important.

Table 1.9 Firm level motives for M&As in the financial sector in the US and selected EU countries (Group of Ten report), Part A

Country	Motives
US	Cost savings due to economies of scale: moderately or very important as a driver of within-segment, within-country mergers and slightly important or not a factor in the case of cross segment mergers and cross-border mergers.
	Revenue enhancement due to product diversification: moderately to very important in motivating cross-segment mergers, both within and across borders.
	Change in organisational focus: mostly unimportant
	Market Power and Managerial empire building: various views.
France	Cost cutting (dominant motive), Revenue enhancement (less important)
Germany	Consolidation within segments at the domestic level: Cost savings and revenue enhancements attributable to size (primary motives), increased market power (second most cited motive).
	Consolidation across segments at the domestic level: Economies of scope (cost savings and revenue enhancement due to product diversification) and improvement in risk management (consolidation of banks with insurance companies), expertise in securities activities (consolidation of investment and commercial banks).
	Not fundamentally different motives in the case of cross-border consolidation.
Italy	Consolidation within segments at the domestic level: Cost savings attributable to increased size (main motive), revenue enhancement due to product diversification and to a lesser extent to increased size, as well as need of banks to increase their market share were mentioned as other relevant motives. Geographical diversification was also mentioned as an important factor for risk diversification and increased market share.
	Consolidation across segments at the domestic level:
	Product diversification (main motive).
	Cross-border operations: Revenue enhancement due to increased size tends to become more important, whereas the cost saving argument loses some of its relevance.
UK	Consolidation within sectors: Cost savings attributed to increased size (most important), increased market power and managerial empire building.
	Across sectors: Revenue enhancement due to size and due to product diversification were most important; managerial empire building continued to rate as an important motive costs savings due to size dropped to slightly important.
	Cross-border: revenue enhancement due to increased size and managerial empire building.

Table 1.9 Firm level motives for M&As in the financial sector in the US and selected EU countries (Group of Ten report), Part B

Country	Motives
Belgium	The leading motive was a combination of cost savings and revenue enhancement. Risk reduction and managerial empire building were not found to be very relevant.
Netherlands	Cost savings and revenue enhancement were the main motives, product diversification was also important particularly for consolidation across segments, though it last was connected to revenue enhancement rather than economies of scope or risk reduction.
	Psychological motives have been moderately important, particularly the fear of becoming a takeover target, as was the shareholders pressures to create value.
Spain	The most important factor has been cost savings due to economies of scale. Attainment of critical mass for three main reasons: face the upcoming European consolidation, increase market share, defend against possible hostile acquisitions.
	Cross-border: revenue enhancement was the main motive, cost savings (economies of scope) was also important. Mixed opinions regarding risk reduction.
Sweden	Economies of scale was one of the main motives for consolidation. Shareholder pressures and the shift to offering retail customers more comprehensive service and integrated asset and liability management were additional motives. Empire building and psychological factors were also cited as potential main motives.
	Cross-border consolidation: mention was made of revenue enhancement due to geographic expansion.

Source: Group of Ten (2001)

Turning to within-country, across-segment mergers, the most important motive appears to be revenue enhancement due to product diversification, or the ability to offer customers "one-stop shopping". The desire to achieve economies of scope was perceived by interviewees to be the second most important motive. Economies of scale, revenue enhancement due to increased size, risk reduction due to product diversification, change in organizational focus, market power and managerial empire building and entrenchment were all considered to be slightly less important factors.

With regard to within-segment, cross-border consolidation, the strongest motives were the desire to achieve increased market power and revenue enhancement through both size and product diversification.

Finally, with regard to cross-segment, cross-border consolidation, revenue enhancement was considered to be a strong motivator, but increased market power was viewed as only slightly important.

Table 1.10 Recent external causes of M&As in US and selected EU countries (Group of Ten report), Part A

Country	External factors
US	Domestic consolidations- Most important: improvements in information and communications, technology, deregulation (especially interstate banking), bailouts (particularly in the last 1980s and early 1990s) and the climate of capital markets. Cross-border consolidation: Expansion of domestic and international capital markets.
France	Information technology, deregulation and privatisation.
Germany	Consolidation within segments at the domestic level: Technology was underlined by all interviewees, expansion of domestic and international capital markets was mentioned by all participants, euro was often cited as an important factor as well. Consolidation across segments at the domestic level: far lesser role of technology due to technological discrepancies and euro also loses much of its significance. Cross-border consolidation: euro was widely cited as an essential encouraging factor, deregulation is important as well, role to technology decreased.
Italy	Information technology (primary factor), euro (second important factor) were the most important external factors. Deregulation has also played an important role over the last years, though it has in current times exhausted its effect. Privatisation was regarded as an additional important factor. Across segments: institutionalisation of savings tends to become more important Cross-border operations: Globalisation was more important compared to other less important such as privatisation and resolution of crises.
UK	Within segments and across segments: Information & Communication technology and e-commerce were ranked highest, while deregulation and privatisation and the creation of euro were insignificant. Across borders: the creation of euro and institutionalisation of savings were ranked highest, followed by e-commerce, deregulation and privatisation.

Table 1.10 Recent external causes of M&As in US and selected EU countries (Group of Ten report), Part B

Country	External factors
Belgium	Introduction of euro and globalisation and favourable climate of capital markets. The development in information technology and disintermediation were also identified as factors.
Netherlands	The development of technology was identified as one of the main factors. Deregulation was also commonly mentioned. Of the factors related to globalisation, the introduction of the euro and the process of European integration in general were mentioned. One interviewee highlighted the high stock prices.
Spain	Bailouts, deregulation and the creation of euro, were the main forces. Expansion of domestic and international capital markets was also cited, as was the climate of capital markets. Mixed opinions regarding technology issues. Cross-border consolidation: deregulation, privatisation and bailouts were mentioned as the most important forces. Regarding technology issues, the opinions were mixed.
Sweden	Globalisation was thought to be a minor factor, while deregulation and privatisation were not regarded as important forces in 1990s.

Source: Group of Ten (2001)

Turning to external forces encouraging consolidation, technological advances were considered to be the most important force, especially with regard to within-country, within-segment combinations. Among them, improvements in information and communications technology were ranked the most important, followed by financial innovation, while electronic commerce was viewed as less important. Over half of the respondents also indicated that deregulation was equally important as a factor encouraging consolidation for domestic, within-segment institutions (with over one third ranking it as a very important factor). The responses regarding other types of consolidation were more or less the same. Globalisation of the non-financial sector did not rate as an important factor encouraging financial consolidation, while the institutionalization of savings was considered to be somewhere between "moderately important" to "very important" factor encouraging consolidation (by 50% to 60% of respondents for each type of consolidation considered). Finally, with respect to the influence of euro, the responses were mixed with the views varying among locations. Interviewees from euro area countries tended to rank this factor much higher than those outside the euro area. Nevertheless, some respondents indicated that the euro was likely to become a more significant force in the future than it has been to date.

1.4 Studies on Banks' M&As

This section provides a brief review of the empirical studies that have examined other aspects of banks' M&As. According to Berger *et al.* (1998) the majority of these studies can be classified into the following categories: (1) studies that examine the characteristics of the banks involved in M&As, (2) studies that examine the determinants of the premium paid for the target, (3) Studies that examine the consequences of M&As on operating performance, (4) Event studies of the merged banks' stock performance around the M&A announcement date, and (5) The consequences of banks M&As on other firms.

A large body of literature exists for each of the above areas. Since our empirical focus is confined to the development of acquisition prediction models, it is only appropriate to discuss the main conclusions of a selection of studies under the categories above[3], and refer the reader to Rhoades (1994, 1998) and Berger at al. (1998) for detailed surveys of the empirical evidence. However, we shall also discuss separately (in the last sub-section) a few studies that have focused on the EU banking sector.

1.4.1 Characteristics of banks involved in M&As

Studies that fall within this category are those of Hannan and Rhoades (1987), Moore (1996), Hadlock *et al.* (1999) and Wheelock and Wilson (2000, 2004).

Hannan and Rhoades (1987) examined the relationship between banks performance and the likelihood that a bank will be acquired. They

---

[3] We discuss just four of the five categories as the last one examines the impact of banks M&As on other firms (e.g. customers) and not on banks themselves.

also examined the influence of additional bank and market characteristics on the likelihood of acquisition. Their sample consisted of 201 acquired banks (in Texas between 1970 and 1982) and 845 non-acquired banks, and they employed multinomial logit analysis to account for the fact that any bank could experience the following three events: (a) acquired by a bank operating within its market, (b) acquired by a bank operating outside its market, (c) not be acquired. Their results can be summarized as follows: (1) no evidence was found to support the argument that poorly managed banks were more likely to be acquired than well managed banks, (2) market concentration was found to reduce the likelihood of being acquired from within the target bank's market, but not from outside the market, (3) high capital asset ratios were found to reduce a bank's attractiveness as an acquisition target, (4) larger market share and operation in urban areas increased a bank's attractiveness as a target, to banks not operating in the same market.

Moore (1996) also employed multinomial logit analysis to examine the characteristics of US banks acquired between June 1993 and June 1996. His results showed that the probability of being acquired tended to be higher for banks with low profitability, slow asset growth, low market share, low capital to asset ratio, and low ratio of non-small business loans to total loans. Small business loans per se and bank size, on the other hand, were not found to have a significant influence on the probability of being acquired.

Hadlock *et al.* (1999) examined a sample of 84 US banks that were successfully acquired between 1982 and 1992 and compared them to a matched sample of 84 banks that were not acquired. The authors analysed the effect of variables related to management incentives, corporate governance and performance on the likelihood of a bank's acquisition. Both univariate and multivariate methods were employed. They examined the mean and median values of the variables to identify any systematic differences between the two sample groups. They also estimated, in addition, four logit models using different explanatory variables and subsamples. They found that banks with higher levels of management ownership are likely to be acquired, especially in acquisitions where the managers of the acquired banks leave their job following the acquisition. They also found little evidence for other incentive, governance or performance variables to support the probability of a bank's acquisition.

Wheelock and Wilson (2000) attempted to identify the characteristics that increased the probability for a US bank to disappear either by being acquired or by failing, focusing especially on how managerial efficiency affected the likelihood of either outcome. Unlike the previous studies that used logit modes, they used proportional hazard models with time-varying covariates to examine a large dataset of US banks with assets over $50 million. They found that banks which were more close to failing were those that: (1) were less well capitalized, (2) had high ratios of loans to assets, (3) had poor-quality loan portfolios, (4) had low earnings, (5) were not located in states where branching was permitted, (6) had inefficient management as reflected in measures of cost or technical efficiency. As for the probability of acquisition, they found it to be higher for banks that: (1) had lower capitalization, (2) had lower return on assets, (3) were characterised by cost efficiency, (4) were located in states permitting state-wide branching.

In a later study, Wheelock and Wilson (2004) used a two-part hurdle model to investigate the determinants of the expected number of mergers and the volume of deposits a bank absorbs through a merger within a fixed interval of time. The sample consisted of all U.S commercial banks with available data that were involved in over 3,000 mergers, which occurred between the second quarter of 1987 and the first quarter of 1999, while numerous explanatory variables were used as proxies of regulatory process, market characteristics, capital adequacy, asset quality, management, and earnings. The authors concluded that: (1) regulatory approval process served as a constraint on bank merger activity, (2) the quality of a bank's management, as reflected in the CAMEL component rating for management was positively related to the expected number of mergers while downgrade in CAMEL and Community Reinvestment Act (CRA) ratings reduced the expected number of mergers a bank will engage in, (3) the expected number of mergers fell with an increase in the concentration in the market that a bank is headquartered, (4) location in an urban market greatly increased the expected number of mergers a bank will engage over time, (5) a bank's size strongly influenced the expected number of mergers a bank will engage in, and (6) an increase in core deposits, and increases in some indicators of asset risk, raised the expected number of mergers.

1.4.2 Premium paid on banks' M&As

Several studies have examined the size of the merger premium paid in the bank M&As literature. These studies have used purchase price-to-book value or similar ratios of the target bank and other key characteristics of the banks to investigate the determinants of the magnitude of premiums paid.

Early studies are those of Beatty *et al.* (1987), Cheng *et al.* (1989), Rhoades (1987), Fraser and Kolari (1987), Rogowski and Simoson (1987), and Hunter and Wall (1989). Beatty *et al.* (1987) examined the purchase price-to-book ratio of bank takeovers in 1984 and 1985. Cheng *et al.* (1989) investigated 135 mergers in the Southeast US that occurred between 1981 and 1986 and related the merger premiums to the characteristics of both acquirers and targets. Rhoades (1987) examined 1,835 bank mergers for the period 1973 to 1983. Fraser and Kolari (1987) examined the impact on pricing of 217 mergers in 1985 while Rogowski and Simonson (1987) studied pricing in 264 bank mergers between the beginning of 1984 and the third quarter of 1985. Hunter and Wall (1989) differentiated their study by using cluster analysis, examining a sample of 559 bank mergers that occurred during the period 1981-86 to reveal the financial characteristics that were highly valued by acquiring banks and systematically associated with attractive purchase prices. They found that the most valued characteristics in target banks included above-average profitability, faster deposit and asset growth, a higher ratio of loans to earning assets and judicious use of financial leverage.

Table 1.11 summarises the findings of some recent studies that have examined the determinants of bank merger pricing, these being conducted mainly over the period covering the last two decades. The majority of these studies suggest that acquirers are willing to pay more for targets that operate with lower overhead expenses and generate higher returns. Furthermore, variables such as bank growth, market growth, method of accounting (purchase or pooling), type of deal (intrastate or interstate), and market concentration were found to be significant in explaining the magnitude of acquisition premiums.

Table 1.11 Summary of studies on premium paid in bank M&As conducted over the last decade, Part A

Author(s)	No of bank mergers	Period studied	Main Results
Adkisson & Fraser (1990)	174	1985-86	Capital ratio, deal term (percent of acquisition price paid in cash), target bank's ROA and change in population in the target market area were significant at the 10% level.
Frieder & Petty (1991)	164	1984-86	Profitability (measured by ROE) and growth (measured by market characteristics – state deposit growth and expected future population) were significant positive determinants of premiums paid in mergers. Charge-offs to total loans had a negative impact on the premiums and was significant at the 1% level.
Palia (1993)	137	1984-87	Merger premium was related to the characteristics of both acquirer and target banks and the regulatory environments in both acquirer and target bank states. The separation of ownership and control in acquirer and target banks had also a significant effect on merger premiums.
Shawky *et al.* (1996)	320	1982-90	Higher merger premiums were paid for (i) smaller size targets (ii) targets with higher return on common equity (iii) targets with higher leverage (iv) targets in a different state than the bidder (v) transactions carried out through exchange of stock as opposed to cash purchase.
Hakes *et al.* (1997)	868	1982-94	The presence of state deposit caps reduced the premium paid. The impact of deposit caps was not constant across different sized banks. The premium paid to moderate size targets (assets between $77 million and $204) was greatly reduced while that paid for small and large banks was reduced less consistently.

Table 1.11 Summary of studies on premium paid in bank M&As conducted over the last decade, Part B

Jackson & Gart (1999)	200	1990-96	Target core deposits, target leverage, target ROA, accounting method, and a factor representing the target's state deposit cap restrictions were found statistically significant at the 1% level. Furthermore, target's non-performing assets, an intra-state variable and a combined factor of intra-state variable and relative size were significant at the 5% level.
Scarborough (1999)	243	1989-96, 1997-98 and 1989-98	Four variables were significant for all three periods. These were: accounting method, deal size, target's equity to total asset ratio, target's bank ROAA. Three more variables (target's size, percent of non-performing assets, whether the merger was intra-state or inter-state) were found to be statistically significant for at least one period.
Jitpraphai (2000)	214	1989-98	Five variables were statistically significant in explaining merger premiums (i) target bank's ROA, (ii) capital asset ratio, (iii) type of deal (interstate or intrastate merger), (iv) accounting method (purchase or pooling), (v) time trend variable.

1.4.3 Evidence on merged banks' operating performance

Studies in this category have typically examined changes in accounting data, before and after the mergers to determine if there have been any significant changes in the merged banks' operating performance (OP). In these studies, statistically significant improvements in profitability, increases in operating efficiency, rapidly growing interest revenues, reduction in costs, more efficient asset management and decreased risk in the post-merger institutions are assumed to be indicators of successful mergers and potential reasons for the M&As themselves. Rhoades (1994) provides a review of 19 operating performance studies that were conducted between 1980 and 1993, while Berger *et al.* (1999) provide a review of more recent ones. These studies can be distinguished between those that use univariate t-tests and those that estimate efficiency usually measured by the best-practice cost or profit efficiency frontier.

Univariate T-Test

These studies employ univariate t-tests to compare profitability ratios such as return on assets (ROA) and return on equity (ROE) and cost ratios such as costs per employee or assets before and after M&As (e.g. Spindt & Tarhan, 1992; Rhoades, 1986, 1990; Rose, 1987; Srinivasan, 1992; Srinivasan & Wall, 1992; Cornett & Tehranian, 1992; Linder and Crane, 1993; Peristiani, 1993; Vander Vennet, 1996). Some of these studies have found improved ratios associated with M&As although others have found little or no improvement in these performance ratios. For example, Rose (1987) examined 106 bank mergers between 1970 and 1985 and found that profitability did not increase for the acquiring banks post-merger. Similar results were obtained by Linder and Crane (1993), who examined 47 M&As that occurred between 1982 and 1987 and found no improvement in either ROA or growth in operating income. By contrast, Cornett and Tehranian (1992) found improvements in return on equity as well as operating cash flow owing to increases in employee productivity, asset growth, loans and deposits. Spindt and Tarhan (1992) examined 79 small mergers and 75 medium-to-large mergers and found improvements in ROE, margin and employee cost or sizes of mergers compared to a control sample. Peristiani (1993) found some improvement in ROE for the combined entities following merger but no improvement in cost ratios.

A problem with drawing conclusions from these studies is that simple ratios (either profit or cost) incorporate both changes in market power and changes in efficiency, which cannot be disentangled without controlling for efficiency. In addition, the use of cost ratios does not account for the fact that some product mixes cost more to produce than others (Berger *et al.*, 1999).

Efficiency Studies

In an attempt to overcome the problems associated with the use of simple ratios, a number of studies have examined the effect of M&As on banks performance using an efficiency frontier function methodology, such as the econometric frontier approach (EFA), the thick frontier approach (TFA), the distribution free approach (DFA), and the data envelopment analysis (DEA).

The cost-efficiency studies employ cost functions to control for input prices, product mix and other factors. Berger *et al.* (1999) argue that cost-efficiency studies are superior to the cost ratios studies, in that by controlling for prices, they are able to disentangle efficiency changes from changes in market power, which may be incorporated into prices. Nevertheless, despite the differences in methodology from the univariate cost ratio studies, the results of most cost-efficiency studies have been quite similar. As Berger *et al.* (1999) point out, the studies of US banking generally show very little or no cost-efficiency on average from the M&As on the 1980s (e.g. Berger & Humphrey, 1992; Rhoades, 1993; DeYoung, 1997, Peristiani, 1997) while the studies that use data from the early 1990s provide mixed results (e.g Rhoades, 1998; Berger, 1998). Probably the potential gains from consolidating branches, computer operations *etc.*, may have been offset by managerial inefficiencies or problems in integrating systems (Huizinga *et al.*, 2001).

The studies on profit efficiency consequences of M&As are related to the scale scope, product mix and efficiency effects for both costs and revenues and might also include at least some of the diversification effects. The theoretical appeal of working with the profit function is that it accounts for the revenue effects as well as the cost effects of operating at incorrect levels or mixes of inputs and outputs (Akhavein *et al.*, 1997). Akhavein *et al.* (1997) analysed a sample of mega-mergers (involving banks with assets exceeding $1 billion) that occurred in the 1980s and found that on average, mergers helped to improve profitability especially when both banks were relatively inefficient prior to the merger. The improvement in profit efficiency was mainly caused by risk diversification following a change in the output mix in favour of more loans and fewer securities holdings. Nevertheless, their measure of profit did not account for changes in risk that could result from such a portfolio switch, assuming that equity markets would recognise and account for any such change. Berger (1998) found similar results in a study that included all US bank mergers, both large and small, from 1990 to 1995.

Overall Assessment of Operating Performance Studies

As Houston *et al.* (2001) mention the mixed results of the literature that examines changes in the operating performance (OP) of merged banks are not surprising given the numerous empirical difficulties associated with these studies. The time period considered is one of the problems. Rhoades (1994) points out that the OP studies typically analyse performance for a period of one to six years after a merger occurs and during these years, many factors unique to the merged firm, other than the merger itself, may affect the firm's efficiency or general performance. Similarly, even if mergers improve performance, accounting based studies can fail to detect it because the flags between the completion of mergers and the realisation of operating improvements can be long and varied (Houston *et al.*, 2001). In their study, Linder and Crane (1993) found that merging banks did not improve their operating profit margins significantly during the first 2 years following the merger, while improvements began to occur after 3 years. A selection bias problem also exists with respect to the industry benchmark since it is difficult to construct benchmarks of non-merged banks in a rapidly consolidating industry (Houston *et al.*, 2001). Finally, the potential inaccuracies of accounting information in measuring economic value and accounting rules governing valuation of assets may also affect the observed results (Went, 2003). Nevertheless, despite these shortcomings, as Rhoades (1994) argues, the OP studies have the advantage of focusing on actual observed operating results of a merger rather than the expectations around the announcement date as event studies do.

1.4.4 Evidence on merged banks' stock market performance

Event studies typically examine the impact of merger announcement on share prices of the acquiring banks and/or the target banks and/or the combined entities around the announcement period. Changes in share prices, adjusted using a marked model for changes in the overall stock, provide an estimate of the anticipated effect of M&As on the future profits of the consolidate institutions. Positive abnormal returns reflect a positive view of the event, while negative abnormal returns reflect the opposite. Although the underlying procedures for estimating the performance effects are more standardised in event studies than in operating performance studies, the former exhibit a great deal of variation with respect to sample size, number of merger announcements studied, period of time over which the market model is estimated, period of time over which abnormal returns are calculated and so on (Rhoades, 1994). The results for the US are mixed, and the outcome basically depends on whether it examines the share price of target bank, acquirer bank or the combined entity (on an aggregate basis).

Rhoades (1994) provides a comprehensive summary of 39 US bank M&As performance studies published during 1980-39, 21 of which used event study methodology. The author concludes that the main findings of these event studies are not consistent. For target banks, only one study found no abnormal returns while eight studies found significant positive abnormal returns. For acquiring banks, seven studies found that a merger announcement had a significant negative influence on the returns to shareholders, while seven others found no significant effect on the acquiring bank's stock return, three studies found positive returns, while four found mixed results.

More recent studies have examined not only the returns of targets or acquirers but also the net wealth changes in stock prices by incorporating both stock returns of the acquiring and the target bank during the event period as well. This net wealth effect is usually calculated as some type of market value weighted sum of the acquirer and the target. Table 1.12, taken from Beitel and Schiereck (2001), presents the findings of some event studies conducted between 1990 and

2000[4]. In general, these studies confirm the findings of earlier studies as it concerns the returns to bidders' and targets' shareholders. Furthermore, a large part of the recent empirical research also aims at explaining empirically the observed results. Among others such studies are those of Hawawini and Swary (1990), Houston and Ryngaert (1994), Madura and Wiant (1994), Becher (2000), DeLong (2001), Zolo and Leshchinkskii (2000), and Banerjee and Cooperman (1998).

Table 1.12 Findings of recent event studies on banks M&As, Part A

Authors (year)	Country	Period	Sample	Event window (days)	CAR[a] Bidder	CAR Target	CAR combined entity
Hawawini & Swary (1990)	USA	1972-87	123	[0, +5]	-1.7%	+11.5%	+3.1%
Baradwaj et al. (1990)	USA	1980-87	53	[-60, +60]	n.s.	25.9 – 30.3%	N.A
Allen & Cebenoyan (1991)	USA	1979-86	138	[-5,+5]	n.s.	N.A	N.A
Cornett & De (1991)	USA	1982-86	152	[-15, +15]	n.s.	+9.7%	N.A
Baradwaj et al. (1992)	USA	1981-87	108	[-5, +5]	-2.6%	N.A	N.A
Houston & Ryngaert (1994)	USA	1985-91	153	[-4L; +1A]	-2.3%	+14.8%	+0.5%
Madura & Wiant (1994)	USA	1983-87	152	[0, 36M]	-27.1%	N.A	N.A
Palia (1994)	USA	1984-87	48	[-5, +5]	-1.5%	N.A	N.A
Seidel (1995)	USA	1989-91	123	[-20, +20]	+1.8%	N.A	N.A
Zhang (1995)	USA	1980-90	107	[-5, +5]	n.s.	+6.9%	+7.3%

---

[4] Some of the studies have been published after 2000. The dates of publication have been updated in Table 2.5 and may therefore not match exactly the ones in the study of Beitel & Schiereck (2001).

Table 1.12 Findings of recent event studies on banks M&As, Part B

Authors (year)	Country	Period	Sample	Event window (days)	CAR[a] Bidder	CAR Target	CAR combined entity
Hudgins & Seifert (1996)	USA	1970-89	160	[-1, +1]	n.s.	+7.8%	N/A
Siems (1996)	USA	1995	19	[-1, +1]	-2%	+13%	N/A
Pilloff (1996)	USA	1982-91	48	[-10, 0]	N/A	N/A	+1.4%
Houston & Ryngaert (1997)	USA	1985-92	209	[-4L, +1A]	-2.4%	+20.4%	N.A
Subrahmanyan et al. (1997)	USA	1982-87	263	[-1, +1]	-0.9%	N.A	N.A
Banerjee & Cooperman (1998)	USA	1990-95	92	[-1, 0]	-1.3%	+13.1%	N.A
Toyne & Tripo (1998)	USA	1991-95	68	[-1, 0]	-2.2%	+10.9%	-0.7%
Cyree & DeGannaro (1999)	USA	1989-95	132	[-1, 0]	n.s.	N.A	N.A
Kwan & Eisenbeis (1999)	USA	1989-96	3844	[-1, 0]	N.A	N.A	+0.8%
DeLong (2001)	USA	1988-95	280	[-10, 1]	-1.7%	+16.6%	n.s.
Tourani Rad & Van Beek (1999)	Europe	1989-96	17targ. & 56 bid.	[-40, +40]	n.s	+5.7%	N.A
Cornett et al. (2003)	USA	1988-95	423	[-1, +1]	-0.78%	N.A	N.A
Cybo-Ottone & Murgia (2000)	Europe	1987-98	46	[-10, 0]	n.s.	+16.1%	+4.0%
Becher (2000)	USA	1980-97	558	[-30, +5]	-0.1%	+22.6%	+3.0%
Brewer et al. (2000)	USA	1990-98	327	{0, +1]	N.A	+8.3%-14%	N.A
Houston et al. (2001)	USA	1985-96	64	[-4L, 1A]	N.A	N.A	+3.1%
Kane (2000)	USA	1991-98	110	[0]	-1.5%	+11.4%	N.A
Karceski et al. (2004)	Norway	1983-96	39	[-7, 0]	n.s	+8.4%	N.A

Table 1.12 Findings of recent event studies on banks M&As, Part C

Authors (year)	Country	Period	Sample	Event window (days)	CAR[a] Bidder	CAR Target	CAR combined entity
Zollo & Leshchinskskii (2000)	USA	1977-98	579	[10, +10]	N.A	N.A	N.A

[a]CAR = cumulated abnormal returns; n.s. = not significant, N.A= not research in the study· [b] Combined entity of the target and the bidder [c] The authors study hostile (25.9%) and friendly (30.3%) takeovers· [d] The authors only study different sub-samples without representing results for the entire sample· [e] 4 days prior to the leakage date to 1 day after the announcement ·[f] No tests for significance· [g] Completed deals.
Source: Beitel & Schiereck (2001)

Hawawini and Swary (1990) examined 123 US bank M&As that occurred between 1972 and 1987 and found M&As to be more favourable for bidders when the targets were small relative to bidders. Hawawini and Swary (1990) also found that mergers between the two banks located in the same state create more value than mergers between banks located in different states, as did Madura and Wiant (1994). Becher (2000) examined the impact of the method of payment on M&As success and found that bank M&As create more shareholder wealth for bidder's shareholders in cash transactions as compared to stock transactions. DeLong (2001) examined 280 US bank M&As over the period 1988 to 1995 and found that increased product/activity focus had a significantly positive effect on M&As success of US banks. Zolo and Leshchinkskii (2000) studied 579 US bank M&As from the period 1977-88 and found that the size of the bidder had a significant negative impact on the acquirer's M&A success. Banerjee and Cooperman (1998) examined a sample of 20 acquirers and 62 targets that were involved in M&As in the US between 1990 and 1995 and found acquirers to be more successful if they were more profitable than their targets, thus providing support to the earlier studies of Hawawini and Swary (1990) and Houston and Ryngaert (1994) that had reached at the same conclusion.

Overall, the empirical evidence from event studies on bank M&As indicates that bank mergers do not create a statistically significant net increase in stock market value. Whereas the shareholders of targets earn positive cumulative abnormal returns, the shareholders of the acquirers earn zero or negative cumulative abnormal returns suggesting a wealth transfer from the acquirer to the target shareholders in bank mergers. Due to the fact that acquirers often pay rather high premiums, these results are not surprising. Furthermore, the negative announcement return of bidding firms can reflect disappointment that the bidding banks is less likely to be acquired in the future (Houston *et al.*, 2001).

Overall Assessment of Event Studies

As Dunis and Klein (2005) mention, event studies are widely used to measure the effect of M&As announcements. Possible reasons are that stock price data are easily available, the calculations are straightforward and these studies do not rely on potentially misleading accounting data. Nevertheless, Rhoades (1994), Berger *et al.* (1999), Houston *et al.* (2001) and Dunis and Klein (2005) point out a number of problems that are associated with event studies. These can be summarized as follows: (1) Information may have leaked prior to the M&A announcement or markets may anticipate M&As prior to their announcements. These problems may be particularly severe during "merger waves"; (2) The period around the announcement event day for which abnormal returns are analysed varies greatly from study to study, and the results often appear to be sensitive to the time period chosen; (3) It is difficult to select a reasonable benchmark in a rapidly consolidating industry; (4) The analysis assumes efficient markets that immediately incorporate new information and relies on the assumption that the market expectations are a good prediction of the long-term effects of an event; (5) The samples are usually small as this method is limited to publicly traded banks. Nevertheless, many merging banks are of course not publicly traded, thus results based on publicly traded stocks are not necessarily representative of all bank mergers; (6) It is impossible to differentiate between the specific value of consolidation and other wealth transfer effects associated with the transaction and to separate the effect of the merger from the company specific events. This is especially true in the case of multiple acquisitions or where new shares are issued to finance the acquisition. It is also difficult to distinguish if gains come from efficiency gains or market power.

1.4.5 Evidence on European banks M&As

Vander Vennet (1996)

Vander Vennet (1996) used a sample of 422 domestic and 70 cross border acquisitions of European Community (EC) credit institutions that occurred over the period 1988-1993 to examine the performance effects of M&As. The analysis consisted of a univariate comparison of the pre- and post-merger performance of merging banks and covered a period starting three years before and ending tree years after a takeover. The results of the study can be summarized as follows: First, domestic mergers among equal-sized partners significantly increased the performance of the merged banks. Second improvement of cost efficiency was also found in cross-border acquisitions. Third, domestic takeovers were found to be influenced predominantly by defensive and managerial motives such as size maximization.

Tourani Rad and Van Beek (1999)

Tourani Rad and Van Beek examined a sample of 17 target and 56 bidding European financial institutions (i.e banks, investment funds, building societies, and insurance companies) that merged between 1989 and 1996. Using event study methodology with daily data and the market model, the authors found that target's shareholders experienced significant positive abnormal returns while abnormal returns to biddings' shareholders were not significant. Furthermore, the results suggested that returns to bidders were more positive when the bidder was larger and more efficient. They also found that cross-border mergers did not outperform domestic ones. Finally, there was no significant difference between mergers before the implementation of the EU-second banking directive and those that took place after the implementation.

Cybo-Ottone and Murgia (2000)

Cybo-Ottone and Murgia also employed an event study methodology to examine a sample of 54 very large deals (above $100mn), covering 13 European banking markets of the EU plus the Swiss market, that occurred between 1988 and 1997. It should be noted that the sample is not limited to bank mergers but also contains 18 cross-product deals in which banks expand into insurance or investment banking. The authors found a positive and significant increase in value for the average merger at the time of the deal's announcement. However, the results were mainly driven by the significant positive abnormal returns associated with the announcement of domestic deals between two banks and by product diversification of banks into insurance. Deals that occurred between banks and securities firms and between domestic and foreign institutions did not gain a positive market's expectation.

Huizinga, Nelissen and Vander Vennet (2001)

Huizinga *et al.* (2001) examined the performance effects of European bank M&As using a sample of 52 bank mergers over the period 1994-1998. The authors first investigated the existence of economies of scale in European banking. They also estimated the level of operational and profit efficiency for the European banking sector and for the banks involved in M&As. In addition, they used the efficiency analysis to reveal information about the ex ante conditions that predict whether a particular merger was likely to yield significant gains. Finally, they investigated whether or not merging banks were able to reap benefits from an increased use of market power on the deposit market. The authors found evidence of substantial unexploited scale economies and large X-inefficiencies in European banking. Comparing merging banks with their non-merging peers, they found that large merging banks exhibited a lower degree of profit efficiency than average, while small merging banks exhibited a higher level of profit efficiency than their peer group. The dynamic merger analysis indicated that the cost efficiency of merging banks was positively affected by the merger, while the relative degree of profit efficiency improved only marginally. Finally, they found that deposit rates tended to increase following a merger, suggesting that the merging banks were unable to exercise greater market power.

Beitel and Schiereck (2001)

In a recent study, Beitel and Schiereck examined the value implications of 98 large M&As of publicly traded European banks that occurred between 1985 and 2000. The perspectives of the shareholders of the targets, the acquirers and the combined, aggregate entity of the target and the bidder were considered. In addition to the entire sample, the authors also examined a number of sub-samples in an attempt to reveal the impact of geographic diversification, product/activity diversification, geographic and product/activity diversification, size, and time period on the abnormal returns. Furthermore, they also examined the deals between 1998 and 2000 using ordinary least square (OLS) regression analysis.

The authors report that for the entire sample the shareholders of targets earned significant positive cumulated abnormal returns in all intervals studied, while the shareholders of the bidding banks did not earn significant cumulated abnormal returns. From a combined view of the target and the bidder, European bank M&As were found to significantly create value on a net basis. Beitel and Schiereck argue that given the insignificant results for the bidding European banks the manager-utility-maximization hypothesis and the hubris-hypothesis cannot be supported in the case of Europe. They mention structural differences between Europe and the US such as the legal frameworks and the corporate governance structure of banks as the potential reasons of these differences between EU and US. Nevertheless, while examining the most recent deals that occurred between 1998 and 2000, they found significant negative cumulated abnormal returns and argue that it could be explained as a shift in these "European results". The results of the sub-sample analysis can be summarised as follows: (1) Cross-border bank-bank transactions with a European focus significantly destroy value; (2) M&As leading to "national champions" that aim at maintaining the existing market power in known markets and thus with a narrow geographic focus are valued higher by the capital markets than growth oriented international transactions that contribute to a single European market; (3) The product/activity diversifying M&As from a target and an aggregate point of view have more favourable value implications than transactions between banks; (4) Deals with targets of a manageable size seem to have a significant positive impact on value.

Beitel, Schiereck, Wahrenburg (2002)

The study of Beitel *et al.* (2002) builds on and extends the study of Beitel and Schiereck (2001), by examining the same data set but with a different objective. The authors analysed the impact of 13 factors that include relative size, profitability, stock efficiency, market-to-book ratio, prior target stock performance, stock correlation, M&A-experience of bidders and the method of payment on M&A-success of European bank mergers and acquisitions, in an attempt to identify those factors that lead to abnormal returns to target shareholders, bidders shareholders, and the combined entity of the bidder and the target around the announcement date of M&A. To accomplish this task they used dichotomisation analysis with mean-difference tests and multivariate cross-sectional regression analysis.

Their results showed that many of these factors have significant explanatory power, leading the authors to the conclusion that the stock market reaction to M&A-announcements can be at least partly forecasted. More important, the returns to targets' shareholders are higher when the target: (i) is small compared to the bidder; (ii) has a good cost to asset ratio relative to the bidder, and (iii) has a poor past stock performance track record. The abnormal returns to bidders' shareholders are higher when a transaction is more focused and involves targets: (i) with higher growth rates; (ii) with a high market to book ratio, and (iii) less profitable than bidders. Finally, the returns for the combined entity were high for non-diversifying transactions, when the bidder was engaged in relatively few M&A transactions, and when the target exhibited: (i) a high market to book ratio and (ii) a poor past stock performance.

Diaz, Olalla, Azofra (2004)

Diaz *et al.* (2004) examined the bank performance derived from both the acquisition of another bank and the acquisition of non-banking financial entities in the European Union. The sample consisted of 1,629 banks, where 181 acquisitions were noted over the period 1993-2000. Using a panel data methodology, Diaz *et al.* (2004) found that the acquirer obtains some efficiency gain in bank mergers. They also found some evidence on the impact of the takeover on the acquirer when acquiring non-bank firms and when the sample was split by type of acquirer (i.e. commercial banks, savings banks, cooperative banks). In particular the results reveal that the acquisitions of financial entities by European banks can increase their profitability. However, a lag of at least two years between the acquisition and the increase in performance was observed. The acquisition of other banks had an effect on acquirers' ROA as was revealed by the increase in the long-term profitability.

Lepetit, Patry, Rous (2004)

Lepetit *et al.* (2004) examined stock market reactions in terms of changes in expected returns to bank M&As that were announced between 1991 and 2001 in 13 European countries, by distinguishing between different types of M&As. More specifically, M&As were classified into several groups depending upon activity and geographic specialisation or diversification. To overcome some of the limitations of previous event studies they employed a bivariate GARCH methodology that allows for some beta movements. The results showed that there was, on average, a positive and significant increase in value of target banks, as well as, that the market distinguishes among the different types of M&As. A probit estimation that was used to further explore the sample by crossing the criteria of M&As classification revealed that the combination of activity diversification and geographic specialisation decreased the probability of having a negative abnormal return.

Dunis and Klein (2005)

The underlying approach in the study of Dunis and Klein (2005) was to consider an acquisition as an option of potential benefits. Hence, assuming semi-efficient capital markets, the market capitalisation reflects the market participant's view on the value of those benefits once the merger is announced. In this case, the share price, equivalent to the option, is the cumulated market value of target and acquirer prior to the announcement of the deal terms, while the exercise price is the hypothetical future market value of both companies without the merger. Therefore, the option premium gives the value of this option and should be equivalent to the takeover premium. This call option is in the money if the market value of the merged entity exceeds the expected future market value of the two separate companies. The authors applied this real option pricing theory model to a sample of 15 European bank mergers announced between 1995 and 2000 to examine if these were possibly overpaid. The results showed that the option premium exceeded the actual takeover premium suggesting that, those acquisitions were not on average overpaid. Further analysis, assuming the option premium equalled the takeover premium, showed that either the implicitly assumed volatility was too low, the assumed time to maturity was very short and/or the assumed subsequent market performance was too optimistic.

Chapter 2

Studies on the Prediction of Acquisition Targets

2.1 Introduction

This study is concerned with the prediction of acquisition targets in the banking sector and since (to the authors' best knowledge) there have been no prior studies developing prediction models solely for banks, the literature reviewed in this chapter covers those that have dealt with the prediction of acquisition targets for sectors other than banking. Even this literature has not been surveyed, and thus our aim in this chapter is to provide coverage of 30 studies that we have been able to identify covering the last 30 years.

The approach in empirical studies of acquisition, as with predictions of corporate failures or bankruptcy, has generally been to determine whether information from the data (financial or non-financial) taken prior to the event can provide signals of that impending event. Following Altman's (1968) pioneering study in bankruptcy prediction, discriminant analysis has been widely used in acquisition predictions where combined information drawn from data is used to construct a weighted index (z-score) of acquisition proneness. This approach has been criticised on a number of grounds (e.g. Lo, 1986) and so researchers have also used logit/probit estimation to develop binary choice models in determining the probability/likelihood of acquisition. These two approaches, statistical and econometric, have dominated the field, both having been extended to multivariate frameworks, although more recently other quantitative techniques such as neural networks, recursive partitioning, and multicriteria methods have also been applied in the dichotomous classification of firms.

For the purpose of this chapter, we attempt to classify these studies into three groups, related to the method employed. The first group, therefore, includes studies that have employed statistical techniques (discriminant analysis), the second group incorporate econometric studies, and in the third group we include all other studies, including those that have utilised non-parametric methods and those that have employed various methods or a combination of them. This distinction conveniently classifies the studies on the basis of the methodology employed, but we also seek to discuss the evidence for each of the 30 studies identified in the literature.

2.2 Studies Employing Statistical Techniques

Simkowitz and Monroe (1971)

Following Altman (1968), Simkowitz and Monroe (1971) were the first to use multiple discriminant analysis (MDA) in acquisition prediction specifically to address the following questions: (1) What was the financial profile of firms absorbed by conglomerate firms during the period April - December 1968?, and (2) Does financial characteristics of the absorbed firms provide a useful criterion for identifying those firms with a high probability of subsequently being acquired by a conglomerate?

Four groups of US firms were used in this study. The first two, considered as part of the analysis sample, consisted of 25 randomly chosen non-acquired firms and 23 firms that were acquired during 1968. This sample was used to develop the discriminant function that separated the acquired firms from the non-acquired firms. The other two groups of firms were used as a holdout sample, in order to test the classification accuracy of the discriminant function. The firms in the holdout sample were chosen with financial characteristics observed over the same time period of study and consisted of 65 non-acquired and 23 acquired firms.

The authors used an iterative process of selecting a set of financial variables to discriminate between groups. Twenty-four variables were initially chosen to provide quantitative measurements covering the following aspects of a firm's financial condition: (1) growth, (2) size, (3) profitability, (4) leverage, (5) dividend policy, (6) liquidity, and (7) stock market variables. Using stepwise discriminant analysis based on a maximisation principle with F-test values as a selection criterion, they reduced their initial choice of 24 to a set of 7 variables that achieved the best discrimination between the acquired and the non-acquired firms in the analysis sample. These seven variables were: (1) Market turnover of equity shares, (2) Price-earnings ratio, (3) Sales volume, (4) Three year average dividend payout, (5) Three year average percentage change in common equity, (6) Dummy variable for negative earnings, and (7) Three year average common dividend divided by common equity from the most recent year.

Their discriminant model classified correctly 77 percent of the firms in the analysis sample. This high classification accuracy is not unusual since the classification is based on the discriminant function derived from the same sample. A more appropriate test of the prediction model is how well it performs in the holdout sample. In this case, their model achieved a classification accuracy of 63.2 percent.

The above analysis assumes that (during the period of investigation) there are specific financial characteristics that permit the discrimination between acquired and non-acquired firms. Simkowitz and Monroe concluded that the following four financial ratios were the most important (based on the standardised coefficients of the discriminant function): (1) price-earning ratios, (2) dividend payout rates, (3) growth rates in equity, and (4) sales volume. In their study, the acquired firms (relative to the non-acquired) were smaller in size, and had lower price-earnings ratios, dividend payout and growth in common-equity.

One can find three limitations in the study of Simkowitz and Monroe. Firstly, their study was limited to conglomerate mergers. Secondly, the developed model was not tested in a holdout sample that relates to a different period rather than the same period used for the development of the prediction model. A different period holdout sample is more appropriate in order to examine the stability of the prediction model over time. Thirdly, it was not tested whether the normalisation of data by industry would add to the discrimination ability of the model.

Tzoannos and Samuels (1972)

Tzoannos and Samuels (1972) also used discriminant analysis to predict corporate acquisitions in the UK. Using a sample of 36 mergers that occurred between July 1967 and March 1968, and 32 companies that were not subject of takeover bids, they attempted to identify the financial characteristics of the type of company that became involved in merger and takeover activity. They used 11 variables as quantitative measurements of various aspects of a firm's financial condition and found that the characteristics of the companies taken over (differentiated from the non-taken-over) were a higher absolute level of capital, a higher rate of increase in the capital gearing, a slower increase in profits, a lower price earnings ratios, a slower rate of increase in dividends and a great variation over time in the rate of dividends. Acquirers were characterised by an above average downward trend in capital gearing, a higher than average increase in profits to capital employed, a higher than average increase in the trend of dividends and a lower absolute level of capital gearing.

From the 30 firms in the bidding sample, 21 were given a probability greater than 0.5, while from the 36 firms in the taken-over sample only 17 were given a probability greater than 0.5. This led the authors to conclude that the bidding firms were predicted with a higher degree of certainty compared to taken-over firms.

The major limitation of their study is that the same set of companies was used for both the estimation and testing of the model, resulting in a potential upward bias in the prediction of the bidding firms. It is obvious that in order to have a more meaningful indication of the models' ability to predict mergers and acquisitions it should be tested on a holdout sample of firms.

Stevens (1973)

In another study of US firms, Stevens (1973) corrected two of the limitations discussed above in Simkowitz and Monroe (1971) study. First, his study was not limited to conglomerate mergers, and second his holdout sample was taken from a different time period than the one used to develop the model. Stevens analysed a group of 40 firms acquired (during 1966) and a group of 40 non-acquired firms, thus making a total of 80 firms for the analysis sample. Unlike Simkowitz and Monroe (1971) who selected their sample of non-acquired firms randomly, Stevens matched the acquired firms to the non-acquired by size.

Stevens initially chose 20 variables to measure firm's liquidity, profitability, leverage, activity, price-earnings and dividend policy to develop a model that discriminated the acquired group from the non-acquired, using multiple discriminant analysis. To overcome potential multicollinearity problems encountered in previous studies that used discriminant analysis (Altman, 1968; Simkowitz and Monroe, 1971), he used factor analysis to reduce the dimensionality of 20 factors to 6 ones that accounted for 82.5 percent of the total variance. Thus, six of the original ratios, one from each factor were used as an input to the model. Finally, the discriminant function was derived based on the following four ratios: earnings before interest and taxes divided by sales (x_1), net working capital to assets (x_2), sales to assets (x_3), long term liabilities to assets (x_4), suggesting the following form of the model:

$$Z = 0.108\ x_1 - 0.033\ x_2 + 0.987\ x_3 + 0.111\ x_4$$

The model achieved a total correct classification accuracy of 70% when applied in the same firms that were used for its development. When a split sample validation technique was employed (with half of the original sample used to develop the model and the other half used to test its classification ability) the total accuracy fell to 67.5%. Stevens also attempted a second type of validation to examine the stability of the model over time. He calculated the same ratios for two new samples of 20 firms each, taken from the acquisition years 1967 and 1968, and found that the model achieved 70 percent accuracy, which indicated the model's potential ability to predict over time.

Based on the findings, Stevens argued that financial characteristics alone provided a means by which acquired firms can be separated from others and therefore, no matter whatever the stated motive for merger, financial characteristics were either explicit decision variables or were directly reflected in non-financial decisions for acquisitions. However, it should be noted, as Stevens points out, that the financial ratios that were found to be important in his study were not the same as those found in the Simkowitz and Monroe (1973) study.

Belkaoui (1978)

Belkaoui (1978) was the first to examine the prediction of acquisitions in Canada. His sample consisted of 25 firms acquired between 1960 and 1968 compared with 25 non-acquired industrial firms that were still in existence in 1973. Thus, like Stevens (1973), Belkaoui matched acquired and non-acquired firms by size. Sixteen predictor ratios were calculated for each of the 50 firms and a discriminant function was derived for each of the five years prior to the acquisition. These ratios were: cash flow divided by net worth (x_1), cash flow divided by total assets (x_2), net income divided by net worth (x_3), net income divided by net assets (x_4), long-term debt (plus preferred stock) divided by total assets (x_5), current assets divided by total assets (x_6), cash divided by total assets (x_7), working capital divided by total assets (x_8), quick assets divided by total assets (x_9), current assets divided by current liabilities (x_{10}), quick assets divided by current liabilities (x_{11}), cash divided by current liabilities (x_{12}), current assets divided by sales (x_{13}), quick assets divided by sales (x_{14}), working capital sales (x_{15}), and cash sales (x_{16}).

The correct classification rates for the model were 72%, 80%, 84%, 78% and 80%, respectively for the years one to five prior to the acquisition. To examine the prediction ability of the model, Belkaoui used a holdout sample of 11 acquired and 11 non-acquired firms (chosen from the same time period). The model achieved the following classification rates for years one through five: 70%, 76%, 85%, 76%,

75%, indicating on average slightly lower classification accuracy as expected.

Wansley and Lane (1983)

Wansley and Lane also used discriminant analysis to identify the financial profile of merged firms and predict acquisition targets in the late 1970s. They studied a sample of 44 U.S. acquired firms during the period 1975-1976, and an equal number of randomly selected non-acquired firms. In addition, a holdout sample of 39 merged firms in 1977 was used to test for the predictive power of the model in identifying acquisition candidates.

They considered 20 variables initially, to select the following aspects of a firm's financial profile: (1) profitability, (2) liquidity, (3) leverage, (4) size, (5) price-earnings, (6) stock market characteristics, (7) market valuation, (8) growth, (9) activity, and (10) dividend policy. The existence of multicollinearity among the variables led them to investigate the relative importance of individual variables using various approaches examined by Eisenbeis *et al.* (1973), Karson and Martell (1980) and Mosteller and Wallace (1963) to rank the variables such as the univariate F-test, the scaled coefficients, the Mosteller-Wallace approach of variables selection, and the forward stepwise method. This led to 5 variables finally entered in the discriminant function: natural log of net sales (x_1), market value of share to book value (x_2), three years average growth in net sales (x_3), long-term debt to total assets (x_4), price-earnings ratio (x_5), giving the following function

$$Z = 0.0953 \, x_1 + 0.2080 \, x_2 - 0.8158 \, x_3 + 0.5315 \, x_4 + 0.0047 \, x_5$$

Their model suggests that acquisition targets relative to non-targets were smaller in size, were growing more rapidly, had smaller market value and smaller price-earning ratios, and used less debt. Their classification accuracy was 75% in the training sample and 69.2% on the holdout sample.

Rege (1984)

Rege (1984) examined a sample of 165 firms in Canada, consisting of three groups of 55 firms each, the first comprising domestic taken-over firms, the second foreign taken-over firms, and the third non-taken-over firms matched by industry classification, the year of the takeover and asset size. Rege used both univariate and multiple discriminant analyses to test three hypotheses: the *Domestic Hypothesis (DH)*, according to which a foreign taken-over firm can be distinguished from a non-taken-over firm on the basis of liquidation, leverage, payout, activity and profitability; the *Foreign Hypothesis (HD)*, which states that a foreign taken-over firm can be distinguished from a non-taken-over firm on a similar basis-; the *Relative Hypothesis (RH)*, according to which a foreign taken-over firm can be distinguished from a domestic taken-over firm, also on the same basis as the other two hypotheses. Table 2.1 presents Rege's results of the discriminant analysis for all three hypotheses, with two sets of data, from 1962-73 and from 1968.

Table 2.1 Rege (1984) study-coefficients of discriminant variables

Hypothesis	Liquidity	Leverage	Payout	Activity	Profitability
I. 1962-73 Sample					
DH	-0.17	0.38	0.40	-0.54	-0.15
FH	-0.33	0.07	0.56	0.53	-0.02
RH	-0.50	-0.43	0.15	0.14	-0.07
II. 1968 Sample					
DH	-0.37	0.41	0.85	0.44	0.10
FH	0.43	-0.06	0.67	0.64	-0.32
RH	1.04	-0.25	-0.00	-0.13	-0.11

The results indicated that the financial characteristics of the firm were not sufficiently significant to discriminate between the three hypotheses, i.e. between either domestic and non-taken-over, foreign and non-taken-over, or foreign and domestic firms. Rege suggested further examination as to whether characteristics based on forecasted data would be more powerful than those based on historical data in locating takeover targets.

Bartley and Boardman (1986)

Bartley and Boardman have used multivariate discriminant analysis to test the hypothesis that the valuation ratio, defined as the market value of the firm divided by the net current value of its individual assets and liabilities, is the main determinant of whether a firm will be an acquisition target or not.

Thirty-three acquired firms were matched with 33 non-acquired firms in 1978 by industry and size of total assets. Seven variables, including the valuation ratio, were selected to measure five financial aspects: performance, leverage, liquidity, profitability and valuation using both replacement cost and historical cost data for their computation. Two variables were measured at two different rates. Price to earnings and valuation ratios were calculated using each acquired firm's stock price eight and twelve months prior to the announcement of acquisition. Five models were developed in the analysis: two using historical cost measures, differing only with respect to the dates for which the price-earnings and valuation ratios were calculated; and two using replacement cost measures of leverage, liquidity, profitability and the valuation ratio for the same two dates. The fifth model was developed using a stepwise procedure. Using both historical and replacement cost measures meant a total of 14 independent variables all together, but only three were finally included in the discriminant function that gave the model the highest classification accuracy, thereby offering a direct comparison of historical costs and replacement cost measures.

The fifth model had the following form:

$$Z = 0.63 \text{ Valuation} + 0.48 \text{ Historical Cost Leverage} - 0.61 \text{ Replacement Cost Leverage}$$

where:
Valuation = Total market value of common stock / Stockholders' equity plus total replacement cost adjustment
Historical Cost Leverage = Total debt / Stockholders' equity

Replacement Cost Leverage = Total debt / Stockholders' equity plus Total replacement cost adjustment.

The classification accuracy of the model was tested using a one-at-a-time holdout procedure described by Lanchenbruch (1967, 1975). This approach can be described as follows: One observation is omitted at a time, while the remaining are used for estimating the discriminant model. Then the omitted observation is classified using the previously developed model. The above steps were repeated until 66 models were estimated. After all replications were performed, an unbiased estimate of the true classification rate was obtained as the average accuracy of all discriminant models estimated. The classification accuracy of the fifth model was 64%.

Bartley and Boardman (1990)

In a latter study Bartley and Boardman (1990) also used multivariate discriminant analysis to determine whether current and historical cost data combined with real (constant dollar) financial accounting data had the potential to improve the predictive ability of models classifying firms as takeover targets. In addition, the authors introduced three innovations. First, unlike most of the previous studies, they used financial data from one year (1979) to classify companies based on takeover attempts during a period of three years suggesting that "*most of prior studies have identified companies that were takeover targets during a single year and then obtained financial data from the financial statements immediately preceding the date of the takeover"..." By examining a period as short as one year, some companies are included in the nontarget group even though they have the characteristics of a target company and actually become targets shortly after the classification period*" (p. 59). Second, while most prior studies (with the exception of Hasbrouck (1985) and Bartley and Boardman (1986)) were based on whether a takeover was successful or not in order to classify the company as a target or non-target, Bartley and Boardman (1990) studied takeovers irrespective of their ultimate outcome. The authors argued that there are other exogenous factors affecting whether a takeover attempt will be successful or not, such as managerial resistance, size of the bid premium *etc.* Furthermore, investors can earn abnormal returns from predictions of takeovers attempts regardless of their success, as the abnormal returns is observed around the announcement date and not the completion date of the deal. Thirdly, based on evidence that positive abnormal returns were produced by investment attempts for as little as 5% of a company's outstanding stock (Bradley *et al.*, 1983; Harris and Risk, 1983), the authors decided to include all companies that were subject to investment attempts exceeding 5% of ownership in the target group, unlike prior studies which included only investments of more than 50% in their target group.

The authors examined a sample of 41 targets, which were subject of a takeover bid during the period 1979 to 1981, combined with 153 non-targets, in the US. Several variables representing performance, earning power, long-term solvency, short-term solvency and other characteristics were used to develop three models, based on Historical Cost (HC), Current Cost (CC) and Constant Dollar (CD) data respectively, as well as a fourth model that combined these measures. Because of the large number of variables that could potentially enter a model, they used a stepwise MDA method to reduce the number finally entering each model. Thus, of the 26 variables, only 12,11,10 represented the HC, CC and CD models respectively, while 18 entered the combination model. Interest coverage, growth rate of sales and total market value were important discriminating factors, and target companies were found to have lower interest coverage, higher growth rates and smaller size, compared to non-targets.

The classification ability of the models was tested using the Lachenbruch method. They obtained classification accuracies between 69.9% (HC model) and 79.9% (combination model) using equal prior probabilities. They argued that "*because the target and nontarget groups are greatly unequal in number, the use of actual prior probabilities would result in a large percentage of the sample companies being classified as nontargets irrespective of the statistical fit of the model. The high prior probability of a company being a nontarget could overwhelm subtle difference in the accuracy of the alternative sets of accounting data. The solution to this problem is to compare classificatory accuracy using equal prior probabilities*" (p. 64). Nevertheless, the authors also tested their model using actual priors for a preliminary sample of 233 companies in which 24% were targets and 76% were no-targets. Almost all models (with the exception of the HC models) were found to be more accurate than a benchmark proportional chance model based on actual priors that classified correctly 65% of the firms in the sample. In the case of the combination model, the total classification accuracy was as high as 82.5%.

Barnes (1990)

Barnes used a sample of 92 targets, subject of successful takeover bids of UK quoted companies in 19 industries over the period 1986-87, and 92 non-targets matched by industrial sector and market capitalization prior to the merger period, in an attempt to develop a model that would predict acquisition targets in the UK.

Nine financial ratios were obtained for each company for two years prior to the merger. For each of these 9 ratios, the *"industry-relative ratio"*, defined as *"the ratio between it and the relevant sector average"* was used to avoid the stability problem across industries. Furthermore, factor analysis was used to reduce the effects of multicollinearity and overlapping of the 9 ratios and five factors where found to explain 91.48% of the variance in the original data matrix. The following five ratios were chosen to represent the five factors and used as inputs in the multiple discriminant model: quick assets divided by current liabilities (x_1), current assets divided by current liabilities (x_2), pre-tax profit margin (x_3), net profit margin (x_4), and return on shareholders' equity (x_5).

Barnes (1990) discriminant model had the following form:

$$D = -1.91218 + -1.61605\ X_1 + 4.99448\ X_2 + 1.11363\ X_3 - 0.70484\ X_4 - 0.11345\ X_5$$

The classification accuracy of the model was 68.48% when tested on the analysis sample, but this increased to 74.3% in a holdout sample of 37 acquired and 37 matched, non-acquired companies. The holdout sample, however, was from the same period as the one used for the development of the model. Barnes argued that the reason for not using a holdout from a subsequent period was that it coincided with the collapse of the stock markets that brought an immediate halt to the merger activity that could potentially lead to a misleading evaluation of the model.

Kira and Morin (1993)

Following up earlier studies of Canada (Belkaoui, 1978; Rege, 1984), Kira and Morin (1993) selected a sample of 34 public Canadian firms acquired during 1990 and matched them with 34 non-acquired firms by industry and market capitalization.

Ten financial ratios were selected, calculated for the year prior to the takeover for each company. As in Barnes (1990), data were normalised prior to the analysis using the industry-relative technique employed by Platt and Platt (1990). Then, factor analysis was performed to extract 5 factors explaining 88.1% of the variation in the data set. The following five industry-relative ratios were finally used in the discriminant analysis: quick ratio (QR), net profit margin (NPM), return on equity (ROE), debt/equity (D/E), sales / assets (S/A).

Their discriminant function has the following form:

$$D = -0.52445 \ QR + 1.84699 \ NPM + 1.58662 \ ROE + 1.30537 \ D/E$$

with the S/A ratio not being statistically significant and therefore not included in the function. By contrast, the D/E and QR ratios were the most significant discriminating variables (high D2), the former having the higher sensitivity of the two (i.e. largest absolute standardised coefficients).

The classification accuracy was 79.4% and 82.4% for the targets and non-targets respectively, with an overall accuracy of 80.77%. The jack-knife method was then used to test the validity of the model; the classification accuracy achieved using this method was reduced to 64.7% and 67.6% for the targets and non-targets accordingly, with an overall accuracy of 66.17%. The authors concluded that despite some limitations of their study, takeover targets were predictable one year prior to the takeover using historical financial data with some degree of accuracy.

2.3 Studies Using Econometric Techniques

Harris, Stewart, Carleton (1982)

Harris *et al.* (1982) were the first to introduce probit analysis to study the financial characteristics of acquired firms and to predict future corporate acquisitions in the US. Instead of using equal-sized samples of acquired and non-acquired firms, they used data reflecting the percentage of acquired and non-acquired firms in the population.

The sample used in their study consisted of manufacturing firms, of which 45 were acquired during the period 1974-1975, 61 were acquired during 1976-1977, and approximately 1,200 non-acquired firms traded as of May 1979. The data for all these firms were included in the COMPUSTAT database. Seventeen variables measuring aspects of firm liquidity, indebtedness, profitability, activity, internal versus external financing, dividend policy, price-earnings ratio, size, valuation plus two "additional variables", normalised by industry averages, were used to estimate various specifications of the probit model.

Despite estimating probit specifications with significant explanatory power, suggesting measurable characteristics that could affect the probability of acquisition, none were satisfactorily capable of providing substantive discriminatory power. The models for the years 1976-1977 reported extremely low probabilities of acquisition assigned to acquired firms. More specifically, the probit model predicted that, on average, 6.62% of the firms with the characteristics of the mean acquired firm would be acquired. Similarly, the model covering the period 1974-1975 predicted that, on average, 4.43% of firms with the characteristics of the mean acquired firms would be acquired. Based on these results, Harris *et al.* did not explore further the prediction ability of their model, arguing that *"Given our results, however, there does not appear to be a sound basis for out-of-sample attempts at predicting mergers based on the variables studied here"* (p. 239).

It could be argued that the small discrimination ability of their model is partly due to the sample they employed in their study. A sample comprising roughly the same ratio of acquired to non-acquired as in the population may be appropriate for testing the predictive ability of the model, however, as Palepu (1986) argues, the "information content of such a sample for model estimation is quite small, leading to relatively imprecise parameter estimates".

Dietrich and Sorensen (1984)

Dietrich and Sorensen (1984) were the first who applied logit estimation to predict the probability that a given firm will be a merger target. They selected a sample of 106 firms from four industries: food and beverages, chemicals, electronics, and transportation. However, after eliminating 17 firms due to missing data, the sample used in their study comprised 30 firms acquired in the years 1969 to 1973, and 59 randomly selected non-acquired firms matched by industry and year. Their selection criterion was to ensure that firms in the non-merged sample were not mergers targets for a two-year period immediately after the 1969 to 1973 period. Thus, 24 of the acquired firms and 43 of the non-acquired, randomly selected firms were finally used in estimating the logit model. The remaining firms were used as a holdout sample for prediction testing.

Apart from their choice of logit estimation, Dietrich and Sorensen emphasized the selection of financial variables with regard to their potential impact on a net present value (NPV) basis. The use of this principle suggests that factors (or variables) tending to increase the NPV of cash flows of a potential target were expected to increase the attractiveness of a particular merger candidate, while factors increasing the cash outflows associated with a merger were expected to reduce its attractiveness. All variables relating to the non-merged firm's characteristics over the five-year period were calculated as a five-year average departure from the mean value for all non-merged firms in the

sample (from the same industry over the same period). The variables
reflecting the characteristics of merged firms were expressed as percent
departures from the average performance for the industry in the last year
for which data for the merged firms were available.

Table 2.2 presents their estimated results. Model 1 shows the
estimates of all the variables, including those that are individually
insignificant although overall the model is statistically significant at the
0.01 level and capable of predicting correctly 92.54% of the firms in the
holdout sample.

Table 2.2 Dietrich and Sorensen (1984) study-logit estimation results

Variables	Coefficients Model 1	Coefficients Model 2
Price earnings	0.43	-
Profit margin	0.35	-
LT debt / Total assets	-3.37^d	-1.33^d
EBIT / Interest payments	-1.38	-
Dividends / Earnings	-0.81^b	-0.74^a
Capital Expenditure / Total assets	-0.24	-
Sales / Total assets	-14.80^a	-11.64^a
Current Ratio	2.24	-
Market Value of Equity	-7.24^b	-5.74^a
Trading volume in the year of acquisition	4.15^c	2.55^c
Constant	-14.36^b	-10.84^a

[a] Variables statistically significant at the 0.01 level, [b] Variables
statistically significant at the 0.05 level
[c] Variables statistically significant at the 0.10 level, [d] Variables
statistically significant at the 0.20 level

The authors tested further the sensitivity of the model by re-
estimating it to exclude all the variables not found to be significant in the
first model. The prediction ability of Model 2 using a holdout sample of
22 firms showed that it correctly classified approximately 91% of the
target and non-target firms in the sample. These findings imply that the
probability of a firm being acquired increased as dividend payout,
turnover, size and leverage decreased, and activity increased.

Palepu (1986)

The study of Palepu (1986) is well known for providing a critique of the procedures followed by earlier studies. Palepu identified three methodological flaws that made previously reported prediction accuracies unreliable: (1) the use of non-random equal size target and non-target samples for estimation leads to biased or inconsistent estimates of the acquisition probabilities, unless appropriate modification is made to the estimators, (2) the use of equal-size samples in prediction tests leads to error rate estimates, which fail to represent the model's predictive ability in the population, and (3) the use of arbitrary cut-off probabilities in prediction tests make the computed error rates difficult to interpret.

The author attempted to correct the above methodological problems by (1) applying the appropriate estimation procedure that accounted for the sampling scheme employed, (2) conducting prediction tests on a group of firms, which approximated the population over which the model would be used in a realistic forecasting application, and (3) testing the predictive ability of the model in the context of a specific forecasting application, using the relevant payoff function and prior probabilities to determine the optional cutoff probability in the prediction tests.

Palepu used a sample of 163 firms acquired between 1971-1979 and 256 non-acquired firms (as of 1979) from mining and manufacturing industries to estimate four different logit models with various independent variables (see Table 2.3). The independent variables were chosen on the basis of the following six hypothesis suggested in the literature, as likely reasons for companies to become acquisitions targets: (1) inefficient management hypothesis (i.e. firms with inefficient management are likely acquisition targets), (2) growth-resources imbalance hypothesis (i.e. firms with a mismatch between their growth and the financial resources at their disposal are likely acquisition targets), (3) industry disturbance hypothesis (i.e. firms in an industry that is subjected to economic shocks are likely acquisition targets), (4) size hypothesis (i.e. the likelihood of acquisition decreases with the size of the firm), (5) market to book hypothesis (i.e. firms whose market values are low compared to their book values are likely to be acquisition targets), and (6) price-earnings hypothesis (i.e. firms with low price earnings ratios are likely acquisition targets).

Table 2.3   Estimates of Palepu's (1986) logit acquisition likelihood models

Variables	Model 1	Model 2	Model 3	Model 4
Average excess return	-1.332 [a]	-1.338 [a]		
Return on equity			0.003	0.005
Growth-Resource dummy	0.5467 [a]	0.4432 [b]	0.4616 [a]	0.4024 [b]
Annual rate of change in the firm's net sales		- 0.0245 [a]		-0.0261
Net liquid assets/ Total assets		-0.005		-0.008
Long term debt / Equity		-0.0035 [a]		-0.0034 [a]
Industry dummy	-0.7067 [a]	-0.6900 [a]	-0.5802 [a]	-0.5608 [a]
Total net book value of a firm's assets	-0.0005 [a]	-0.0005 [a]	-.00004 [a]	-0.0004 [a]
Market value of the common equity / Book equity	-0.0044	0.0117	-0.0051	0.0126
Price-earnings ratio	0.0065	0.0099	0.0031	0.0041
Constant	-2.1048 [a]	-2.1096 [a]	-2.1533 [a]	-2.1898 [a]

[a]Significant at the 0.05 level, two tailed-test, [b]Significant at the 0.10 level, two tailed-test.

Table 2.3 shows the parameter estimates of the four different versions of the model. Model 1 is estimated with six variables, corresponding to the six hypotheses listed above. Model 3 differs from model 1 only by the use of return on equity instead of average excess return. Models 2 and 4, are simply re-estimates of models 1 and 3, respectively, with the inclusion of three additional variables measuring growth, liquidity and leverage. Although all models are statistically significant their explanatory power is small. Model 2 has the largest explanatory power and was used for further analysis. The predictive ability of the model was tested on a holdout group of firms consisting of 30 targets and 1087 non-targets. The model correctly identified a high percentage of actual targets, since from the 30 firms in the group that were actually targets, 24 (or 80%) were accurately predicted. But the model also erroneously predicted a large number of non-targets as targets, since from the 1087 non-targets only 486 (45%) were correctly predicted. Palepu also examined the possibility of earning abnormal returns from investing in the stocks of predicted targets. Unsurprisingly, the large number of firms erroneously classified as targets significantly reduced the overall economic usefulness of the model's prediction. On this basis, the author concluded that the model did not predict non-targets accurately and that the estimated model's ability to predict targets was not superior to that of the stock market.

However, there are possible explanations for the poor results of Palepu's study. First of all, the set of independent variables used is not exhaustive, there being only six variables based on six hypotheses supposed to affect the acquisition likelihood. The literature is inconclusive as to what are the main determinants of mergers and acquisitions (Ali-Yrkko, 2002). Second, Palepu defined as observation year (in the case of target firms) the year in which they were acquired while he defined 1979 as the observation year for all non-acquired firms. By following such a procedure, the author did not consider the problem of the potential instability of financial ratios over time and assumed that the value for a given variable remained constant across years (1971-1979). It should be obvious that a value for a variable in year 1979 need not necessarily be the same as for the year 1971 when an acquirer makes the decision to acquire firm X instead of firm Y. As Barnes (1990) correctly points out, it is unreasonable to expect the distributional cross-sectional parameters of financial ratios to be stable over time due to inflationary effects, technological and numerous other reasons, such as changing accounting policies. It is therefore important to ascertain as far as possible that the years of observation be the same for acquired and non-acquired firms.

Ambrose and Megginson (1992)

Ambrose and Megginson (1992) extended the logit model of Palepu (1986) using a larger sample of target and non-targets firms, over the period 1981-1986. Despite having a broader coverage compared to the mining and manufacturing firms used by Palepu (1986), their sample selection criteria, however, excluded public utilities and financial firms. They found that the explanatory power of the Palepu model was much reduced when re-estimated over their sample, reporting that *"none of the variables in the Palepu update were significant and the overall model had negligible explanatory power and was not significant"*. They extended Palepu's models by adding more variables, such as insider and institutional shareholdings, the importance of tangible assets in a firm's production process and the presence of formal takeover defences. The results of their estimations are presented in Table 2.4.

Table 2.4 Estimated coefficient values of Ambrose & Megginson (1992) models

Variables*	Model 1	Model 2	Model 3
Intercept	-1.058	-1.109	-1.096
Average excess return	-22.007	-13.215	-3.796
Growth-resource dummy	-0.072	-0.048	-0.098
Growth	-0.540	-0.516	-0.585
Liquidity	0.050	0.111	0.098
Market-to-Book ratio	0.020	0.025	0.026
Price-earnings ratio	-0.0017	-0.0012	-0.0015
Size	-0.0001	-0.0001	-0.0001
Tangible (fixed) assets to Total assets	0.914	0.999	1.022
% of Institutional investor shareholdings	0.0030	0.034	0.466
Change in institutional shareholdings	-6.7488	-3.815	-6.103
% of officer and director shareholdings	0.3273	0.330	0.195
Poison pill	-	-0.226	-0.268
Anti-takeover charter amendments	-	-0.120	-
Classified boards	-	-	0.238
Fair-price requirements	-	-	-0.695
Voting rights	-	-	2.246
Supermajority requirements	-	-	0.515
Black-check preferred-stock authorizations	-	-	-1.053
Dual-class recapitalisations	-	-	-0.068
No of observations (no of targets in parentheses)	331 (117)	327 (115)	327 (115)

* For details on the calculations of the variables see original article, Table 2, page 579.

The only model that is statistically significant is model 3 (with a chi-square value of 33.22 (p-value = 0.016), and a high explanatory power, given by a likelihood ratio index of 0.078). The results of this study shows that the probability of receiving a takeover bid is positively related to tangible assets, and negatively related to firm size and the net change in institutional holdings. Blank-check preferred stock authorisations are the only common takeover defence, being significantly (negatively) correlated with acquisition likelihood. The authors did not provide information regarding the classification accuracy of their model.

Walter (1994)

The study of Walter (1994) is one of the few that have tested the ability of the model to earn abnormal returns and hence is useful for an investment strategy that aims to "beat the market" and earn abnormal returns. Walter estimated two logit models, one with current cost (CC) data and another with historical cost (HC) data. In both cases, data were averaged over a two-year period and standardised by industry average. A total of 11 independent variables were constructed, including nine quantitative financial ratios and two categorical variables. Each one was associated with a different characteristic hypothesised to be related to acquisition likelihood. The models were estimated using a sample of 33 firms acquired over the period 1981 to 1984 and 274 non-acquired firms, using a backward stepwise technique. The models were then tested in a holdout sample of 10 companies acquired during 1985 and 81 non-acquired companies. The HC model classified correctly 60% of acquired firms and 74.1% of non-acquired while corresponding accuracies for the CC model were 40% and 69.1%. The predictions were then used to form two portfolios, for which the 250-day portfolio cumulative abnormal returns were calculated. The historical cost portfolio under-performed both the current cost portfolio and the entire prediction sample. The current cost portfolio on the other hand earned a statistically significant abnormal return compared to the prediction sample consisting of 9.2% of the population of firms that disclosed current cost data, but the model could only barely outperform the entire population of firms in the database irrespective of whether they disclosed current cost data or not.

Walter's study is interesting for three reasons. First, he used industry relative ratios, in an attempt to enhance comparability and the stability of the model. Second, he compared historical with current cost data, adding to the limited studies that had examined this issue. Third, he actually tested the ability of the model to earn abnormal returns, this being another issue that had received little attention in the literature. The only drawback of his study is the small sample size that was used for the acquired firms both in the estimation (33 firms) and the testing sample (10 firms). As Walter points out, this limits the generalisability of the findings (p. 375).

Meador, Church and Rayburn (1996)

Meador *et al.* (1996) also used logit analysis to examine the US case. The innovation in their study was the development of models to examine separately horizontal and vertical mergers. The authors collected data for 100 acquired firms, 50 horizontal and 50 vertical mergers, completed between 1981 and 1985 that were matched (using asset-size and industry) by an equal sample of 100 non-acquired firms. After removing firms with missing data and their matching counterparts, the final sample used for estimation consisted of 160 firms.

Drawing upon previous studies, variables representing liquidity, profitability, size, leverage, activity, growth, price-earnings, stock market characteristics, market valuation and dividend policy, were chosen. Stepwise binary logit regression was then used to the whole sample as well as for the horizontal and vertical sub-samples of merged companies. Table 2.5 shows the results.

For the combined sample the prediction accuracy was 63.75% and the overall model was significant at the 1% confidence level. However, only the variables Long Term Debt to Total Assets and Long Term Debt to Market Value were significant (at the 5% and 10% level respectively). The model for vertical acquisitions showed a higher predictive ability (67.07% overall) and was significant at the 1% level, but with only one variable, dividend policy to common shareholders, significant at the 10% confidence level. Finally, the model for horizontal acquisitions showed the highest predictive ability (78.21% overall). This model also has more significance, with long term debt to total assets, long term debt to market value of equity and market value to book value per share all significant at the 5% confidence level, and furthermore, asset growth and sales growth, also found to be significant at the 10% confidence level. The classification accuracy of this model was also tested using a holdout sample consisting of 10 firms merged in 1986, 12 firms merged in 1987 and 10 non-merged firms. Although the model correctly predicted 19 of the 22 merged firms (86.36%), it classified correctly only 3 of the 10 non-merged firms (30%). Based on the finding that the model predicted better horizontal rather than vertical M&As, the authors concluded that future studies should consider these types of business combinations as well as the role of qualitative variables on the acquisition decision.

Table 2.5   The logit models of Meador *et al.* (1996)

Variable	Coefficients		
	Total	Horizontal	Vertical
MT[1]	0.060	-	-
Cash available + marketable securities (CA)	0.011	0.044	0.000
Current ratio (CR)	-0.066	-0.321	0.354
Net working capital / Total assets (WTCA)	1.472	4.594	1.833
Net working capital / Sales (WCS)	-0.627	-5.062	-2.843
Earnings before interest and taxes (EBITS)	4.593	7.458	-1.113
Net income / Total stockholders equity (ROE)	-6.950	-9.868	-10.424
Net income / Total assets (NIA)	0.670	5.036	8.160
Net sales (NS)	-0.000	-0.003	0.000
Total assets (TA)	0.000	0.003	-0.002
Long term debt / Total assets (LDTA)	9.857*	20.367*	4.760
Long term debt / Net stockholders equity (LDSE)	-0.461	-1.116	-0.416
Total liabilities / Total assets (TLTA)	-3.933	-7.523	0.602
Long term debt / Market value of equity (LDMV)	-0.928**	-1.711*	-0.402
Sales / Total assets (STA)	0.454	0.178	-0.378
Costs of goods sold / Inventory (CGSI)	0.049	0.046	0.055
2 Year growth in sales (SGR)	0.000	0.013**	0.003
2 Year growth in assets (AGR)	-0.002	-0.027**	0.006
2 Year growth in EPS (EPSGR)	0.155	0.054	0.232
Market price / EPS common (PE)	0.001	0.010	0.000
Common shares traded / Common shares outstanding (CTSO)	0.462	1.547	0.454
Market price per share / Book value per share (MVBV)	-0.453	-1.122*	-0.143
2 Year percentage change in share price (SPGR)	-0.001	0.001	-0.000
Cash Dividends common / Earnings Available to common shareholders (DPCS)	-0.150	-0.634	1.784**
Intercept	0.287	2.119	-1.188
Prediction (Percent Correct)	63.75	78.21	67.07

[1]The authors do not provide any information about this variable but is presumed to be a dummy distinguishing the two types of mergers
*Significant at 5%, ** Significant at 10%

Powell (1997)

Powell's study had three specific purposes. First, to explore the potentially separate roles for the characteristics of the firm and those of the industry to which that firm belongs to in understanding the takeover likelihood of a firm. Second, to investigate whether the various models of takeover likelihood developed were robust over time. Third, and probably most interesting, to investigate whether segregating targets into those subject to hostile bids and those subject to friendly bids improved models of takeover likelihood.

Powell used a sample of 411 targets and 532 non-targets over the period 1984-1991 and employed a multivariate logit probability model for estimation. In contrast to studies that initially chose a large set of variables that were consequently reduced using factor or stepwise procedures (e.g. Wansley and Lane, 1983; Barnes, 1990), Powell based his selection of variables on takeover theories, hence following the approach of Palepu (1986), Ambrose and Megginson (1992) and others. Eight variables were selected corresponding to six takeover theories noted earlier (i.e. replacement of inefficient management, firm undervaluation, free cash flow, firm size, real property, growth-resource mismatch). These variables were: accounting rate of return (x_1), market to book ratio (x_2), operating cash flow divided by total assets (x_3), log of total assets (x_4), tangible fixed assets divided by total assets (x_5), average sales growth (x_6), cash and marketable securities divided by total assets (x_7), and debt divided by the sum of total share capital and reserves (x_8).

Powell estimated four logit models to achieve the three specific purposes highlighted above. Most notable, the specifications and samples used sought to distinguish between the models as to whether they aggregated targets into a single group or treat hostile and friendly targets as separate, and whether raw or industry relative variables were used. The estimation sample, for example, consisted of a pooled sample of targets and non-targets drawn from the period 1984-1991, which was then sub-divided into two sub-samples: one drawn from the period 1984-1987 and another drawn from the period 1988-1991. A noteworthy aspect related to the sample of data is that Powell reconstructed as near as possible the true historical populations of firms, thus addressing the criticisms of previous studies that suffered from survivorship bias.

There are four main contributions of Powell's study, according to Thomas (1997). First, it confirmed, for the UK, some of the findings of Morck *et al.* (1988) that examined the US case. Second, it also confirmed that, as in the US, the characteristics relating to the takeover likelihood of firms in the UK are not robust over time. Third, the study revealed that the industry characteristics of a firm that is taken over could play a separate role (from the characteristics of the firm itself) in explaining the takeover likelihood of that firm. Fourth, and most interesting, the results provided evidence that hostile and friendly targets are viewed differently. Thus, the study provided a new insight that treating friendly and hostile takeovers as belonging to a single homogenous group of takeovers can produce misleading inferences about the effect of firm and industry characteristics on takeover likelihood.

Unfortunately, Powell does not provide any indication of the predictive ability of the developed models, using either the holdout sample or the estimation sample. In addition, Thomas (1997) highlighted the need for a statistical test before one could be confident that there is any temporal variation in the characteristics of those firms that are taken over. He also raised the issue of distinguishing between takeover bids and completed takeovers that were used interchangeably in the study of Powell.

Barnes (1998)

Another interesting study by Barnes (1998) examines several issues using a sample of UK firms. First, the author develops and compares industry-relative models and industry-specific models. Second, he examines whether the inclusion of anticipated share price changes as an input in regression would improve the predictive accuracy of the models developed using accounting data alone. Third, Barnes examines the following three alternative methods to determine the cut-off points when using a logit model: (1) a weighted cut-off point based on historical experience, (2) a cut-off based on the minimisation of errors estimated form the period used for models' estimation and (3) a cut-off based on the maximisation of returns.

Forty-two variables corresponding to three hypotheses of takeover likelihood (inefficient management, growth-resource mismatch, and size) were initially considered. Of these, the following 17 were finally selected taking account of possible multicollinearity problems (variables with correlations above 0.65 were dropped) while retaining full representation of the hypotheses: profit before tax divided by sales (x_1), profit before tax divided by shareholder's equity (x_2), growth of profit before tax over last 3 years (x_3), price (2 months before) divided by earnings (x_4), average divided for last 3 years divided by shareholders' equity (x_5), dividend growth over last 3 years (x_6), market capitalization divided by shareholders' equity (x_7), sales divided by total assets (x_8), total remuneration divided by sales (x_9), sales growth over last 2 years (x_{10}), sales growth over last 3 years (x_{11}), current assets divided by current liabilities (x_{12}), (current assets less current liabilities) divided by total assets (x_{13}), long-term debt divided by total assets (x_{14}), (profits before tax plus interest paid) divided by interest paid (x_{15}), long-term debt divided by shareholders' equity (x_{16}), market capitalization 2 months before the bid (x_{17}).

Four models were estimated in total. The first model, referred as the non-share price model was estimated across all industrial classifications based on industry relative ratios using the full set of 17 variables above. The second model included the effect of anticipatory share price changes (x_{18}) in addition to the 17 variables of the first model. The third and fourth models are simply the first two models re-estimated for each of the two industrial sectors (determined according to the first two digits of the SIC).

The estimation sample consisted of a group of firms that were the subject of both successful and unsuccessful bids during 1991-1993. As the population of some sectors was small the industry-specific models were estimated over the period 1991-1993 using a sample size of 323 bids in total. The general model was estimated using data from 82 targets that were the subject of a bid during 1993 matched with 82 non-targets. A holdout sample of 1185 UK quoted companies at January 1st 1994, of which 16 experienced a takeover bid during 1994, was used to test the predictive ability of the general models. In the case of the industry specific models the holdout sample was reduced to 874 non-targets and 13 targets.

The results of this study can be summarised as follows: First, in the first two models (i.e. both the general non-share price and the share price models), four variables (x_1, x_2, x_9, x_{10}) were significant, indicating that profitability, sales growth and shareholders' equity were the important discriminatory factors. Second, the difference between the likelihood values of these two models was negligible, implying that that the addition of the anticipated share price did not improve the goodness of fit (i.e. the effect of adding the latter variable ($x18$) in the second model was not significant and the predictive accuracy was only minutely improved). Third, the general model performed better than the industry-specific models in terms of overall classification (both targets and non-targets). However, none of the models was successfully in identifying targets. Fourth, predictions could not be significantly improved by the choice of cut-off point, as they were not sensitive to it, especially as it concerns the number of successful target predictions that is necessary to generate the excess returns.

Kim and Arbel (1998)

Kim and Arbel (1998) also used logit analysis but differentiated their study by focusing on the hospitality industry. A sample of 38 hospitality firms that were merger targets during the period 1980-1992, were combined with a sample of 78 firms that were not merger targets as of 1992, to develop their models.

They identified nine independent variables (see Table 2.6) as proxies for the following nine hypotheses suggested by the literature as reasons for M&As: (1) The firm size hypothesis, (2) The inefficient management hypothesis, (3) The financial leverage hypothesis, (4) The liquidity hypothesis, (5) The growth-resources imbalance hypothesis, (6) The relative capital expenditure hypothesis, (7) The dividend payout hypothesis, (8) The stock market trading volume hypothesis, and (9) The asset undervaluation hypothesis.

Among several models they estimated the best one predicted correctly 76% of the firms. Table 2.6 shows the variables used and the coefficient estimates of this model. Four variables, price-to-book ratio, growth-resource imbalance dummy, firm size and capital expenditure ratio were found to be significant in predicting which hospitality company is likely to become a merger target. With the exception of size, the remaining three variables were significant at the 5% level or better.

Table 2.6   Kim and Arbel (1998) logit model

Variable	Coefficient Estimate
Size (log of sales)	0.34^{*}
Asset Turnover	-0.39
% Average trading volume to shares outstanding	-0.01
Dividend Payout ratio	0.005
Price-to-Book ratio	-0.48^{***}
Leverage (Long-term debt / equity)	-0.05
Growth-resource imbalance (dummy variable)	1.47^{**}
Liquidity (current ratio)	-0.16
Capital Expenditure	5.20^{**}

*Significant at 10% level, **Significant at the 5% level, ***Significant at the 1% level

The predictive ability of the model was also tested in a holdout sample of 14 targets and 31 non-targets. From the 14 targets, 11 firms (79%) were predicted correctly; while from the 31 non-targets 23 (74%) were correctly classified as non-targets. The authors compared their results with the model of Palepu (1986), which had significantly lower predictive ability (around 46%). However, despite their high classification accuracy the authors concluded that because of the low likelihood ratio (the pseudo R^2 which was 0.28), the model could be used only as a supplementary decision-supporting tool and suggested the use of additional information and judgment. The main reason for this was probably the fact that other characteristics not reflected in the nine financial characteristics used in their study, play important roles in mergers.

Cudd and Duggal (2000)

Cudd and Duggal replicated the study of Palepu (1986) for a latter period in order to re-investigate (1) the usefulness of the six acquisition hypotheses in predicting takeover targets, and (2) the importance of using industry-specific distributional characteristics in determining classification accuracies.

A sample of firms acquired between 1988-1991 and a random sample of firms not acquired as of 1991 were used for the estimation of the acquisition model. After randomly selecting a group of non-acquired firms and screening for data availability, their final sample consisted of 108 acquired and 235 non-acquired mining and manufacturing firms listed either on the American Stock Exchange or the New York Stock Exchange. A holdout sample consisted of 13 firms acquired in 1992 and 460 non-acquired firms.

The authors used the same variables as in Palepu (1986) to generate three models, with coefficient estimates shown in Table 2.7. The first model (Model 1) applied Palepu's financial variables unaltered as defined in Palepu's study. The second model (Model 2) applied an adjustment factor to the financial variables to capture the distributional effects unique to each firm's industry. Previous studies in acquisition prediction that used industry relatives calculated the adjusted ratios by simply dividing the value of the ratio with the corresponding average value of the industry. Cudd and Duggal followed a different procedure by calculating the adjusted ratios as follows: $D_i = (R_{ij} - N_j)/\sigma_j$ where: R_{ij} is the value of the financial ratio of firm i in industry j, N_j is the industry average financial ratio value of industry j, σ_j is the standard deviation of R_{ij} values within industry j, and D_i is the adjusted financial ratio deviation from the industry norm for firm i. The third model (Model 3) was identical to Model 2 but with the disturbance variable redefined to reflect acquisition activity occurring during the 12 months immediately preceding the month of acquisition (as opposed to on a calendar year basis).

The results (Table 2.7) show that, without adjustment for industry-specific distributional characteristics (Model 1), the findings are consistent only with the size hypothesis. However, after adjusting for distributional properties (Model 2), the findings are consistent, in addition with the inefficient management and growth-resources-mismatch hypotheses. Finally, Model 3 results also show the significance of the industry disturbance hypothesis.

Table 2.7 – Logit models of Cudd and Duggal (2000)

Variable	Model 1	Model 2	Model 3
ROE	0.0066**	-0.3740**	-0.3826**
Growth-Resource-mismatch dummy	0.5630**	0.6534**	0.6950**
Growth	-0.204**	-0.1236	-0.1499
Liquidity	-1.3123**	0.0501	-0.1132
Leverage	-0.0009*	-0.0316	-0.0258
Industry disturbance dummy	0.0384	0.1269	1.2505**
Size	-0.0001**	-0.3209**	-0.3039**
Market-to-book	-0.0331	-0.0766	-0.0661
Price-earnings	0.0001	0.0209	0.02042
Constant	-1.1934**	-0.8065**	-1.1468**

*Indicates statistical significance at the 5% level, **Indicates statistical significance at the 1% level.

Based on these results and a t-test to access the differences in prediction accuracies between the models the authors concluded that the adjusted model produced classification accuracy significantly higher than chance, and significantly greater than that observed for the unadjusted model. However, it should be noted that although Model 3 achieved the highest overall classification accuracy, it also achieved the lowest correct classification of acquired firms (7.69% compared to 61.53% achieved by Model 1).

Powell (2001)

In line with the studies of Palepu (1986) and Cheh *et al.* (1999), Powell (2001) examines whether it possible to "beat the market" and earn abnormal returns by investing in the stocks of the predicted targets. The author argued that Palepu (1986) applied a classification rule, which resulted in his portfolio comprising a large number of non-target firms incorrectly predicted as targets. Palepu included in his portfolio all firms with positive expected abnormal returns, no matter how small. Nevertheless, investing in such a large portfolio is unlikely to yield abnormal returns since the abnormal returns to the small number of actual targets in the portfolio are diluted by the near zero abnormal returns to the large number of firms not taken over. Similar procedure with the one of Palepu (1986) was also followed in the study of Cheh *et al.* (1999).

Thus, in his attempt to "beat the market", Powell (2001) followed another procedure to construct the portfolios. He examined the concentration of target firms within portfolios constructed from the estimation sample of target and non-target firms. Ten portfolios were constructed by sorting each firm in the estimation sample in descending order by its probability of takeover. The classification rule (cut-off point) was derived from the portfolio that had the highest concentration of targets firms (G-ratio). Applying this classification rule to the population of firms, results in smaller portfolios with higher average takeover probabilities.

The estimation sample consisted of a pooled sample of non-financial firms (targets and non-targets) listed on the London Stock Exchange, drawn from the true population of firms for the period 1986 to 1995. As in Powell (1997), the author again reconstructed the considered sample to reflect, as near as possible, to the "true population of firms". A total of 471 targets met data requirements and were included in the sample, while an equal number of non-targets were randomly selected from the same period. After removing outliers, the estimation sample comprised of 444 targets and 422 non-targets.

Two logit models, distinguished on the basis of the independent variables used, were estimated. The first model used only firm values for characteristics examined as independent variables. The second model used industry-relative ratios, where industry-weighted values were scaled by economy-weighted values. The variables employed in estimating the models were the same as in Powell (1997), corresponding to the same takeover theories.

The within sample total classification accuracy of the first model (Model 1) was between 50.35% and 58.31% depending on the cut-off point, while corresponding accuracies for Model 2 were between 51.39%

and 59.12%. For Model 1, the highest G-ratio (0.66) was achieved using a cut-off point equal to 0.55 that resulted in correct classification accuracy equal to 56.35% in total, and 62.89% of targets in the portfolio. The latter (% of targets in the portfolio) corresponds to the number of target firms correctly classified by the model divided by the total number of firms in the portfolio. For Model 2, the highest G-ratio (0.67) was achieved using a cut-off point equal to 0.64 that resulted in correct classification accuracy equal to 51.96% in total, and 67.06% of targets in the portfolio.

The predictive ability of the developed models was tested using the population of firms on 1st January 1996, the day on which the portfolios of predicted targets were formed. The sample used consisted of 971 non-targets and 29 targets. To "beat the market", the portfolios were formed by applying the previously determined cut-off probabilities, nevertheless for comparison purposes portfolios were also formed using Palepu's rule of minimising the total error rate. The models predicted quite well on average predicting about 84% of targets and non-targets correctly, with Model 2 outperforming Model 1. Both models outperform those of Palepu (1986) whose best model correctly predicted only 46% of firms in the population. However, Powell (2001) acknowledges that if the same classification rule as in Palepu had been used in his study, it would have resulted in a much lower predictive accuracy (47%) than the one achieved. On this basis, the models failed to clearly identify target firms from the total population. For example, of the 209 firms predicted as targets in Model 1, only 7 were in fact targets (3.24%). This percentage was even lower in the case of the Model 2 (2.08%).

Despite the low predictive ability of the models, Powell (2001) examines whether abnormal returns could be earned from the predicted takeovers. Abnormal returns were measured in two ways: (1) as the difference between the return on a firm and the return on the market portfolio (the Market Adjusted Model or MAM), and (2) as the difference between the return on a firm and the return on a control portfolio matched by firm size (the Size Adjusted Model or SAM). Ten portfolios were formed and held for a 12-month holding period. The buy and hold abnormal returns calculated on the basis of both MAM returns and SAM returns suggested that it was not possible to earn significant positive abnormal returns by investing in firms predicted by the models to be potential takeover targets. Using the method similar to Palepu also produced negative abnormal returns, however these were smaller in magnitude compared to the method followed by Powell (2001) using the G-ratio as the optimal cut-off.

There are two issues that should be raised at this point, as they could had lead to higher abnormal returns. First, Powell characterised as targets only those firms that were successfully acquired. However, as Bartley and Boardman (1990) point out, investors can earn abnormal returns from predictions of takeover attempts irrespective of their success. Second, although not explicitly mentioned, only full acquisition or acquisitions above 50% were considered in his study. Nevertheless, in the context of developing a predictive model that can be used by investors, large investment attempts that do not seek a controlling ownership interest need also to be considered (Bartley and Boardman, 1990), based on evidence that positive abnormal returns are produced by investment attempts for as little as 5% of a company's outstanding stock (Bradley *et al.*, 1983; Harris and Risk, 1983). As the purpose of Powell's study was also to examine abnormal returns, these issues could turn out to be critical.

2.4 Other Studies

Slowinski, Zopounidis, Dimitras (1997)

A new approach to the prediction of a firm's acquisition was proposed by Slowinski *et al.* (1997). This method, based on the rough set theory, does not need any assumption about data prior to the analysis, unlike parametric methods such as discriminant or logit analysis. The information about the firms is organised in a financial information table, where the financial characteristics of the firms correspond to condition attributes and the classification is defined by a decision attribute indicating whether a firm has been acquired or not. With the rough set approach one can determine minimal subsets of conditional attributes (financial ratios) ensuring an acceptable approximation of the classification of the firms analysed and to obtain decision rules from the information table, which can be used to distinguish between acquired and non-acquired firms.

A sample of 30 acquired Greek firms over the period 1983-1990 as well as 30 non-acquired firms matched by asset size, sales volume, and number of employees, from various sectors (excluding the service sector) were used to develop the model. Ten financial ratios were initially chosen and calculated for up to three years prior to the takeover both for acquired and non-acquired firms. The initial information table was reduced from ten to five columns corresponding to: (1) two profitability ratios: (i) earnings before interest and taxes divided by total sales and (ii) cash flow divided by total assets, (2) two debt capacity ratios: (i) (long term debt plus current liabilities) divided by total assets, and (ii) net worth divided by (net worth plus long-term debt), and (3) one liquidity ratio: quick assets divided by current liabilities, which were used to derive decision rules using data from one year prior to the acquisition. From the 24 decision rules, 13 rules classified acquired firms and 14 classified the non-acquired firms.

The predictive ability of the model was tested using the same firms but data from 2 years and 3 years prior to the acquisition instead of data from 1 year before the acquisition. The classification accuracy was 75% and 66.7% for 2 and 3 years before the acquisition. The authors compared the new methodology with discriminant analysis, using the same five ratios. They reported that the error rates of the discriminant function for 2 and 3 years before the acquisition were higher than those of the rough set approach, and suggested the rough set approach as a reliable alternative to discriminant analysis.

The new methodology presented in the study of Slowinski *et al.* offers a promising non-parametric methodology, as it avoids the assumptions of parametric methods and provides good classification accuracies. Nevertheless, the predictive accuracy of the model should have been tested using some kind of holdout sample or resampling technique. Although the authors used data from years 2 and 3 prior to the acquisition, these data were obtained from the same firms that were used for the development of the model. Given that data from year one prior to the acquisition used for the development are not independent from data from years 2 and 3 prior to the acquisition the comparison of the methods should be extended.

Zanakis and Zopounidis (1997)

Zanakis and Zopounidis (1997) offer a comparison of linear and quadratic discriminant analysis and logit models using industrial and commercial Greek firms that were acquired during the period 1983-1990. Two samples, a training sample of 80 firms, and a holdout sample of 30 firms, with equal number of acquired and non acquired firms matched by asset size, sales volume and number of employees, were used to estimate the parameters of the models and test their predictive ability.

For each one of the firms, 16 financial ratios, representing three basic groups, profitability, managerial performance and solvency, were calculated for the three years preceding the takeover. These ratios were chosen after considering: i) the data availability, ii) existing empirical studies using similar ratios and iii) their popularity in the financial literature. Factor analysis was used prior to the development of the prediction models to identify any multicollinearity among the financial ratios, which transformed the original ratios into a few uncorrelated factors representing the same financial information. Various discriminant models were developed using a combination of factors and procedures involving stepwise discriminant analysis. In addition, four logit models were obtained using as input the sixteen financial ratios for each year separately and combined.

The authors reported mixed results since most models classified correctly a significant proportion of acquired or non-acquired but not both. They partially supported the findings of Mahmood and Lawrence (1987) on quadratic discriminant analysis being more accurate than linear discriminant analysis in classifying acquired firms and also reported that the logit models provided inferior overall predictions compared to those made by linear discriminant analysis. Their best two models, however, were produced by linear discriminant analysis of six ratios.

The first model had a classification accuracy of 70% for the acquired, 65% for the non acquired and 67.5% in total for the training sample, all significant at the 95% confidence level, while the corresponding accuracies in the holdout sample were 66.7%, 62% and 64.3%. The ratios used in this model were: (long term debt plus current liabilities) divided by working capital (x_1), (long term debt plus current liabilities) divided by cash flow (x_2), (long term debt plus current liabilities) divided by working capital (x_3), inventory to working capital (x_4), earnings to total assets (x_5), current assets to current liabilities (x_6). For this model, ratios x_1 and x_2 were obtained using data one year prior to the acquisition, ratios x_3 and x_4 using data two years prior to the acquisition, while for the last two ratios $(x_5$ and $x_6)$ data from three years prior to the acquisition were used.

The second model classified correctly 65%, 68% and 66.5% of the acquired, non-acquired and overall respectively, in the training sample, all significant at the 95% confidence level. The predictions in the holdout sample decreased to 63.5%, 61% and 62.3% respectively. This model using data from one year prior to the acquisition utilised the following ratios: cash flow to total assets (x_1), fixed assets to total assets (x_2), net worth to total assets (x_3), inventory to working capital (x_4), (long term debt plus current liabilities) to cash flow (x_5), quick assets to total liabilities (x_6).

The authors offered three main reasons for not obtaining better predictions: i) the similarity in the financial ratios between acquired and non-acquired Greek firms, ii) the inclusion of different (non-homogenous) sectors in their sample, which they argued made the predictions more difficult than would have been the case if all firms were from a single sector, iii) the use of takeover data from a less developed country like Greece at that period, were takeover practice had appeared only in recent years, hardly favoured the development of highly predictive models. They concluded that probably Greek takeovers were influenced more by strategic (non-financial characteristics) and such variables should be also considered in future studies.

Fairclough and Hunter (1998)

Fairclough and Hunter employed Neural Networks to discriminate between acquired and non-acquired firms. The sample used consisted of 140 acquired firms and a randomly selected group of non-acquired firms (1480 company years of data) from the period 1987 to 1996 that were listed on the London Stock Exchange. This sample was then divided into the following three sub-samples: (1) a state-based training set of 120 firms, randomly selected for model specification, (2) a cross-validation sample of 150 firms randomly drawn from the remaining observations used to evaluate net performance, and (3) the remaining 1350 observations used as a holdout sample.

Motivated by the findings of Palepu (1986) (whose model could classify correctly 80% of acquired firms but only 45.95% of non-acquired firms) the authors attempted to develop a model that would minimise Type II errors (i.e. the misclassification of non-acquired firms, Type I errors being the misclassification of acquired firms). However, by following such a policy, although the best model achieved an overall classification of 94% in the cross-validation sample and 93.33% in the holdout sample, the differences between type I and type II errors were extremely large. The model classified correct only 12.5% of acquired in the cross-validation sample compared to 98.59% of non-acquired, while the corresponding accuracies in the holdout sample were 4.17% and 98.36%.

The authors also compared their model with discriminant analysis. The model developed using discriminant analysis obtained a classification accuracy of 87.5% for acquired firms and 20.74% for non-acquired firms in the holdout sample, and a total classification accuracy of 24.3%. Based on these results the authors concluded that their artificial neural networks was better at ex-ante classification than the discriminant method. However, considering the differences in their obtained classifications between acquired and non-acquired firms the results of the study should be treated with some caution.

Cheh, Weinberg and Yook (1999)

This is another study that investigates the potential of an artificial neural network (ANN) for identifying potential takeover targets and the possibility of yielding positive abnormal returns from investing in the target stocks. Unlike previous studies which found little to support the claim that it is possible to beat the market, Cheh *et al.* found that it was possible to earn daily average returns significantly higher than the market average return based on models' predictions.

Two data sets were used. The first data set consisted of 173 acquired and 1,275 non-acquired firms and was used for model development. Firms were selected from the 1985-1987 time period, that were listed on either the New York or the American Stock Exchange and belonged to non-financial or service industries with at least six years of data available. One of the three sampling years was randomly assigned to each one of the non-acquired firms in order to spread them throughout the same sampling period as the acquired firms. The second data set consisted of 186 acquired firms and 1,338 non-acquired firms listed on the 1988 Compustat Industrial File, and used for validation purposes.

Eight financial variables measuring several aspects of a firm's financial condition (size, leverage, liquidity, growth rate, dividend payout, price-earnings ratio, return on equity, q ratio), and one other variable indicating acquisition activity within industry were used.

A standard feed-forward, back propagation neural network with one hidden layer was designed to accept as input values eight independent variables for a three year period along with the industry code. Of the total of 1,448 firms available for model development a holdout sample of approximately 10% was set aside to be randomly selected for testing during the training phase. Various network parameters were adjusted and the network repeatedly trained and retrained until a Root Mean Square Error of less than 0.10 was achieved, and comparable performance on the holdout set observed. The trained network was then applied to the validation sample set to test its predictive performance. Various network activation levels or decision thresholds were examined to test the model's overall performance. Firms with network activations below the decision threshold were classified as potential takeover targets and included in the portfolio. Two methods were used to describe the network's performance: (1) its misclassification rates, and (2) investment performance of the model portfolio versus a standard benchmark portfolio.

The results show that although the ANN models were able to achieve low Type I errors (i.e identify a firm to be acquired when it is not actually acquired) at all decision thresholds (0.0075-0.0441), Type II (i.e fail to identify an acquired firm) errors were substantial (0.5860-0.8763). To test further the ability of the model, its accuracy was compared with that of a discriminant model. On one hand, the Type I error of the discriminant model was higher than the ANN model's. However, on the other hand, the Type II error rate of the discriminant was lower. This implies that the discriminant analysis is more likely to misclassify firms as acquired than neural network (higher Type I error), but it misses fewer opportunities (lower Type II error).

The authors also investigated whether predictive performance could be improved if the neural network and discriminant analysis were applied together. Two rules were followed. In the first case, firms were classified as targets, if they were identified as targets by discriminant analysis *and* had neural activation less than the decision threshold. In the second case, firms were classified as acquired if they were either identified as targets by discriminant analysis *or* had neural activation less than the decision threshold. The results were promising since the accuracies obtained following the *and* rule were substantially better than those obtained by either method alone.

Finally, the authors examined the ability to earn excess returns when investing in the stock of the firms identified as targets by the ANN model. Stocks were assumed to be purchased at the beginning of 1989 and held until the firms were acquired (for correctly predicted firms that were actually acquired) or at the end of observation period (1993) for non-acquired firms (misclassified firms). Benchmark portfolios, consisting of equal numbers of stocks as the portfolios suggested by the model, in which all stocks were assumed to earn market return were constructed for comparison reasons. Unlikely previous studies that found that it is not possible to beat the market, Cheh *et al.* found that daily average return of the portfolios identified by the neural network were significantly higher than market average return. In addition, when the ANN and discriminant analysis were applied together, the daily average returns were even higher.

Barnes (2000)

In his 2000 study, Barnes compares the logit and discriminant methods using the same sample and the 17 accounting variables as in his 1998 study (Barnes, 1998). Two models were estimated using each technique, a model across all industrial classifications based on industry relative ratios and a set of models estimated separately for each industrial sector.

Barnes came up with 3 overall conclusions. First, although the models predicted better than change, provided that the cut-off was properly selected, their overall forecasting ability over-stated their ability to generate excess returns because they were particularly weak at identifying targets. Actually neither the logit industry-specific nor the general models identified a single target using either of the two alternative cut-off points (i.e. weighted average cut-off and maximization of returns), while the discriminant analysis model classified correct approximately 8% of targets in both cases (i.e. general and specific model). Second, the choice of the statistical technique depended on how well the assumptions of the estimation model fitted the statistical nature of the underlying data. Third, the differences between the distributions of forecasts using the general model and the specific model were greater, suggesting that the choice of data form (industry relative or raw accounting data) may be more important than the choice of statistical technique.

Zopounidis and Doumpos (2002)

In a more recent study, Zopounidis and Doumpos (2002) proposed a new technique based on an iterative binary segmentation procedure, known as Multi-group Hierarchical DIScrimination (MHDIS). The proposed method belongs to the Multicriteria Decision Aid (MCDA) family and is a non-parametric approach to study discriminant problems involving two or more ordered groups of alternatives.

The sample consisted of 30 acquired and 30 non-acquired Greek firms and 10 financial ratios covering various aspects of a firm's financial condition were used to develop the model. These ratios were: earnings before interest and taxes divided by total assets (x_1), cash flow divided by total assets (x_2), net income divided by net worth (x_3), cash divided by total assets (x_4), (long term debt plus current liabilities) divided by total assets (x_5), (long term debt plus current liabilities) divided by cash flow, net worth divided by (net worth plus long term debt) (x_7), quick assets divided by current liabilities (x_8), current assets divided by current liabilities (x_9), and working capital divided by total assets (x_{10}).

The model was developed using data from one year prior to the acquisition (year −1) while years two (year −2) and three (year −3) before the acquisition were used to test its discriminating ability. The model classified correct 58.33% and 61.67% of the firms for years 2 and 3 prior to the acquisition respectively. The authors argued that this poor classification could be attributed to the difficulty of predicting acquisition targets in general, and not necessarily to the inability of the proposed approach as a discrimination method.

To test further the proposed technique its classification accuracy was compared with that of discriminant analysis and another multicriteria method, namely UTADIS (for more details on UTADIS and its comparison with MHDIS, see Chapter 3). The correct classification accuracy obtained using the proposed method was better for all years compared to the one obtained using discriminant analysis. As opposed to the UTADIS method, the classification accuracy under the proposed approach was significantly higher for year −1, equal for year −2 and slightly higher for year −3.

Based on these results the authors concluded that the iterative binary segmentation procedure is able to provide at least favourable comparable results with the ones provided by UTADIS and outperforms discriminant analysis. Nevertheless, while interpreting the results one should keep in mind that the two MCDA models (MHDIS and UTADIS) have many more parameters to be estimated, resulting in an over fitting in the training sample. Although data from previous years were used for models' validation, these data corresponded to the same firms used for model development.

Espahbodi and Espahbodi (2003)

Another recent study that compared a number of methodologies is that of Espahbodi and Espahbodi (2003). The authors proposed the use of recursive partitioning, a non-parametric technique based on pattern recognition, as an alternative technique to discriminate between targets and non-targets, and compared this method with probit, logit, and discriminant analyses.

The authors used a sample of 133 US firms that were taken over during the last six months of 1997. These firms were matched with up to three control firms at random from all the firms listed on the database, based on the fiscal year-end to eliminate the effect of time and SIC codes to reduce the effects of industry-wide factors. Firms were drawn from various sectors, but excluding utilities and financial institutions due to the different conditions under which firms in these industries operate as well as differences in their financial statements. The authors considered a set of 14 financial variables that were based on market and financial statements data. In addition, 4 other non-financial variables were used: (1) existence of poison pills, (2) existence of golden parachutes, (3) percentage ownership of officers and directors, and (4) state legislation.

Both forward and backward stepwise selection techniques were employed to develop the discriminant and logit models. The final discriminant and logit models included four variables whose order and overall significance were exactly the same. The discriminant model classified correctly 63.2% of the targets and 61.3% of the non-targets, while the classification accuracy of the logit was lower with 62.4% and 60.3% accordingly. Since there is no stepwise selection program for probit, the variables that were found to be significant at the logit were used to develop the probit model.

The classification accuracy of the probit model was similar to the other two models with 61.7% of the targets and 61.8% of the non-targets being correctly classified. Table 2.8 presents the coefficients for the three models. The classification accuracies of the recursive partitioning model were 89.5% and 88.1% for the target and non-target groups, thus significantly higher than those of the other three models. The research and development over total firm value, the size, the growth in sales, the price earnings ratio, and the existence of poison pills were the five variables on the basis of which the model separated the acquired and non-acquired firms.

Table 2.8 Coefficients of discriminant, logit and probit Models (Espahbodi & Espahbodi, 2003)

Variables	Discriminant	Logit	Probit
Free Cash Flow over total Assets	1.099	1.428	0.813
	(7.08)	(2.76)	(2.86)
Existence of golden parachutes	0.701	0.612	0.366
	(4.10)	(1.95)	(1.91)
State of Delaware incorporation dummy	0.312	0.340	0.204
variable	(2.26)	(1.61)	(1.65)
Market Value of Equity over total firm value	-0.605	-0.606	-0.353
	(1.72)	(-1.36)	(-1.33)
Constant	0.235	-0.811	-0.508

Notes: t-values in parentheses (F-values in the case of discriminant)

The four models were validated using a holdout sample consisting of 38 firms taken over in the first two months of 1998 and a random sample of 200 non-acquired firms. The classification accuracies (respectively for recursive partitioning, discriminant, logit and probit models) were approximately 66%, 53%, 55%, 55% for target firms, and 66%, 51%, 52%, 52% for non-target firms.

Tartari, Doumpos, Baourakis, Zopounidis (2003)

Following recent studies in bankruptcy prediction that attempted to develop integrated prediction models (e.g. Jo and Han, 1996; McKee and Lensberg, 2002), Tartari *et al.* (2003) were the first to propose such a technique for the prediction of acquisition targets. Although Cheh *et al.* (1999) had used a simple *and/or* rule to combine ANN with discriminant analysis, Tartari *et al.* attempt to accomplish such a combination using a more sophisticated approach. Thus, unlike previous studies that have focused on an appropriate methodology to develop a prediction model and in some cases offered a comparison with other techniques to investigate its efficiency, this study by contrast proposes the integration of different methods using a stacked generalisation approach. This is one of the two approaches to integration of models that is described further and employed in our empirical investigation (Chapter 6).

The sample used by Tartari *et al.* consisted of 48 UK firms, selected from 19 industries/sectors, acquired during 2001 and 48 non-acquired firms matched by principal business activity, asset size, sales volume and number of employees. Twenty-three financial ratios measuring profitability, liquidity and solvency and managerial performance were calculated for each firm for up to three years prior to the acquisition (1998-2000). Factor analysis was then used to account for any multicollinearity among the financial ratios, which resulted in nine factors explaining more than 77% of the total variance. The following ratios had the highest loadings in the 9 factors and were used further in model development: (1) current assets divided by current liabilities, (2) net income divided by net fixed assets, (3) long-term liabilities divided by (long term-liabilities plus net worth), (4) gross profit divided by total assets, (5) total liabilities divided by working capital, (6) cash flow divided by total assets, (7) inventories divided by current assets, (8) current liabilities divided by net worth, and (9) working capital divided by working capital required.

Four classification methods, namely linear discriminant analysis (LDA), probabilistic neural networks (PNN), rough sets theory, and the UTADIS multicriteria decision aid method, originating from different quantitative disciplines (i.e. statistics, neural networks, rule induction, multicriteria analysis) were used at a first stage to develop individual models. The most recent year (2000) was used as a training sample while the data for the other two years (1998 and 1999) were used to test the generalising performance of the proposed integration approach. An 8-fold cross validation approach was employed to develop the base models using the four methods. The obtained classifications of the firms were then used as a training sample for the development of a stacked generalisation model for the prediction of acquisitions targets. The development of the stacked model was performed using the UTADIS method that combined (at a meta-level) the group assignments of all the four methods considered in the analysis. The use of other methods to develop the combined model was also examined; nevertheless the results were inferior to those obtained with UTADIS. Table 2.9 presents the classification results obtained using the four methods and the stacked model.

Table 2.9 - Classification results (overall correct rate in %) in the study of Tartari *et al.* (2003)

Methods	2000 (training)	1999	1998
LDA	58.33	50.00	54.17
PNN	100.00	58.33	62.50
Rough Sets	100.00	57.29	58.33
UTADIS	71.87	57.29	55.21
Stacked model	88.54	60.42	63.54

It becomes immediately apparent that the stacked model performed better (in terms of the overall correct accuracy rate) than any of the four methods upon which it was based, throughout all years of the analysis. Furthermore, the results indicated that the stacked model provided significant reductions in the overall error rate compared to LDA, rough sets and UTADIS, although less significant compared to PNN.

The authors concluded that future research needs to be directed to an investigation of the similarities and differences between the assignments made by the models developed using the different classification models and the use of alternative approaches for models integration such as bagging and boosting algorithms.

Doumpos, Kosmidou, Pasiouras (2004)

Doumpos *et al.* (2004) illustrate the use of UTADIS method to develop a model for the prediction of UK acquisition targets. The classification ability of the UTADIS model was compared against the classification ability of models developed using discriminant analysis (DA), logistic regression (LR) and artificial neural networks (ANN).

The sample included 76 firms operating in manufacturing, construction, production, and mining-quarrying-extraction industries that were acquired during the period 2000-2002. These firms were matched by industry and size with 76 non-acquired firms. Thus, the total sample consisted of 152 firms.

Twenty-nine financial ratios were initial candidates for model development, representing profitability, efficiency, activity, financial leverage, liquidity and growth. To avoid problems associated with dimensionality and multicollinearity, the authors sought to reduce the number of variables using a t-test. They argued that although factor analysis provided a reduced number of distinct factors, they do not provide any useful information about the importance of individual variables in a specific research problem. It is possible, using factor analysis, that one may exclude variables that are significant in terms of discriminating the firms between the two groups (acquired and non-acquired). Using the t-test, the following six variables were found to be significant at the 5% level: current ratio, solvency ratio, gearing, debtors collection period, net assets turnover and salaries divided by turnover. The correlation between these six variables were low to moderate, hence allowing the use of all 6 variables in model development.

The UTADIS model was first developed using data drawn from the most recent year prior to the acquisition (i.e. year -1). The results showed that distinction between acquired and non-acquired was primarily based on the gearing ratio, the net assets turnover and the salaries to turnover ratio. The developed model was then applied to data from 2 and 3 years prior to the acquisition (years −2 and −3). The average accuracies were 74.34% and 78.95% respectively.

The models developed using DA, LR and ANN, were tested following the same procedure. More specifically, based on the same 6 ratios, the models were developed using the sample data from one year prior to the acquisition and then applied on the data of the years −2 and −3. The specification for the ANN model was achieved through a trial and error process involving several experimentations that led to the use of a back propagation, feed-forward architecture with one hidden layer of six nodes. The results showed that the UTADIS method outperformed both

DA and LR, and were found comparable or better than those of ANN when tested using data from years –2 and –3.

While comparing the results of different methods in this study, one should note that UTADIS and ANN approaches are non-parametric and both significantly different from each other as well as from DA and LR methods, resulting in a-priori data fitting superiority in the training sample (year –1). Although the authors assume that by using data from years –2 and –3 for testing they overcome this problem, it is also possible that this *a-priori* fitting might not be totally eliminated when using such a back-testing analysis to compare the models, as variables come from the same firms used for training.

2.5 Conclusions

This section has reviewed a good number of empirical studies that have developed models for the prediction of acquisition targets. A number of conclusions can be drawn.

(1) The majority of these studies have employed discriminant or logit analysis and only more recently have studies emerged employing alternative classification techniques (i.e. neural networks, multicriteria decision aid, rough sets, *etc.*). Consequently, as Espahbodi and Espahbodi (2003) point out, not many have attempted to compare the ability of various classification procedures in predicting corporate takeovers. In this context, our knowledge regarding whether some classification methods may be more effective (in terms of classification accuracy) than others appears to be quite limited. For example, on the basis of our literature review, there are only eight studies that offer a comparison of various methods, of which four compare just two methods while the remaining 4 compare either 3 or 4 methods. At the same time, drawing conclusions among studies is not possible since researchers usually use different independent variables and examine different time periods, industries, countries, *etc.*; while validation techniques used to access the ability of the models also differ across studies. In our empirical study, we will attempt to answer the question whether model

development technique has an impact on prediction ability. To accomplish this task, we compare seven different methodologies, which are almost double in number compared to most previous studies did. In addition, two of these methodologies have not been previously employed for the development of acquisition prediction models.

(2) So far, there has been only one study (Tartari *et al.*, 2003) in the literature on the prediction of acquisition targets that has attempted to combine various methods, despite the promising results of integrated methods in similar financial problems like credit scoring (e.g. Doumpos, 2002; Lee *et al.*, 2002) and bankruptcy prediction (e.g. McKee and Lensberg, 2002). As noted earlier, our empirical study will employ the stacked generalisation method of Tartari *et al.* (2003), as well as an additional technique, the majority voting rule (Huang and Suen, 1993). Thus we will not only examine whether integration methods leads to better classification results but also offer a comparison of prediction models based on different methods of integration.

(3) To our best knowledge all previous studies on the prediction of acquisition targets have developed models for non-financial sectors. However, the financial characteristics of the banking sector are different from those of other industries. Thus models developed for other industries cannot be readily applied for the prediction of bank acquisition targets, and therefore it is necessary to develop M&As targets prediction models specifically for the banking industry.

(4) There appears to be a lack of coherence about the sample used to develop and validate the prediction models. After the criticism of Palepu (1986), many researchers have developed and/or validated their models using unequal samples of acquired and non-acquired firms. At the same time, many researchers continued to use matched samples. It is obvious that both procedures have advantages and disadvantages. However, no study has empirically examined whether the classification accuracy of a model tested in a matched sample is significantly different from that of the same model tested in an unequal sample. The present study will

compare the classification ability of the developed models by validating them in equal and un-equal holdout samples.

(5) Finally, all studies reviewed above have examined individual countries, with the majority of them focusing on the US and UK market. To our knowledge there exists no study that seeks to develop models for prediction based on firm level data across countries. Our empirical study is the first that attempts the development of prediction models with a sample of banks drawn from 15 EU countries.

Chapter 3

Methodological Framework for the Development of Acquisition Targets Prediction Model

3.1 Introduction

The prediction of acquisition targets is essentially an application of classification techniques, which classify firms into two groups (i.e. acquired and non-acquired). Other well-known areas of classification in finance and accounting are bankruptcy prediction, credit risk assessment, and auditing. In general in any classification task, there is a set $X = \{x_1, x_2, ... x_n\}$ of n alternatives (e.g. firms) described over a set $g = \{g_1, g_2, ... g_m\}$ of m independent variables (e.g. financial ratios) to be classified into a set $C = \{C_1, C_2, ... C_q\}$ of q predefined groups. The classification problem refers to the development of a model that will assign the alternatives into the predefined groups as accurately as possible. The process is not automatic. As shown in Figure 3.1, the process for the development of acquisition prediction models consists of four main steps: (i) construction of an observation set, (ii) selection of input variables, (iii) selection of classification methods to develop the model, and (iv) evaluation of the developed model. This methodological framework is adopted in this study and, consequently, in this chapter we seek to explain each of these steps in detail. Thus, section 3.2 deals with the construction of sample and examines issues such as the definition of acquisition, the splitting of sample into training and testing sub-samples, and the use of equal or unequal sub-samples of acquired and non-acquired firms for training and testing. Section 3.3 explains the procedures for dealing with variables selection and summarises the methods for reducing and selecting input variables from a potentially large data set of candidate variables for model development. Section 3.4 presents methods for developing prediction models for acquisition targets, covering classical statistical and econometric methods, operational research methods, and machine learning methods. Finally, section 3.5 explores issues dealing with the evaluation and assessment of classification methods. It should be noted that some of the issues raised above were already discussed in Chapter 2, but the aim of this chapter is to illustrate the procedures.

3.2 Sampling Considerations

3.2.1 Definition of acquisitions

There are two issues relevant to the definition of acquisitions that affect the construction of the sample. The first is related to the percentage of ownership that is subject to the investment attempt. The second is whether both successful and unsuccessful attempts will be ultimately characterised as acquisitions. These two issues are discussed below.

Practitioners and academics often use the words "mergers" and "acquisitions" interchangeably or refer to the acronym M&As without actually distinguishing between these two events. In principle, a merger between two firms A and B occurs when these two firms amalgamate to form a new legal entity C, while an acquisition occurs when firm A buys part of firm B. An acquisition can take one of the following three forms: full (i.e. when A acquires 100% of B), majority (i.e. when A acquires between 50.01% and 99.99% of B), and minority (when A acquires less than 50% of B). It is obvious that the choice of which definition of "acquisition" to adapt will influence the construction of the sample and subsequently the development of the model.

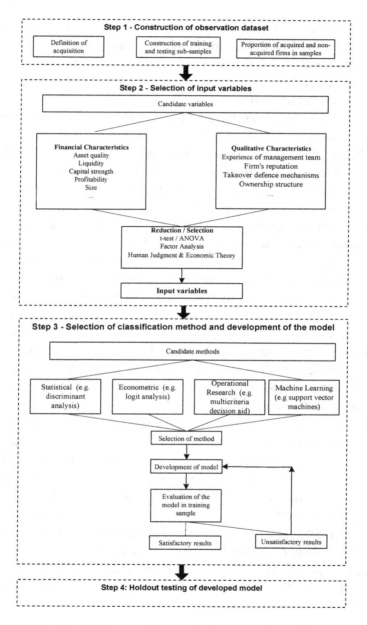

Figure 3.1 Methodological framework for the development of acquisition targets prediction models

For example, if we decide to classify as "acquired" firms only those that were involved in full acquisitions, then firms involved in majority acquisitions will be considered as non-acquired. Nevertheless, the characteristics of these firms may resemble those of the "acquired" firms rather than the "non-acquired" ones.

Most of the studies examined in Chapter 2 had samples in which acquired firms were involved in majority or full acquisitions. Nevertheless, there are a few exceptions such as Hasbrouck (1985) and Bartley and Boardman (1990) that considered as acquisitions investment attempts as low as 5% of ownership. Bartley and Boardman (1990) argue that there two reasons for which investment attempts that do not seek a controlling ownership interest need to be considered. First, attempts to gain control of a firm may involve a series of investments that are ultimately intended to achieve control. Consequently, any dichotomy of large investment attempts and takeover attempts is arbitrary since it is not possible to be confident that an investment attempt, seeking less than 50% ownership is not part of a takeover attempt. Second, if the model is to be used by investors to form portfolios, since there is evidence that positive abnormal returns are produced by investment attempts for as little as five percent of a company's outstanding stock (Bradley et al., 1983; Harris and Risk, 1983), then the model should not be limited to investments above 50%.

Another issue is whether firms subject to both successful and unsuccessful acquisition attempts should be considered as acquired. Most of the studies classify successful acquisitions as acquired and unsuccessful acquisitions as non-acquired. However, some studies (e.g. Bartley and Boardman, 1990; Barnes, 2000) examine attempted acquisitions without regard to their ultimate outcome. Bartley and Boardman (1990) justify their choice by arguing that the success of an acquisition attempt is mostly dependent on factors others than the financial characteristics of the target firm, and a model for predicting successful acquisitions that includes only financial data for successful acquisitions can be miss-specified.

3.2.2 Training and testing samples

An important issue of concern in evaluating the classification ability of a prediction model is to ensure that it has not over-fit on the training (estimation) dataset. As Stein (2002) notes, "A model without sufficient validation may only be a hypothesis". Prior research shows that when classification models are used to reclassify the observations of the training sample, the classification accuracies are "normally" biased upward. Thus, it is necessary to classify a set of observations that are not used during the development of the model, using some kind of testing sample.

Although the measures of model's performance will be discussed in a latter section, it is necessary to examine at this point how we can split the data set into training and testing samples. Taking into account the nature of the problem and the availability of data, the decision maker can consider a number of alternative techniques. The simplest technique for "honestly" estimating error rates is using the holdout method that represents a single train-and-test experiment. Re-sampling techniques such as cross-validation, jack-knife and bootstrap also exist that obviate the need for a separate test sample. However, a drawback of resampling techniques is that they cannot take population drifting into account.

3.2.2.1 Holdout sample

As mentioned above, the simplest way of avoiding the bias in the error rate, is to use a holdout sample as considered by Highleyman (1962) among others. Studies in the prediction of acquisition targets have used holdout samples either from the same period (Barnes, 1990) or from a future period (Barnes, 2000; Espahbodi & Espahbodi, 2003). Using a future period entails the case of a drifting population (i.e. change of population over time) and allows determining if the variables in the prediction model and their coefficients remain stable over other time periods[1].

---

[1] The case of drifting population and its relevance to the prediction of acquisitions will be discussed more detailed in section 3.2.2.3.

If a holdout sample from the same period is used, then all available cases (or data) are randomly split into training and testing samples. The classification model is developed using the data from the training sub-sample and then tested on the holdout sub-sample.

When a holdout sample from a future period is used, all available cases (data) are first ordered by time. Then the training cases are taken from a given period (up to a specified time), and the testing cases are taken from the following period. The length of the time periods for both training and testing samples depends on the knowledge of the application and the availability of data. Because the population may change with time, this approach provides a closer simulation of the task of prediction, train from the current period to predict a future period.

Generally speaking the larger the training sample, the better the classifier, although the effect begins to diminish after a certain volume of training data. On the other hand, the larger the testing sample, the more accurate is the error rate estimation. Owing to constrained data availability in any real world application, the researchers is therefore faced with the following dilemma: to get a good classification model, by using as much of the data as possible for training or to get a good error estimate by using as much of it as possible for validation. Since a classification model developed with insufficient cases will generally lead to an inaccurate model, the majority of cases are usually used for training and the remainder for testing. Typically 2/3 of the total sample is used for training and 1/3 for testing (Weiss and Kulikowski, 1991).

3.2.2.2 Resampling techniques

It was mentioned above that three well known resampling techniques are the jack-knife, the bootstrap and the k-fold cross validation. Quenouille (1949) proposed a technique, latter named the jack-knife, to estimate the bias of an estimator by deleting one element each time from the original data set and recalculating the estimator based on the rest of the data. The bootstrap, introduced by Efron (1979) and investigated further in a series of articles (Efron, 1981a,b, 1982, 1983, 1985, 1987, 1990), is an estimation technique that uses sampling with replacement to form the training set. Today it is widely used for the estimation of classification error rates, the selection of classification models, as well as for the comparison of classification methods (Doumpos and Zopounidis, 2002a). There are numerous bootstrap estimators, but the two that so far have yielded the best results for classification are known as the e0 and the .632 bootstrap. Those interested in most detailed explanations and proofs for the jack-knife and bootstrap techniques can find an excellent discussion in Efron (1982), who exhibits the close theoretical relationship between them, as well as Shao and Tu (1995) who provide a systematic introduction to the theory of the jack-knife, the bootstrap and other resampling methods.

We now turn to k-fold cross validation technique that will be used in the empirical part of the study. One way of almost eliminating the bias in the apparent error rate is through the leave-one-out technique (like jack-knife, although the rationale is different) as described by Lachenbruch and Mickey (1968) or through cross validation as discussed in a wider context by Stone (1974) and Geisser (1975). In general, during a k-fold cross-validation the complete sample X, consisting of n observations (e.g. firms), is initially randomly split into k mutually exclusive sub-samples (folds) $X_1, X_2, \ldots, X_k$ of approximately equal size. Afterwards, k models are developed, with each fold in turn used for validation and the remainder left for training (i.e. estimation). The average error rate over all k folds is known as the cross-validated error rate. Typically, the number of folds k ranges between 1 and 20, although it can also be set equal to n (in the case of leave-one-out cross-validation), but the latter can be computationally expensive with large samples. The most widely used value for k in cross-validation is 10 (thus known as 10-fold cross-validation). The 10-fold cross validation process is best described as follows (see Abrahams, 2004):

Step 1: The data are randomly split into 10 sub-samples (folds)

Step 2: In each one of the 10 rounds, 9 sub-samples are used for training and one for validation.

Step 3: When all 10 rounds are completed, the average error is used to access the classification accuracy of the developed model. The standard deviation of these estimates can also be calculated to obtain a confidence interval for the overall estimate.

Figure 3.2 below provides a schematic presentation of Rounds 1-10.

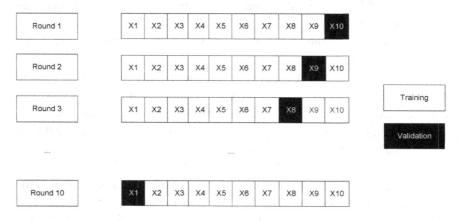

Figure 3.2   A 10-fold cross validation procedure

3.2.2.3 Population drift

Classification ability is likely to overstate predictive ability as suggested by those studies that use a holdout sample from a latter non-overlapping period (Taffler, 1982). Thus a superior approach would require that the model be validated against a future period, as this approach more closely reflects a "real world" setting. As Espahbodi and Espahbodi (2003) state "After all, *the real test of a classification model and its practical usefulness is its ability to classify objects correctly in the future. While cross-validation and bootstrapping techniques reduce the over-fitting bias, they do not indicate the usefulness of a model in the future*" (p. 571).

If the models are stable then their classification ability will equal their predictive ability (Barnes, 1999). However, there are many reasons why the model may not be stable over time. As Barnes (1990) points out, given inflationary effects, technological and numerous other reasons, including changing accounting policies, it is unreasonable to expect the distributional cross-sectional parameters of financial ratios to be stable over time.

Business failure models have been found to be highly unstable and their predictive accuracy is thereby considerably reduced (Mensah, 1984; Wood & Piesse, 1987; Barnes, 1987; Platt and Platt, 1990). Barnes (1999) suggests that if the stability of the model is a problem in the business failure prediction studies, this is likely to be even a greater problem in takeovers and mergers for three reasons. First, although failing firms have some general and basic financial characteristics during the period of failure, such a consistency both across firms and across time as to the characteristics of targets may not be the case. Second, stability assumes consistency of takeover reasons and motivations. However, there are many different motives and reasons for which M&As occur over the same period and in similar industries. Finally, stability also assumes that the parameters of the explanatory variables (accounting ratios), are stable across industries, which is highly unlikely.

3.2.3 Proportion of acquired and non-acquired firms in sample

We now turn to three other issues, related to sampling, that have received a lot of attention in the acquisitions (and bankruptcy) prediction literature. These are: (i) the proportion of acquired to non-acquired firms (bankrupt/non-bankrupt, respectively) that should be used in the training sample, (ii) the proportion of acquired to non-acquired firms that should be used in testing samples, and (iii) the criteria on which acquired and non-acquired banks could be matched.

(i) Groups' proportions in training sample

The majority of the studies on the prediction of acquisitions have used training samples with equal numbers of acquired and non-acquired firms, known as state or choice based sample. There are two primary reasons for following this procedure. The first is the lower cost of gathering data compared to an unmatched sample (Zmijewski, 1984; Bartley and

Boardman, 1990). The second and most important is that a state based sample provides higher information content than a random sample (Cosslett, 1981; Palepu, 1986). Given that the number of acquired firms is relatively small compared to non-acquired, random sampling will consequently result in a sample comprising of many non-acquired firms and only a few (if any) acquired firms, which from an estimating procedure perspective, is inefficient[2]. Thus, it is essential to select the sample in a way that will ensure that acquired firms in the training sample represent an adequate proportion. Manski and Lerman (1977) and Manski and McFadden (1981) point out that such a state based sample will provide more efficient estimates than a random sample of the same size, while Cosslett (1981) characterises such a sample as a close-to-optimum design.

However, a state-based sample is not representative of the true population if as mentioned above, non-acquired firms exceed by far the acquired ones. As Zmijewski (1984) and Palepu (1986) point out, this will result in biased parameter estimates when the models are developed with estimation techniques that assume random sampling, such as logit and probit analysis. Thus, alternative or adjusted techniques are required to estimate unbiased parameters (Zmijewski, 1984). For example, Palepu (1986) proposed a conditional maximum likelihood estimator in his study. Alternatively, rather than using a conditional maximum likelihood estimator, one can adjust the constant term[3] (Madalla, 1983) or the cut-off probability appropriately to take into account the bias introduced by the state-based estimation sample (Palepu, 1986; Espahbodi & Espahbodi, 2003).

---

[2] See Palepu (1986) and Barnes (1990).

[3] Madalla (1983) has shown that the coefficients are not affected, when a state based sample is being used instead of a random sample. In fact, it is only the constant term that differs by a known value γ. This value can be calculated as follows: $\gamma = \ln P_1 - \ln P_2$, where P_1 and P_2 are the proportions sample from acquired and non-acquired groups respectively.

(ii) Groups' proportions in testing sample

Palepu (1986) also criticised previous studies for using equal samples during testing and argued that such samples fail to represent the model's ability to predict targets. He demonstrated that if Stevens (1973) had used an unequal sample for testing, the overall prediction accuracy of his model would have been 56% instead of 70% as reported by Stevens. Palepu's argument, although correct, may not be as simple, as the difference in the prediction ability of the model could be attributed to the performance measure that was used (i.e. overall accuracy), which is very sensitive to the prevalence of positive cases (i.e. targets) as a percentage of the total sample[4]. For example, in the case of Stevens, using the numbers that Palepu assumed[5], the correct classification accuracy for targets remained 85%, as did the correct classification accuracy for non-targets (55%). Thus, if one had used either of these two measures or the average accuracy of two groups (i.e. calculated on a 50:50 sample[6]) the results would have remained unchanged. Of course, one could also argue that these measures remain unchanged because of the assumptions Palepu made.

(iii) Matching criteria

We now turn to the dilemma of choosing characteristics on which acquired and non-acquired banks should be matched. The matching criteria considered in previous studies were time, size, and industry. Among these, time is considered the most innocuous one (Hasbrouck, 1985) and has been used by almost all the researchers. However, in studies not concerned with merger waves, it seems reasonable to match an acquired firm with a non-acquired firm on the basis of time if

---

[4] This and other issues relative to models' performance measures are discussed in more detail in section 3.5.

[5] Palepu simply assumed that the sample of Stevens could consist of a total of 1,000 firms, 40 targets and 960 non-targets, rather than 40 targets and 40-non targets as used by Stevens, and recalculated the overall accuracy holding the individual groups accuracies constant.

[6] See for example Wilson et al. (1999); Espahbodi and Esphabodi (2003); Doumpos and Pasiouras (2004).

observations are likely to be slowly changing or trending. Furthermore, samples for the development and testing of prediction models are usually pooled along many years and, as Barnes (1990) argues, accounting data are rather more volatile particularly around the period of acquisitions.

Many researchers have, in addition to time, matched firms either by industry (e.g. Espahbodi and Espahbodi, 2003) or size (e.g. Stevens, 1973) or both industry and size (e.g. Barnes, 1990), while Hasbrouck (1985) matched cases separately by industry and size. Bartley and Boardman (1990) argue that matching cases by industry, size or other criterion may be an appropriate control technique when the research objective is to examine the statistical significance of individual causal variables, while, additionally, given the lack of a theoretical model, the choice of variables to be matched is inherently arbitrary. Furthermore, as they point out in an earlier study (Bartley and Boardman, 1986) matching firms by industry and size reduces the classificatory power of the discriminant models.

Another important issue, noted by Hasbrouck (1985), is that if a characteristic is used as a matching criterion, then analysis of its effects will not be possible. For example, matching by size prevents analysis of the effects of size on the likelihood of acquisition. In a similar manner, use of an industry-matched sample will exclude from the analysis any industry-specific effects.

3.3 Variables Selection Process

Barnes (2000) points out that the problem for the analyst who attempts to forecast M&As is simply a matter of identifying the best explanatory/predictive variables. Consequently, the second step in the development of an empirical prediction model is the selection of input variables. Unfortunately, financial theories do not offer much by way of discriminating between the numerous variables regarded as potential candidates in model development.

There are, nevertheless, various factors that should be examined, since the reasons that lead firms to merge with or acquire other firms vary. As outlined in Chapter 1, the causes of M&As can be attributed to internal and external factors. Researchers have mainly used financial ratios to account for these reasons and consequently the majority of the acquisition prediction models are based on the financial characteristics of firms. The common assumption underlying these models is that fundamental economic factors (e.g. inflation, interest rates, etc) and the characteristics of the firm (e.g. management quality, sector, ownership, etc) are reflected in firm's financial statements. Similarly to bankruptcy prediction models, the established practice for acquisitions prediction models is to use financial ratios as an input.

A question that emerges when attempting to select financial ratios for empirical research is what ratios, among the hundreds, should be used? Given the large number of possible ratios, it is important to reduce the list of ratios that enter the final model selection process. Variables selection has long been an active research topic in statistics and pattern recognition. It is important that it can simplify the data description, which results in an easier understanding of problems, and better and faster problem solving. However, there is no easy way to determine how many ratios a particular model should contain. Too few and the model will not capture all the relevant information. Too many and the model will be overfitting the training sample, but under-perform in a holdout sample, and will most likely have onerous data input requirements. As Hamer (1983) mentioned, the variable set should be constructed on the basis of (a) minimising the cost of data collection and (b) maximising the model applicability.

Huberty (1994) suggests three variable screening techniques that should be used: logical screening (i.e. financial theory and human judgement), statistical screening (i.e. test of differences of two group means such as ANOVA) and dimension reduction (i.e. factor analysis). All these techniques have been used in past studies and are outlined below.

3.3.1 Financial theory and human judgement

In this case, the selection of variables is based on the most frequently suggested takeover hypotheses. Well-known studies that followed this procedure for variables selection are Palepu (1986), Powell (1997, 2001),

Barnes (1998, 2000), Kim and Arbel (1998), Cudd and Duggal (2000). However, in most cases, models developed with variables based on this approach have had rather low prediction ability. Powell (1997) mentions two potential explanations for this. The first is that these models are based upon takeover theories that are prevalent in the literature but have little or no validity. The second is that the empirical constructs used fail to capture the implications underlying the theories. Furthermore, some researchers select the variables on the basis of previous empirical findings (e.g. Belkaoui, 1978; Meador et al., 1996) or upon an effort to cover most aspects of a firm's financial condition (e.g. Cheh et al., 1999; Zopounidis and Doumpos, 2002).

3.3.2 Univariate statistical tests of mean differences

To classify the acquired and non-acquired firms effectively, the variables should be able to discriminate between these two groups. Thus, the aim is to make a determination as to what are the critical factors that distinguish the two groups of banks. In other words, to reveal what is different between an acquired and non-acquired bank?

In practice, statistical tests (e.g. t-test, ANOVA, Kruskal-Wallis) are used to compare, on a univariate basis, the financial characteristics of the two groups of acquired and non-acquired firms. The purpose is to analyse individual ratios to examine the discriminating power of many popular candidates for inclusion in the model. In this case, the rule of thumb is to keep the number of variables small and exclude a variable unless its discriminating power is statistically significant (Kocagil et al., 2002). There are at least two ways of determining the discriminating power of predictors in a univariate context (i.e. parametric or non-parametric statistical tests).

The application of a t-test assumes that the data have been derived from normal distributions with equal variance. If this assumption is not valid (in most cases normality does not hold when using financial ratios), then non-parametric tests could be used instead (which do not make such an assumption).

The Kolmogorov-Smirnov (K-S) test is typically used to test for normality of the underlying distribution. This test compares the cumulative probabilities of values in the data set with the cumulative probabilities of the same values in a specified theoretical normal distribution. If the discrepancy is sufficiently large, the test indicates that the data are not well fitted by the theoretical distribution. In other words, the K-S test examines the null hypothesis that the sample has been drawn from a normal distribution.

Once the variables that differ significantly between the two groups have been identified, a correlation analysis can be employed. If two variables are highly correlated, there is multicollinearity and one of them might be dropped from the analysis. Including highly correlated ratios when estimating the optimal weights for a model without careful attention to address the multicollinearity issue can result in imprecise estimates of the weights, which may result in a poor performance of a model when applied outside of the training sample (Kocagil et al., 2002). After all, if two variables measure essentially the same characteristic, there is no reason to enter both into the analysis.

3.3.3 *Factor analysis*

The technique of factor analysis was first described by Spearman in 1904. It is a multivariate statistical method, designed to reduce the number of variables to a small number of factors that are linear combinations of the initial variables. Variables that are correlated with one another but largely independent of other subsets of variables are combined into factors. The first factor accounts for as much variation in the data as possible. Each succeeding factor accounts for as much as variation as possible that is not already accounted for by proceeding factors. In general, the univariate correlations between different factors can be expected to be low. By selecting one "representative" ratio from each factor, the choice can be limited to ratios, which depict the information content of the larger set of ratios. The fundamental idea that underlines factor analysis is shown in Figure 3.3, where eleven variables are clustered into four separate factors. Variables g_1, g_4, g_5, g_8 are clustered together, which means that they are highly correlated with one another and represent a factor. In a similar manner, variables g_3 and g_7 represent another factor, while g_2, g_6, g_9 define a third factor. Finally, variables g_{10} and g_{11} represent the last factor. Thus, by choosing each factor, the analyst will obtain almost as much information as is inherent in the original nine variables. Of course, the present example may be too simple since in practice the derived factors are not so clear-cut as it is presented in Figure 3.3. The reason is that there might be some overlap between the factors since some of the original variables may have some degree of correlation with some of the other variables. However, factors are distinguished by the fact that the set of variables defining one factor are more highly correlated with each another than they are with the variables defining other factors.

Stevens (1973) was the first to apply factor analysis developing a model for the prediction of acquisition targets, followed by Barnes (1990), Kira and Morin (1993), Zanakis and Zopounidis (1997), and Tartari et al. (2003) among others.

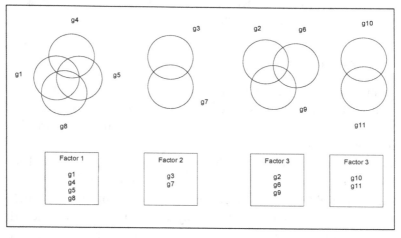

Figure 3.3 An example of eleven variables reduced to four factors

3.4 Method Selection

A variety of classification methodologies are available for developing prediction models. This section discusses seven different methodologies that are implemented in the empirical study. These methodologies originate from different disciplines; including statistics, econometrics, operational research, and machine learning.

3.4.1 Discriminant analysis

Discriminant Analysis (DA) was initially proposed by Fisher (1936) in the 1930s and was the first multivariate statistical classification technique. Although the initial study of discriminant analysis involved applications in biological and medical sciences, in recent years it has become increasingly popular in disciplines such as education, engineering, psychology and finance. Consequently, DA has become the most commonly discussed and widely used statistical technique in modeling classification tasks (Lee et al., 1999).

In the field of finance, DA was introduced by Altman (1968) who used it to develop a bankruptcy prediction model. His work motivated many other researchers to apply DA in various other classification problems in finance, such as credit scoring (Lane, 1972), venture capital decisions (Laitinen, 1992) and prediction of acquisitions (Simkowitz and Monroe, 1971; Tzoannos and Samuels, 1972; Stevens, 1973; Belkaoui, 1973; Rege, 1984; Wansley, 1984; Bartley and Boardman, 1990; Barnes, 1990; Kira and Morin, 1993).

The DA method seeks to obtain a linear combination of the independent variables whose objective is to classify observations into mutually exclusive groups as accurately as possible by maximising the ratio of among-groups to within-groups variance. In the case of acquisition prediction, assume there are two groups of firms (acquired and non-acquired), and m variables, $g_1, g_2, ..., g_m$, for each firm i. The DA method therefore estimates a discriminant function of the following form:

$$D_x = p_0 + p_1 g_1 + p_2 g_2 + ... + p_m g_m$$

where D_x is the score (for a firm i), p_0 is the intercept term and p_j ($j=1,...,m$) represent the slope coefficients associated with the independent variables g_j ($j=1, ..., m$) for each firm.

A cut-off point is calculated according to the a-priori probabilities of group membership and the costs of misclassification. In the final step, each firm is classified into the acquired or the non-acquired firms group, depending on its score and the cut-off point. Firms with discriminant scores greater than the cut-off point are classified into the one group, while firms with discriminant scores less than the cut-off point are classified into the other group. Alternatively, firms can be classified on the basis of the probability of belonging to one of the groups and a cut-off probability point.

The estimation of the constant term and the discriminant coefficients is based on two major assumptions: (a) the independent variables follow a multivariate normal distribution, and (b) the variance-covariance matrices for all groups are equal. Alternatively, a Quadratic Discriminant Analysis (QDA) can be employed when the covariance matrices of the given populations are not equal.

3.4.2 Logit analysis

The Logit method that originates from the field of econometrics has been applied to acquisition predictions by various researchers (e.g. Dietrich and Sorensen, 1984; Palepu, 1986; Ambrose and Megginson, 1992; Meador et al., 1996; Powell, 1997; Cudd and Duggal, 2000).

In the logit analysis the probability of a firm to be acquired is based on a set of independent variables is given by the following function:

$$P_i = \left(\frac{1}{1 + e^{-Z_i}} \right)$$

where

$$Z_i = \ln\left(\frac{P_i}{1 - P_i} \right) = p_0 + p_1 g_1 + p_2 g_2 + \ldots + p_m g_{m,} + \varepsilon_i$$

is the probability that firm i will be acquired, p_0 is the intercept term and p_j ($j = 1,...,m$) represents the coefficients associated with the corresponding independent variables g_j ($j = 1,...,m$) for each firm.

The coefficient estimates are obtained by regression that involves maximising a log-likelihood function (under the usual normality assumption of the random disturbances). The model is then used to estimate the group-membership probabilities for all firms under consideration. The firm is classified as acquired or non-acquired using an optimal cut-off point, attempting to minimise type I and type II errors. For example, in a two group classification problem like the one examined here, one can impose a classification rule of the following form: "classify a firm i into group 1 (acquired) if P_i>cut-off probability, otherwise classify the firm into group 2 (non-acquired). Thus, if the probability of acquisition for a firm is greater than the optimum cut-off point, the predicted firm is classified into the acquired group, otherwise into the non-acquired group. An approach that is commonly used in practice is to set the cut-off point equal to 0.5. Under this classification rule, firms with estimated probability higher than 0.5 are classified as acquired, while those with estimated probability lower than 0.5 are classified as non-acquired. Palepu (1986) proposed the empirical estimation of the optimum cut-off point. Under the classification rule of Palepu, the cut-off point is where the conditional marginal probability densities for acquired and non-acquired banks are equal and is equivalent to minimising the total error probabilities. As an alternative Barnes (1998) proposed the use of a maximization of returns cut-off or a weighted cut-off point based on historical data. Finally, Powell (2001) experimented with various cut-off points and selected the one with the highest ratio of number of targets to the total number of firms in the portfolio.

3.4.3 UTilités Additives DIScriminantes (UTADIS)

The UTADIS multicriteria decision aid method employs the framework of preference disaggregation analysis[7] for the development of an additive utility function that is used to score the firms and decide upon their classification. The UTADIS method has been successfully applied in several fields of finance, such as bankruptcy (Zopounidis and Doumpos, 1999a,b; Doumpos and Zopounidis; 2002a), credit risk (Doumpos and Pasiouras, 2004), auditing (Spathis et. al. 2002, 2003, Pasiouras et al., 2004a), prediction of acquisitions (Doumpos et al., 2004). We provide a brief description of UTADIS below, drawing upon Doumpos and Zopounidis (2002b) where the reader is referred to for more details.

The developed additive utility function has the following general form:

$$U(x) = \sum_{i=1}^{m} p_i u_i'(g_i) \in [0,1]$$

where $g = \{g_1, g_2, ..., g_m\}$ is the set of the evaluation criteria[8], (which in this case correspond to the financial ratios), p_i is the weight of criterion g_i and $u_i'(g_i)$ is the corresponding marginal utility function normalised between 0 and 1. The criteria weights sum up to 1, i.e. $\sum_{i=1}^{m} p_i = 1$, and indicate the significance of each criterion on the developed classification model. On the other hand, the marginal utility functions $u_i'(g_i)$ are used to consider the partial performance of each alternative on the criterion. In

---

[7] Preference disaggregation analysis (Jacquet–Lagreze and Siskos, 1982, 1983, 2001) refers to the analysis (disaggregation) of the global preferences (judgement policy) of the decision maker in order to identify the criteria aggregation model that underlies the preference result. Preference disaggregation analysis uses common utility decomposition forms to model the decision maker's preferences through regression-based techniques. More detailed, in preference disaggregation analysis the parameters of the utility decomposition model are estimated through the analysis of the decision maker's overall preference on some reference alternatives. The problem is then to estimate the utility function that is as consistent as possible with the known subjective preferences of the decision maker.
[8] In multicriteria decision aid, the term "criteria" is used to denote the independent variables. We therefore follow this terminology when describing UTADIS and MHDIS.

other words, the marginal utility functions provide a mechanism for decomposing the aggregate result (global utility) in terms of individual assessment to the criterion level. To avoid the estimation of both the criteria weights p_i and the marginal utility functions $u_i'(g_i)$, it is possible to use the transformation $u_i(g_i) = p_i u_i'(g_i)$. Since $u_i'(g_i)$ is normalised between 0 and 1, it becomes obvious that $u_i(g_i)$ ranges in the interval $[0, x_i]$. Hence, the additive utility function is simplified to the following form:

$$U(x) = \sum_{i=1}^{m} u_i(g_i) \in [0,1]$$

The developed utility function provides an aggregate score $U(x)$ for each firm x along all financial ratios[9]. To classify firms in their original group, it is necessary to estimate the utility thresholds $u_1, u_2, ..., u_{q-1}$, defined in the global utility scale (i.e. between 0 and 1) that distinguish the set of q ordered groups $(C_1, C_2, ...C_q)$ [10]. Comparing the global utilities of a firm a with the utility thresholds, the classification is achieved by using the relations:

$$\left.\begin{aligned}
U(x) \geq u_1 &\qquad \Rightarrow x \in C_1 \\
\cdots\cdots\cdots\cdots\cdots\cdots\cdots\cdots\cdots\cdots \\
u_k \leq U(x) < u_{k-1} &\quad \Rightarrow x \in C_k \\
\cdots\cdots\cdots\cdots\cdots\cdots\cdots\cdots\cdots\cdots \\
U(x) < u_{q-1} &\qquad \Rightarrow x \in C_q
\end{aligned}\right\}$$

---

[9] In the case of acquisitions prediction, this score provides the basis for determining whether the firm could be classified in either the group of acquired firms or the group of non-acquired ones.

[10] The UTADIS as well as the MHDIS, discussed in the next section, make the assumption that the groups are ordered. Therefore C_k is preferred to C_{k+1}, $k=1,2,...q$. In the case of acquisitions prediction where there are two groups, we can assume that C_1 corresponds to the non-acquired firms and C_2 to the acquired ones, as one of the main hypothesis in the literature is that the acquired are less efficient firms.

The estimation of the additive utility model is performed through mathematical programming techniques. More precisely, the following linear programming formulation is employed to estimate the additive utility function and the utility threshold u_1, minimizing the sum of all violations of the above classification rule for all firms:

$$\text{Minimize } F = \sum_{x \in C_1} \sigma^+(x) + \dots + \sum_{x \in C_k} [\sigma^+(x) + \sigma^-(x)] + \dots + \sum_{x \in C_q} \sigma^-(x)$$

s.t.

$$\sum_{i=1}^{m} u_i[g_i(x)] - u_1 + \sigma^+(x) \geq 0 \qquad \forall x \in C_1$$

$$\left.\begin{array}{l} \displaystyle\sum_{i=1}^{m} u_i[g_i(x)] - u_{k-1} - \sigma^-(x) \leq -\delta \\[3em] \displaystyle\sum_{i=1}^{m} u_i[g_i(x)] - u_k + \sigma^+(x) \geq 0 \end{array}\right\} \qquad \forall x \in C_k$$

$$\sum_{i=1}^{m} u_i[g_i(x)] - u_{q-1} - \sigma^-(x) \leq -\delta \qquad \forall x \in C_q$$

$$\sum_{i=1}^{m} \sum_{j=1}^{a_i-1} w_{ij} = 1$$

$$u_{k-1} - u_k \geq s \qquad\qquad k = 2, 3, \dots, q-1$$

$$w_{ij} \geq 0, \ \sigma^+(x) \geq 0, \ \sigma^-(x) \geq 0$$

where:

-a_i is the number of subintervals [g_i^j, g_i^{j+1}] into which the range of values of criterion g_i is divided[11],

-$w_{ij}=u_i(g_i^{j+1})-u_i(g_i^j)$ is the difference between the marginal utilities of two successive values g_i^j and g_i^{j+1} of criterion i ($w_{ij} \geq 0$),

-δ is a threshold used to ensure that $U(x) < u_{k-1}$, $\forall x \in C_k$, $2 \leq k \leq q-1$ ($\delta > 0$)

- s is a threshold used to ensure that $u_{k-1} > u_k$ ($s > \delta > 0$),

- $\sigma^+(x)$ and $\sigma^-(x)$ are the misclassification errors (over-estimation and under-estimation errors respectively).

After the solution F^* of this linear programming problem is obtained, a post-optimality stage is performed in order to identify, as far as possible, other optimal or near optimal solutions, which could provide a more consistent representation of the decision maker's preferences. In this way the robustness of the developed classification models is examined (Zopounidis and Doumpos, 1999a).

3.4.4 Multi-group Hierarchical DIScrimination (MHDIS)

Zopounidis and Doumpos (2000) developed an alternative MCDA non-parametric approach to use utility functions for discrimination purposes, known as Multi-group Hierarchical DIScrimination (MHDIS) method. Similar to UTADIS, MHDIS has also been successfully applied in classification problems in finance, such as bankruptcy prediction (e.g. Pasiouras et al., 2004b), credit risk (e.g. Doumpos et al., 2002) country risk (e.g. Doumpos and Zopounidis, 2001), auditing (e.g. Pasiouras et al., 2004a), M&A's (Zopounidis and Doumpos, 2002). MHDIS distinguishes the groups progressively, starting by discriminating the first group from all the others, and then proceeds to the discrimination between the alternatives belonging to the other groups.

To accomplish this task, instead of developing a single additive utility function that describes all alternatives (as in UTADIS), two additive

---

[11] A basic assumption of the UTADIS involves the monotonicity of the criteria. As this is rather the exception than the rule in real problems, the most common technique to consider such cases, is to divide the range of criterion values into intervals so that preferences are monotone in each of them.

utility functions are developed in each one of the q-1 steps, where q is the number of groups. The first function $U_k(x)$ describes the alternatives of group C_k, while the second function $U_{-k}(x)$ describes the remaining alternatives that are classified in lower groups $C_{k+1},...,C_q$.

$$U_k(x) = \sum_{i=1}^{m} p_{ki} u_{ki}(g_i) \text{ and } U_{-k}(x) = \sum_{i=1}^{m} p_{-ki} u_{-ki}(g_i)$$

$$k = 1,2,...,q-1$$

The corresponding marginal utility functions for each criterion g are denoted as $u_{ki}(g_i)$ and $u_{-ki}(g_i)$ which are normalised between 0 and 1, while the criterion weights p_{ki} and p_{-ki} sum up to 1, i.e. $\sum_{i=1}^{m} p_{ki} = 1$ and $\sum_{i=1}^{m} p_{-ki} = 1$. Throughout the hierarchical discrimination procedure it is assumed that the marginal utility functions $u_{ki}(g_i)$ are increasing functions on the criterion's scale concerning the classification of an alternative in group C_k; while on the other hand the marginal utility of a decision concerning the classification of an alternative, according to criterion g_i, into a lower (worse) group than C_k [denoted as $u_{-ki}(g_i)$] is a decreasing function on the criterion's scale[12]. Denoting as g_i^j and g_i^{j+1} the two consecutive values of criterion g_i ($g_i^{j+1} > g_i^j$, $\forall g_i \in G$), the monotonicity of the marginal utilities, can be expressed in mathematical terms through the following constraints:

$$u_{ki}(g_i^1) = 0 \qquad\qquad u_{ki}(g_i^{j+1}) > u_{ki}(g_i^j)$$

$$u_{-ki}(g_i^{p_i}) = 0 \qquad\qquad u_{-ki}(g_i^{j+1}) < u_{-ki}(g_i^j)$$

---

[12] The set of criteria may include both criteria of increasing (i.e. higher values are preferred) and decreasing (lower values are preferred) preference. Without loss of generality the discussion of this section focuses on criteria of increasing preference. Obviously, as Doumpos and Zopounidis (2001) mention, the criteria of decreasing preference can be transformed into increasing preference through sign reversal.

These constraints can be simplified by introducing a small positive constant t as the lower bound of the difference between the marginal utilities of the consecutive values g_i^j and g_i^{j+1} as follows:

$$w_{kij} \geq t \text{ and } w_{\sim kij} \geq t \text{ }^{13}$$

where:

$$w_{kij} = u_{ki}(g_i^{j+1}) - u_{ki}(g_i^j)$$

$$w_{\sim kij} = u_{\sim ki}(g_i^j) - u_{\sim ki}(g_i^{j+1})$$

Thus, the marginal utility of criterion g_i at point g_i^j can be calculated as

$$u_{ki}(g_i^j) = \sum_{l=1}^{j-1} w_{kil} \text{ and } u_{\sim ki}(g_i^j) = \sum_{l=j}^{p_i-1} w_{\sim kil}$$

As mentioned above, the model is developed in q-1 steps, where q is the number of groups. In the first step, the method develops a pair of additive utility functions $U_1(x)$ and $U_{\sim 1}(x)$ to discriminate between the alternatives of group C_1 and the alternatives of the other groups $C_2,...,C_q$. On the basis of the above function forms the rule to decide upon the classification of any alternative has the following form:

If $U_1(x) \geq U_{\sim 1}(x)$ then x_j belongs in C_1

Else if $U_1(x) \leq U_{\sim 1}(x)$ then x_j belongs in $(C_2, C_3,...,C_q)$

The alternatives that are found to belong into class C_1 (correctly or incorrectly) are excluded from further analysis.

In the next step, another pair of utility functions $U_2(x)$ and $U_{\sim 2}(x)$ is developed to discriminate between the alternatives of group C_2 and the alternatives of the other groups $C_3,...,C_q$. As in step 1, the alternatives that are found to belong to group C_2 are excluded from further analysis. This

---

[13]Upper bounds on the difference between the marginal utilities among the consecutive values g_i^j and g_i^{j+1} can also be set in a similar way (i.e. $w_{kij} \leq$ upper bound and $w_{\sim kij} \leq$ upper bound).

procedure is repeated up to the last stage $q-1$, where all groups have been considered. The overall hierarchical discrimination procedure is presented in Table 3.1:

Table 3.1- The hierarchical discriminant procedure in MHDIS

If $U_1(x) \geq U_{\sim 1}(x)$ then $x_j \in C_1$
Else If $U_2(x) \geq U_{\sim 2}(x)$ then $x_j \in C_2$
....
Else If $U_{q-1}(x) \geq U_{\sim q-1}(x)$ then $x_j \in C_{q-1}$
Else $x_j \in C_q$

(Source: Doumpos and Zopounidis, 2002a)

In contrast to the UTADIS method, as Doumpos and Zopounidis (2002) point out, the utility functions in MHDIS do no indicate the overall performance but rather serve as a measure of the conditional similarity of an alternative to the characteristics of group C_k when the choice among C_k and all the lower groups $C_{k+1},..., C_q$ is considered. However, similarly to the UTADIS, the estimation of the weights of the criteria in the utility functions as well as the marginal utility functions is accomplished through mathematical programming techniques. More specifically, at each stage of the hierarchical discrimination procedure, two linear programming and a mixed-integer programming problems are solved to estimate the utility thresholds and the two additive utility functions in order to minimise the classification error, as summarised in Table 3.2.

Note that each of the three mathematical programming formulations in Table 3.2 incorporates two constraints to ensure the monotonicity of the marginal utilities, as well as to normalise the global utilities in the interval [0,1]. The classification error in LP1 is denoted using the error function e. For an alternative $x \in C_k$ such that $U_k(x) \leq U_{\sim k}(x)$ the classification error is $e(x) = U_{\sim k}(x) - U_k(x) + s$. Similarly, for an alternative $x \notin C_k$ such that $U_k(x) \geq U_{\sim k}(x)$ the classification error is $e(x) = U_k(x) - U_{\sim k}(x) + s$. The small positive real constant s is used to ensure the strict inequalities $U_k(x) > U_{\sim k}(x)$ and $U_k(x) < U_{\sim k}(x)$.

If after the solution of LP1, there exist some alternatives for which $e(x)>0$, then these alternatives are misclassified. However, it may be possible to achieve a "re–arrangement" of the classification errors leading to the reduction of the number of misclassifications. In MHDIS this possibility is explored through a mixed-integer programming (MIP) formulation. Since MIP formulations are difficult to solve, especially in cases where the number of integer variables is large, the MIP formulation used in MHDIS considers only the misclassifications that occur through the solution of LP1, while retaining all the correct classifications. This reduces significantly the number of integer variables, which are associated to each misclassified alternative, thus reducing the computational effort required to obtain a solution. In the MIP formulation used in MHDIS, *COR* denotes the set of correctly classified alternatives after solving LP1, and *MIS* denotes the set of misclassified alternatives. The first set of constraints in MIP ensures that all correct classifications achieved by solving LP1 are retained, while the second set of constraints is applied only to alternatives that were misclassified by LP1. The integer error variables I indicate whether an alternative is misclassified or not.

Through the solution of LP1 and MIP the "optimal" classification of the alternatives is achieved, where the term "optimal" refers to the minimisation of the total number of misclassified alternatives. However, the correct classification of some alternatives may be "marginal", that is, although they are correctly classified, their global utilities according to the two utility functions developed may be very close. The objective of LP2 is to clarify the obtained classification, through the maximisation of the minimum difference between the global utilities of the correctly classified alternatives achieved according to the two utility functions. Similarly to MIP, *COR'* denotes the set of correctly classified alternatives after solving LP1 and MIP, and *MIS'* denotes the set of misclassified alternatives. The first set of constraints in LP2 involves only the correctly classified alternatives. In these constraints d represents the minimum absolute difference between the global utilities of each alternative according to the two utility functions. The second set of constraints involves the misclassified alternatives and it is used to ensure that they will be retained as misclassified.

Table 3.2 Mathematical programming formulations in MHDIS (source: Doumpos and Zopounidis, 2001).

LP1: Minimising the overall classification error	MIP: Minimising the number of misclassifications	LP2: Maximising the minimum distance
$\text{Min } F = \sum e(x)$ s.t. $\left. \begin{array}{l} \sum_{i=1}^{m}\sum_{j=1}^{r_{ki}-1} w_{kij} - \sum_{i=1}^{m}\sum_{j=1}^{r_{ki}-1} w_{-kij} + e(x) \geq s, \ \forall x \in C_k \\ \sum_{i=1}^{m}\sum_{j=1}^{r_{ki}-1} w_{-kij} - \sum_{i=1}^{m}\sum_{j=1}^{r_{ki}-1} w_{kij} + e(x) \geq s, \ \forall x \notin C_k \end{array} \right\} , \ \forall x \in COR$ $e(x), s \geq 0, t \geq 0.$	$\text{Min } F = \sum_{\forall x \in MIS} [I(x)]$ s.t. $\left. \begin{array}{l} \sum_{i=1}^{m}\sum_{j=1}^{r_{ki}-1} w_{kij} - \sum_{i=1}^{m}\sum_{j=1}^{r_{ki}-1} w_{-kij} \geq s, \ \forall x \in C_k \\ \sum_{i=1}^{m}\sum_{j=1}^{r_{ki}-1} w_{-kij} - \sum_{i=1}^{m}\sum_{j=1}^{r_{ki}-1} w_{kij} \geq s, \ \forall x \notin C_k \end{array} \right\} , \ \forall x \in COR'$ $\left. \begin{array}{l} \sum_{i=1}^{m}\sum_{j=1}^{r_{ki}-1} w_{kij} - \sum_{i=1}^{m}\sum_{j=1}^{r_{ki}-1} w_{-kij} + I(x) \geq s, \ \forall x \in C_k \\ \sum_{i=1}^{m}\sum_{j=1}^{r_{ki}-1} w_{-kij} - \sum_{i=1}^{m}\sum_{j=1}^{r_{ki}-1} w_{kij} + I(x) \geq s, \ \forall x \notin C_k \end{array} \right\} , \ \forall x \in MIS$ $s \geq 0, t \geq 0, I(x) \text{ integer.}$	$\text{Max } d$ s.t. $\left. \begin{array}{l} \sum_{i=1}^{m}\sum_{j=1}^{r_{ki}-1} w_{kij} - \sum_{i=1}^{m}\sum_{j=1}^{r_{ki}-1} w_{-kij} - d \geq s \ \ \forall x \in C_k \\ \sum_{i=1}^{m}\sum_{j=1}^{r_{ki}-1} w_{-kij} - \sum_{i=1}^{m}\sum_{j=1}^{r_{ki}-1} w_{kij} - d \geq s \ \ \forall x \notin C_k \end{array} \right\}, \ \forall x \in COR'$ $\left. \begin{array}{l} \sum_{i=1}^{m}\sum_{j=1}^{r_{ki}-1} w_{kij} - \sum_{i=1}^{m}\sum_{j=1}^{r_{ki}-1} w_{-kij} \leq 0 \ \ \forall x \in C_k \\ \sum_{i=1}^{m}\sum_{j=1}^{r_{ki}-1} w_{-kij} - \sum_{i=1}^{m}\sum_{j=1}^{r_{ki}-1} w_{kij} \leq 0 \ \ \forall x \notin C_k \end{array} \right\}, \ \forall x \in MIS'$ $d \geq 0, \ s \geq 0, \ t \geq 0.$

$$w_{kij} \geq t, \ w_{-kij} \geq t \ \text{(monotonicity constraints)}$$

$$\sum_{i=1}^{m}\sum_{j=1}^{r_{ki}-1} w_{kij} = 1, \ \sum_{i=1}^{m}\sum_{j=1}^{r_{ki}-1} w_{-kij} = 1 \ \text{(normalisation constraints)}$$

3.4.5 Classification and Regression Trees (CART)

CART (Breiman et al., 1984) has become one of the most popular machine learning approaches in classification problems over the last years. Instead of developing classification functions or network architectures a binary decision tree is developed. The main idea behind CART is simple: at each brand node, the best splitting value for each independent variable is determined, and the sample is split based on the best of these values. This can be accomplished through a set of if-then split conditions that permit accurate prediction or classification of cases. For each parent node, the left child node corresponds to the points that satisfy the condition, and the right child node corresponds to the points that do not satisfy the condition. Figure 3.4 provides a simple hypothetical example of a decision tree involving three independent variables g_1, g_2, g_3 for the classification of a set of firms as acquired (A) and non-acquired (NA).

Given the hierarchical nature of classification trees, these splits are selected one at a time, starting with the split at the root node (i.e. the top decision node), and continuing with splits of resulting child nodes until splitting stops and the child nodes, which have not been split, become terminal nodes (i.e. points on the tree beyond which no further decisions are made). In general terms, the split at each node will be found that generate the greatest improvement in predictive accuracy. Nevertheless, various split criteria exist such as the Gini, Symgini, Twoing, Ordered Twoing, Maximum Deviance. The Gini index is the measure most commonly used for classification problems and was chosen by Espahbodi and Espahbodi (2003) (also used in the present study). This criterion defines the best splitting value as the one resulting in the smallest node heterogeneity. Consequently, it reaches a value of zero when only one class is present at a node. With priors estimated from class sizes and equal misclassification costs, the Gini index is calculated as the sum of products of all pairs of class proportions for classes present at the node.

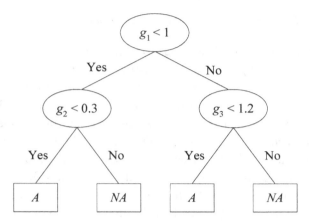

Figure 3.4 An example of a decision tree for classification

Obviously splitting could continue until all cases are correctly classified. However, this would probably result in "overfitting" in a given sample with a reduced ability to classify accurately new observations. One way to control splitting is to continue until all terminal nodes are pure or contain no more than a specified minimum number of cases or objects. An alternative strategy is to continue until all terminal nodes are pure or contain no more cases than a specified minimum proportion of the sizes of one or more classes. The tree obtained from the above procedure can then be pruned to obtain a final tree that has close to the minimum estimated error rate. A k-fold cross-validation is usually employed to perform pruning. Breiman et al. (1984) provides an extended description of this method with discussion of above issues, including theory of binary trees, splitting rules, etc.

3.4.6 Nearest neighbours

Nearest neighbours is a non-parametric density estimation method that has been applied in various problems in finance such as credit risk assessment (e.g. Henley and Hand, 1996; West, 2000; Doumpos and Pasiouras, 2004), bankruptcy prediction (e.g. Tam and Kiang, 1992) and interest rate modelling (Nowman and Saltoglu, 2003). The nearest neighbour rule classifies an object (i.e. firm) to the class of its nearest neighbour in the measurement space using some kind of distance measure like the local metrics (Short and Fucunaga, 1980), the global metrics (Fukunaga and Flick, 1984), the Mahalanobis or the Euclidean distance. The latter is the most commonly used one and is also employed in the present study.

The modification of the nearest neighbour rule, the k-nearest neighbour (k-NN) method that is employed in the present study, classifies an object (i.e. firm) to the class (i.e. acquired or non-acquired) more heavily represented among its k nearest neighbours.

Assuming a firm x described by the feature vector $<g_1(x), g_2(x), ..., g_m(x)>$, where $g_r(x)$ is used to denote the values of the rth characteristic of firm x, the distance between two instances x_i and x_j is estimated as follows:

$$d(x_i, x_j) \equiv \sqrt{\sum_{r=1}^{m} (g_r(x_i) - g_r(x_j))^2}$$

Then, the algorithm for approximating a discrete-valued function of the form $f : \Re^n \to C$, where C is a finite set of classes $\{C_1, C_2, ..., C_q\}$ proceeds as follows:

Step 1: For each training example (i.e. firm) $< x, f(x) >$, add the firm to the list of training examples.

Step 2: Given a query firm x to be classified, let $x_1, x_2, ..., x_k$ denote the k instances from the training examples that are nearest to x.

Step 3: Return $\hat{f}(x) \leftarrow \arg\max_{c \in C} \sum_{i=1}^{k} \delta(c, f(x_i))$, where $\delta(a,b)) = 1$ if $a = b$ and where $\delta(a,b)) = 0$ otherwise.

Thus, the algorithm returns the value $\hat{f}(x)$ as an estimate of $f(x)$, which is the most common value of f among the k training examples nearest to x.

3.4.7 Support Vector Machines (SVMs)

The Support Vector Machines (SVMs) approach has been recently applied in a few financial applications mainly in the areas of time series forecasting (Tay and Cao, 2001, 2002; Kim, 2003; Huang et al., 2005), bankruptcy prediction (Shin et al., 2004) and credit risk assessment (Huang et al., 2004).

SVMs was introduced by Vapnik (1995) and is based on the Structural Risk Minimization (SRM) principle from computational learning theory, that seeks to minimise an upper bound of the generalisation error rather than minimise the training error. A brief description of the SVM approach is given below. A more detailed explanation and proofs can be found in textbooks by Vapnik (1995, 1998) and Cristianini and Shawe-Taylor (2000). SVMs can be used for both regression and classification. Given the purpose of the present study, we will focus on the latter.

SVM uses a linear structure to implement nonlinear class boundaries through extremely non-linear mapping of the input vectors into the high-dimensional space. If the data is linearly separated, SVM finds a special kind of linear model, the optimal separating hyperplane (OSH) that provides the maximum separation between the classes. The training points that are closest to the maximum margin hyperplane are called support vectors. All other training examples are irrelevant for determining the binary class boundaries.

For the linearly separable case, the decision rule defined by an OSH for the binary decision class can be represented by the following equation:

$$y = b + \sum y_i a_i \, x \bullet x_i$$

where y is the outcome, y_i is the class value of the training example x_i, and $\bullet$ is the dot product. The vector x corresponds to an input, the vectors x_i are the support vectors and b and a_i are parameters that determine the hyperplane ($a \geq 0$).

From the implementation point of view, Vapnik (1995) showed how training a SVM and finding the parameters b and a leads to a quadratic optimisation problem with bound constraints and one linear equality constraint. This means that the solution of SVMs is unique, optimal and absent from local minima (Tay and Cao, 2001).

Since most real-world problems seem not to be linearly separable, SVMs can work in combination with the technique of "kernels", that automatically realises a non-linear mapping into a feature space. For the nonlinearly separable case, a high-dimensional version of the above equation is given as:

$$y = b + \sum y_i a_i \, K(\text{x, x}_i)$$

The function $K(\text{x, x}_i)$ is the kernel function for generating the dot products to construct machines with different types of non-linear decision surfaces in the input space. Any function satisfying Mercer's theorem can be used as the kernel. For constructing decision rules, two typical examples are the polynomial kernel function $K(x_i, x_j) = (x_i \bullet x_j + 1)^d$ where d is the degree of the polynomial kernel, and the Gaussian function with kernel $K(x_i, x_j) = \exp(-1/\delta^2 (x_i - x_j)^2)$ where δ^2 is the bandwidth of the Gaussian kernel.

In the general non-separable case the development of an SVM model involves two objectives: the maximisation of the separation margin and the minimization of the misclassifications for the training sample. The relative firms in the importance of the two objectives is taken into consideration through a user-defined constant ($C \succ 0$) representing the importance given to the minimisation of the misclassification as opposed to the margin maximisation objective. Implicitly C defines an upper bound on the coefficients a of the separating function.

3.5 Aspects of Model Evaluation

3.5.1 The classification matrix

The outcome of an acquisitions prediction model is between two discrete alternatives, acquired or non-acquired. The model provides a number of correct as well as a number of incorrect predictions. Obviously, the objective of developing an acquisitions prediction model is in fact straightforward: one wants to classify correct as many firms as possible.

The classification results are usually reported in the form of a classification table, often referred to as a confusion matrix. Although there are other measures of evaluation (e.g. Receiver Operating Characteristics - ROC curves), the confusion matrix is almost universally adopted as the standard error report in supervised classification. It is the only method that has been used in previous studies in the prediction of acquisition targets. This matrix is a convenient way to compare the firms' actual group membership versus their predicted group membership. Usually, the column present the number of firms classified in the group while the rows present the number of firms in the actual groups, although the opposite format may be used (i.e. classified in rows and actual in columns). A confusion matrix, using the former format, is shown in Table 3.3

Table 3.3 The confusion (classification) matrix

		Classified (predicted) by the model		
		Acquired	Non-Acquired	Total
Actual group	Acquired	a	b	$(a+b)$
membership	Non-Acquired	c	d	$(c+d)$
	Total	$(a+c)$	$(b+d)$	N

The notations are defined as:

a: The number of acquired firms that are correctly classified as acquired.
b: The number of acquired firms that are incorrectly classified as non-acquired.
c: The number of non-acquired firms that are incorrectly classified as acquired.
d: The number of non-acquired firms that are correctly classified as non-acquired.

Obviously a perfect model would have zeros for both cells b and c, and the total number of acquired and non-acquired firms in cells a and d

respectively, indicating that it perfectly discriminated between the acquired and non-acquired firms. Based on the differential analysis of elements in the matrix, a number of measures can be computed. Perhaps the most basic tool for understanding the performance of an acquisitions prediction model is the "percentage right". The following are four commonly used measures (calculated as shown on the RHS):

$$\text{Overall correct classification} = (a+d)/N$$
$$\text{Average correct classification} = \{[a/(a+b)]+ [c/(c+d)]\}/2$$
$$\text{Acquired firms correct classification} = a /(a+b)$$
$$\text{Non-acquired firms correct classification} = c /(c+d)$$

Alternatively one can focus on classification errors (or misclassifications) as opposed to correct classifications. For example:

$$\text{Overall error rate} = 1\text{-overall correct classification}$$

Or

$$\text{Overall error rate} = (c+b)/N.$$

Before going into more details about the choice of the appropriate evaluation measure, two issues related to model evaluation need to be addressed. These are (i) the absolute comparison performance, and (ii) the comparative performance.

(i) Absolute comparison performance

In general, an absolute evaluation compares the performance of a model to some exogenous metric (i.e. the model should obtain a correct classification accuracy of at least 70% to be characterised as effective). Of course this metric depends highly on the area of application (i.e. for example, bankruptcy prediction models have historically achieved higher accuracies than acquisitions prediction models). Therefore, the most critical question is whether the results of the prediction model are better than the ones that could be obtained by chance assignment. For example, if we had a sample of 50 acquired firms and 50 non-acquired firms, it would be reasonable to expect then, that by using the flip of a coin to decide firm group membership, we could classify about 50% of the firms correctly. The critical question then would be, if by using a classification model we could classify correct more than 50% of the firms.

One way to address this issue is to use the odds ratio. However, this ratio has an unfortunate characteristic of being infinite when either b or c is 0. Hence, it has the same value when the model is perfect or lacks one type of error. An alternative is to use the Kappa Index (Huberty, 1994).

The Kappa index was initially proposed by Cohen (1960) to compare the observed agreement to the one expected by change, between two or several observers or techniques when the judgments are qualitative, contrary to the coefficient of Kendall for example that evaluates the degree of agreement between quantitative judgments. Kappa can therefore express the proportionate reduction in error generated by a classification process, compared with the error of a completely random classification. It can take values between −1 and +1, with 1 indicating perfect agreement and 0 indicating no better than chance agreement. Finally, negative values occur when agreement is weaker than expected by chance. Kappa is often multiplied by 100 to give a percentage measure of classification accuracy. For example, a value of 0.7 would imply that the classification process was avoiding 70% of the errors that a completely random classification would generate.

Kappa can be calculated as follows:

$$Kappa = (P\_Observed - P\_Expected) / (1 - P\_Expected)$$

where P_Observed = $(a+d) / N$
and P_Expected = $(((a+c) * (a+b)) + ((b+d) * (c+d))) /$ sq (N)

Cohen's Kappa can be expressed as:

$$Kappa = 2\,(ad - bc) / ((a+c)(c+d) + (b+d)\,(a+b))$$

Cohen's Kappa is a widely accepted calculation that, although not commonly used in finance, has been characterised as the touchstone for assessing the quality of diagnostic procedures (Faraone and Tsuang, 1994). An issue that one should consider when evaluating a model with Cohen's Kappa is that when the sample size of one group far exceeds the other Kappa fails and tends to be quite low[14].

Byrt et al. (1994) proposed a solution to the possible bias of Cohen's Kappa, known as "Prevalence-Adjusted-Bias Adjusted Kappa" (PABAK). PABAK has the same interpretation as Cohen's Kappa and can be calculated following the three steps below:

1. Calculate the mean of a and d: $n = (a+d) / 2$
2. Calculate the mean of b and c: $m = (b+c) / 2$
3. Use means m and n from steps 1 and 2, Cohen's Kappa formula and the table below to calculate PABAK.

Table 3.4 Calculation of PABAK

		Predicted	
		Acquired	Non-acquired
Actual	Acquired	n	m
	Non-acquired	m	n

PABAK is the value that kappa would take if there were no systematic one-side variations between the ratings and the categories were of equal prevalence.

(ii) Comparative performance

Comparative performance gives an indication of whether model A is better than model B. Obviously, a researcher may be interested in comparing the effectiveness of two classification models using a given dataset. The models may be developed using different classification techniques or the same technique but different predictor variables. For

---

[14] The decrease becomes larger especially when the model provides unbalanced classification accuracies between the groups.

example, in the case of acquisitions prediction, it may be of interest to compare the results of discriminant analysis with those of logit analysis, or to compare the results of using raw with industry adjusted data.

Probably the most important issue when comparing classification models is to use a testing sample. The reason is that some methods such as neural networks, multicriteria decision aid, support vector machines, among others, have different parameters to be estimated compared to each other and significantly more than discriminant and logit, resulting in some of them having an a-priori data fitting superiority in the training sample.

3.5.2 Issues to consider when choosing evaluation measure

We have so far discussed six measures of a model's evaluation performance. It should be mentioned at this point that these measures have different characteristics, and in particular some are sensitive to the prevalence of positive cases (e.g. acquired, bankrupt) as a percentage of the total sample. For example, in the case of acquisition targets prediction, the acquired firms are always much less in the population, and also in the sample, than the non-acquired ones. Tables 3.5 and 3.6 show the effect of prevalence on the measures of evaluation using a hypothetical example. The first table shows the classification of firms obtained by the model. The second shows the six measures for each one of the examples.

It is obvious from Table 3.6 that three measures are not being affected by prevalence while the rest are positively or negatively affected. In particular, the individual correct accuracies for the acquired and non-acquired are not changing. As a result, the average accuracy also remains stable. When the observations in the two groups are equal (i.e. prevalence 50%), the overall accuracy equals the average one. However, the overall correct classification accuracy is negatively related to prevalence. As the number of acquired firms in the sample decreases, the overall correct classification increases. The example could be even more extreme considering that, even if none of the acquired firms had been classified correctly in the third example, the overall classification accuracy would have been 98.37% by assigning all cases to the non-acquired group. Cohen's Kappa and PABAK are positively and negatively related accordingly. As in the case of overall and average accuracies, when the prevalence is 50% these two measures of Kappa are equal. When the prevalence decreases, Cohen's Kappa tends to decrease while PABAK tends to increase.

Table 3.5 Hypothetical classification matrices for different prevalence of acquired firms in sample

		Classified (predicted)		
Example 1 (prevalence = 50%)		Acquired	Non-Acquired	Total
Actual	Acquired	60	40	100
	Non-Acquired	20	80	100
	Total	80	120	200
Example 2 (prevalence = 14.28%)				
	Acquired	60	40	100
Actual	Non-Acquired	120	480	600
	Total	180	560	700
Example 3 (prevalence = 1.63%)				
	Acquired	60	40	100
Actual	Non-Acquired	1200	4800	6000
	Total	1260	4840	6100

Table 3.6 Effect of prevalence on evaluation measures

	Example 1	Example 2	Example 3
Prevalence	50%	14.28%	1.63%
Evaluation measure			
Overall correct classification accuracy	70%	77.1%	79.7%
Correct Classification of acquired firms	60%	60%	60%
Correct Classification of non-acquired firms	80%	80%	80%
Average Correct Classification Accuracy	70%	70%	70%
Cohen's Kappa Index	40%	30%	6%
PABAK Index	40%	54.3%	59.3%

The selection of the measure of performance depends on the cost of each type of error as well as the prior probabilities. As mentioned above, the error can be used as a measure instead of correct classification. Obviously classification inaccuracies can result in one of two ways, as shown in Table 3.7. First, the model can indicate a firm as acquired, when in fact, it is not acquired (known as Type II error). Second, the model can indicate a firm as non-acquired, when in fact, it is acquired (Type I error).

Table 3.7 Type I and Type II errors of an acquisition targets prediction model

		Classified by the model	
		Acquired	Non-Acquired
Actual	Acquired	Correct prediction	Type I error
	Non-Acquired	Type II error	Correct prediction

The issue of model error cost is a complex and important one. It is often the case, for example, that a particular model will perform better under one set of cost assumptions, but it will not do so under a different set of assumptions (Provost and Fawcett, 1997; Hoadley and Oliver, 1998). Obviously different users may have different cost structures, making it difficult to present a single cost function that is appropriate across all of them. This leads Altman (1993) to argue that when dealing with costs, one needs to specify exactly who the user is and what costs are relevant. For example, as Cheh *et al.* (1999) point out, in the context of an investment application (i.e. developing a model to predict acquired targets and form portfolios to earn abnormal returns), there are a number of diversified strategies that an investor could follow by changing the trade-off between type I and type II errors.

Turning to the evaluation measures, for reasons of simplicity, thief the two types of classification inaccuracies (i.e. Type I and Type II errors) incur the exact same loss, as is often assumed, then a single overall classification rate can be used for model evaluation. In that case, the selection of the "best" model is easy, since the one with the highest overall classification rate is selected. However, when the costs are known with some degree of certainty or we simply know that one type of error is more costly than other, but we cannot quantify it, then the best model could be selected based upon the individual classification rates (of the acquired and the non-acquired firms). Consequently, although it is possible for some models to commit less of one type of error than the other, users of models seek to keep the probability of making either type of error as small as possible. Unfortunately, minimising one type of error usually comes at the expense of increasing the other type of error (Sobehart *et al.*, 2000). Thus, as the probability of making a Type II error increases, the probability of a Type I error decreases. For that reason, the average accuracy offers a good alternative that is not affected by prevalence.

Turning to Kappa measures, PABAK is similar to overall accuracy, as it is negatively related to prevalence. Since Cohen's Kappa is positively related to prevalence, a good approach could be to calculate and consider both of them.

It was mentioned above that the prior probabilities should also be considered prior to the selection of the appropriate measure of performance. If the prior probability of one of the two groups is very high, the model will achieve a strong prediction rate if all observations are simply classified into this class. However, when a group has a low probability of occurrence (e.g. acquisition, bankruptcy) it is far more difficult to assign these low probability observations into their correct class. This particular difficulty of accurate group assignments of rare events will not be captured if the overall classification is used as an evaluation method. Therefore, as in the case of costs above, one might prefer to examine the individual group classifications or the average classification.

3.5.3 Out-of-sample performance — model's testing

It was mentioned in section 3.2.2 that when classification models are used to reclassify observations of the training sample, the classification accuracies are normally biased upward and the testing of the model in a holdout sample is necessary.

According to Gupton and Stein (2003), the primary goals of testing are to: (1) determine how well a model performs, (2) ensure that a model has not been over-fit and that its performance is reliable and well understood, and (3) confirm that the modelling approach, not just an individual model, is robust through time. Obviously, the same measures are calculated to access the performance of the model in the testing sample. Therefore if the developed model performs satisfactory in the training sample, when evaluated with the other measures discussed above, it can used to decide upon the classification of a set of new alternatives.

3.6 Conclusion

In this chapter we have presented a general methodological framework for the development and the evaluation of an acquisition targets prediction model. The chapter began with a discussion of several sampling issues that should be considered at the early stage of data collection and preparation. We then discussed the reasons and techniques for selecting a small set of input variables among the numerous financial variables that could be included in the model. Three most commonly used techniques for selecting the final set of input variables were discussed. Then, we presented seven well-known classification methodologies, and finally discussed several issues relating to the evaluation of a prediction model. The procedures and issues explained in this chapter will be used in the following chapters for empirical analyses, including the selection and preparation of data as well as the development and evaluation of the prediction models.

Chapter 4

Data and Preliminary Analysis

4.1 Introduction

This chapter begins with a discussion of the data sources and the samples used for our empirical work, and then goes on to discuss some criteria for determining and identifying potential candidate variables for inclusion in model development. Despite the potential importance of non-financial considerations in decisions affecting M&As, we shall in common with the majority of previous studies on acquisition predictions consider only financial variables, that will reflect capital strength, asset quality, liquidity, profit and cost efficiency, as well as growth, size and market power. Although certain firm specific characteristics (such as management quality) may be proxied by financial variables, it is in practice difficult to allow explicitly for other immeasurable influences on banks' probability of acquisition, such as acquisition takeover defences, or agency and hubris motives. Furthermore, while qualitative influences may contribute to higher discrimination ability, the development of such a model would impose onerous data requirements on decision makers who face unrelenting pressures to deliver quick results.

As we explained earlier, our sample size is restricted to commercial banks in the EU, and we have considered a time span of bank acquisitions covering the period 1998-2002, matched with non-acquired banks operating as at the end of 2002. This allowed us to collect financial data on a total of 734 banks, of which 168 were acquired and 566 non-acquired (in accordance with the criteria defined below). In general, collecting a larger sample size requires a longer time span.

However, as the literature suggests, acquisition likelihood models are not robust over time (e.g. Barnes, 1990; Powell, 1997), since the characteristics of firms and the motives for acquisitions change as the economic environment changes. Thus, as Espahbodi and Espahbodi (2003) argue, in order to minimise the time series distortion in the models, it is essential to limit the analysis to the shortest period of time possible. Further, as Beitel and Schiereck (2001) point out, during the period 1998-2000, more M&A deals occurred in the EU banking industry than during the previous 14 years, and therefore the time-span we have chosen (1998-2002) seems to be appropriate permitting the use of an adequate sample size for both model development and testing without sacrificing the stability of a short time horizon. To preserve sufficient homogeneity while extending coverage to 15 EU countries, we have excluded other types of banks (e.g co-operative banks, building societies, etc) from our analysis, leaving this extension for future research.

The remainder of this chapter is structured as follows. Section 4.2 outlines the data sources for the sample. Section 4.3 discusses the requirements for sample selection and the construction of various sub-samples, distinguished by the construction of variables and the number of (acquired and non-acquired) banks. Section 4.4 deals with issues defining the choice of candidate variables providing the basis for discrimination between the acquired and the non-acquired banks. Finally, section 4.5 employs a selection procedure incorporating the use of descriptive statistics and the application of a non-parametric test, backed up by correlation analysis, in order to reduce the number of potential candidate variables for model development. The selection procedure aims to narrow down the number of candidate variables to those significantly able to discriminate between the two groups of banks, and the final set of input variables selected on this basis appear to be robust across the range of samples considered.

4.2 Data Sources

The development of a prediction model requires a sample of banks, some that were acquired and some that were not, together with data corresponding to a set of variables that discriminates between the acquired and the non-acquired banks. The data sources along with the requirements that the two groups of banks had to meet in order to be included in the sample are outlined below.

(i) Acquired banks

Three data sources were used to construct a list of acquired banks operating in the EU during the period 1998 to 2002. These sources were:

a. Bankscope Database of Bureau van Dijk's company, which is a specialised database that contains information for approximately 12,000 banks around the world.
b. BANKERSalmanac.com is another specialised database that contains bank level data and M&As information for financial institutions.
c. Zephyr Database of Bureau van Dijk's company, which is a special source on M&As, IPO and venture capital deals.

In order to be included in the sample, acquired banks had to meet the following criteria:
a. They were acquired between January 1, 1998 and December 31, 2002.
b. The acquisition represented the purchase of 50% or more of ownership of the acquired bank[1].
c. They operated in one of the 15 EU countries (Austria, Belgium, Denmark, Finland, France, Germany, Greece, Ireland, Italy, Luxembourg, Netherlands, Portugal, Spain, Sweden, UK).

---

[1] The Bankscope and BANKERSalamanac.com provide information only for full acquisitions and, therefore, we had to rely only on Zephyr for the selection of data relative to majority acquisitions. Consequently, whether our list is complete or not, depends highly on the availability of information in Zephyr.

d. All were classified as commercial banks in the Bankscope database.
e. All had financial data available for two years before the year of acquisition (in Bankscope).

A total of 168 banks met the above requirements and were included in the group of acquired banks.

(ii) Non-acquired banks

In order to be included in the sample, non-acquired banks had to:
a. Operate in one of the 15 EU countries.
b. Be classified as commercial banks in the Bankscope database.
c. Had financial data available (in Bankscope) for the period 1996-2002. This requirement of a longer period for the non-acquired banks was placed for two reasons. First, it ensures than an acquired bank, if not identified in the sources of acquisitions, could not be wrongly considered as non-acquired. (It is obvious that if a bank was 100% acquired in a given year, e.g. 1998, it could not have had data from the following years, i.e. 1999, 2000, etc.). Second, with available data for all non-acquired banks for all years the possibility of randomly matching with an acquired bank in any fiscal year is ensured.

The above procedure yielded a total of 566 non-acquired banks that were included in the sample.

4.3 Samples Construction

As discussed in Chapter 3, after the model is estimated, it is necessary to test its out-of-sample prediction ability, in order to classify a set of observations that were not used during model development. Hence, the total sample must be split into a training sub-sample, used for model development, and a testing sub-sample, used to determine the model's ability to classify observations out-of-sample. The testing sub-sample can be created using either a holdout method or a resampling technique, such as cross-validation, bootstrap and jack-knife. Requiring that a model be validated against a "future" period is more appropriate for comparing classification methods, as this approach more closely reflects a "real world" setting due to population drifting.

In this study, a training sample is constructed using banks acquired between 1998 and 2000, randomly matched with non-acquired banks, while the testing sample is constructed using banks acquired during 2001 and 2002, randomly matched by non-acquired banks not used in the training sample[2]. Because prediction of acquisitions is very difficult (see, e.g. Palepu, 1986), the models are only intended to predict acquisitions in a given year based on data of the prior year. Although the year of acquisition is not common for all banks in the sample, the usual practice is to take them to be acquired in year "zero", considered as the year of reference. The year of activity prior the "zero" year is then coded as "year −1" (one year prior) and refers to the latest financial reports that were issued prior to acquisition[3].

After obtaining the two sub-samples for the acquired banks, the next step was to match the non-acquired banks with the acquired banks. It was noted in section 3.2 that the acquired and non-acquired banks should be matched only by fiscal year[4]. Using this approach, financial data for the non-acquired banks were taken from the same fiscal years as the corresponding acquired banks. For example, suppose bank A1 was acquired in 1998, then data for "year −1" were obtained from year 1997 for both A1 and its matching non-acquired bank NA1.

For a comparative evaluation of the classification methods, the following 4 sub-samples were constructed:

---

[2] Acquisitions from two years were used in the validation samples for two reasons. First, to provide an adequate number of observations that would ensure the proper testing of the model (as discussed in Chapter 3, we follow the recommendation of 1/3 of total observations to be used for validation purposes when a holdout sample is used). Second, to ensure that the observed results are not biased by the performance of the model in a single year.

[3] Actually, for a few acquired banks in sample, " year −1" refer to financial statements issued for two fiscal years prior to the year of acquisition, as data for the actual year −1 were not available.

[4] Since the literature suggests that size is an important explanatory variable in acquisitions, it was preferred in this study to use size as an independent variable rather as a matching characteristic.

Training Sample A

An equal matched training sub-sample consisting of 109 banks acquired between 1998 and 2000, and 109 non-acquired banks. The 109 non-acquired banks were randomly selected from the initial list of 566 non-acquired banks and matched by fiscal year with the acquired banks.

Training Sample B

A double matched training sub-sample consisting of the same 109 banks that were included in training sample A, and 218 non-acquired banks (i.e. 109 non-acquired banks of training sample A plus another 109 non-acquired banks randomly selected, from the remaining 457 non-acquired banks).

Testing Sample A

An equal matched testing sub-sample consisting of 59 banks acquired during 2001 and 2002, and 59 non-acquired banks randomly selected from the remaining 348 non-acquired banks not used for model development (i.e. 566 non-acquired banks in the initial observation set minus 218 banks used in the two training sub-samples *A* and *B* for the development of the models).

Testing Sample B

An unequal testing sub-sample consisting of 59 banks acquired during 2001 and 2002, and the 348 non-acquired banks not used for model development.

Table 4.1 provides a summary of these samples, and the following tables (Tables 4.2 and 4.3) give a more detailed picture, by classifying the banks in training and testing samples by country and year. As Tables 4.2 and 4.3 show, a significant proportion (more than double) of the observations in the training samples are from year 2000 (112 in training sample A and 168 in training sample B), nevertheless an adequate number of observations is also used from 1998 and 1999. With respect to the geographical distribution of the identified acquisitions, France, Italy, Spain, Germany, Luxembourg and Greece are the 6 countries with above average acquired banks included in the samples.

Table 4.1 Summary of training and testing sample

Sample	Year of Acquisition	Number of acquired banks	Number of Non-acquired banks
Total (initial)	1998-2002	168	566
Training sample *A**	1998-2000	109	109
Training sample *B* *	1998-2000	109	218
Testing sample *A* **	2001-2002	59	59
Testing sample *B* **	2001-2002	59	348

Notes: * The same acquired banks were used in both training sample A and training sample B. The non-acquired banks in training sample B sum up to 218 by adding another 109 non-acquired banks to the 109 non-acquired banks of training sample A.
** The same acquired banks were used in both testing sample A and testing sample B. The 348 non-acquired banks of testing sample B are calculated as 566 (initial set) minus 218 (used for development purposes). The 59 non-acquired banks of testing sample A were randomly chosen from the 348 non-acquired banks of testing sample *B*.

Table 4.2 Training sample A (1:1 matching)

Country	Acquired				Non-acquired			
	1998	1999	2000	Total	1998	1999	2000	Total
Austria	2	0	0	2	1	1	3	5
Belgium	3	0	3	6	3	1	1	5
Denmark	0	2	2	4	0	3	8	11
Finland	0	0	1	1	0	0	0	0
France	10	9	7	26	4	9	15	28
Germany	3	3	4	10	3	2	12	17
Greece	0	3	4	7	0	0	0	0
Ireland	0	1	0	1	1	1	0	2
Italy	1	5	14	20	0	4	4	8
Luxembourg	1	1	7	9	3	2	6	11
Netherlands	0	1	1	2	4	0	1	5
Portugal	0	0	4	4	1	0	0	1
Spain	3	3	6	12	2	2	4	8
Sweden	0	0	0	0	0	0	0	0
UK	1	1	3	5	2	4	2	8
Total	24	29	56	109	24	29	56	109

Not surprisingly the acquisition activity in the four out of the five principal EU banking sectors represents about 62% of the acquired banks included in the sample[5]. However, no single country dominates the sample. Non-acquired banks come mostly from the same countries with banks from the four countries (France, Italy, Spain, Germany) representing almost 56% in training sample A and 58% in training sample B.

Table 4.3 Training sample B (1:2 matching)

Country	Acquired				Non-acquired			
	1998	1999	2000	Total	1998	1999	2000	Total
Austria	2	0	0	2	2	2	3	8
Belgium	3	0	3	6	6	2	2	10
Denmark	0	2	2	4	0	6	12	18
Finland	0	0	1	1	0	0	0	0
France	10	9	7	26	8	18	30	56
Germany	3	3	4	10	6	4	26	36
Greece	0	3	4	7	0	0	1	1
Ireland	0	1	0	1	1	1	1	3
Italy	1	5	14	20	1	9	10	20
Luxembourg	1	1	7	9	5	4	10	19
Netherlands	0	1	1	2	8	0	2	10
Portugal	0	0	4	4	2	0	0	2
Spain	3	3	6	12	5	4	5	14
Sweden	0	0	0	0	0	0	0	0
UK	1	1	3	5	4	8	9	21
Total	24	29	56	109	48	58	112	218

We now turn to the testing samples (see Table 4.4). The observations from the two years were almost equal, with 28 banks identified as acquired in 2001 (and met the other criteria for inclusion in the sample) and 31 for 2002. For the non-acquired banks, in the equally matched sample (testing sample A) equal number of observations were drawn from the corresponding years, while for the unequal sample (testing sample B), care was taken to keep a similar proportion. Thus, 165 non-

---

[5] UK is the fifth large sector in the EU. However, the UK banking sector had experienced a large number of M&As in a previous period than the one considered in the present study.

acquired banks were assigned to acquired banks from 2001 and 183 non-acquired banks were assigned to acquired banks from 2002 respectively[6].

Table 4.4 Number of banks in testing samples A and B by country and year

| | Acquired banks | | | Non-acquired banks | | | | | |
| | | | | Testing sample A | | | Testing sample B | | |
	2001	2002	Total	2001	2002	Total	2001	2002	Total
Austria	1	1	2	2	1	3	6	6	12
Belgium	0	3	3	1	2	3	5	4	9
Denmark	3	3	6	2	1	3	10	13	23
Finland	1	0	1	0	0	0	1	2	3
France	3	6	9	8	7	15	39	46	85
Germany	5	1	6	3	4	7	23	29	52
Greece	0	1	1	0	0	0	0	5	5
Ireland	0	0	0	1	1	2	6	2	8
Italy	3	9	12	2	3	5	14	13	27
Luxembourg	7	2	9	4	1	5	19	19	38
Netherlands	0	0	0	0	4	4	4	9	13
Portugal	2	0	2	0	3	3	3	4	7
Spain	1	4	5	1	2	3	16	11	27
Sweden	1	0	1	0	0	0	4	0	4
UK	1	1	2	4	2	6	15	20	35
Total	28	31	59	28	31	59	165	183	348

Concerning the geographical distribution of the acquired banks, Italy, France, Luxembourg, Germany, Denmark and Spain, are the 6 countries with above average acquired banks included in the testing sample. The number of acquired banks from the four of the five principal EU banking sectors remains high, reaching 54% of the total. Non-acquired banks come mostly from the same countries with banks from the above mentioned four countries, representing almost 51% in testing sample A and 55% in testing sample B.

---

[6] This was calculated as follows: Acquired banks in 2001 and 2002 as a proportion of total acquired in 2001 and 2002 equals 47.46% and 52.54% respectively. Thus, from the total of 348 non-acquired banks, 47.46% and 52.54% should be assigned to 2001 and 2002, that is 165 and 183 banks accordingly.

4.4 Identification of Candidate Variables

After the initial groups are defined and banks are selected, candidate variables need to be identified and the final set of input variables selected. In the present pan-European setting, the need for comparable data from different countries imposes strong restrictions on the type of variables one can use. To minimise possible bias arising from different accounting practices, broad variable definitions as provided by Bankscope were used. Using Bankscope has two main advantages. Firstly, it has information for a very large number of banks, accounting for about 90% of total assets in each country (Claessens et al., 2001). Secondly, and most important, the financial information at the bank level is presented in standardised formats, after adjusting for differences in accounting and reporting standards. The data compiled by Bankscope uses financial statements and notes found in audited annual reports. Each country in the Bankscope database has its own data template, thus allowing for differences in the reporting and accounting conventions. The data are then converted to a "global format" using a globally standardised template derived from the country-specific templates. The global format contains 36 standard ratios, which can be compared across banks and between countries. Therefore, Bankscope is the most comprehensive database that allows cross-country comparisons (Claessens et al., 2001). Studies that have used the Bankscope data to perform cross-country analyses in European banking include, among others, DeBandt and Davis (1999), Focarelli and Pozzolo (2001), Diaz et al. (2004), Pasiouras and Kosmidou (2005).

The various motives for acquisitions suggest a variety of financial characteristics possessed by the ideal target company. These motivations are not independent of one another, which make the testing of alternative theories problematic. Thus, it is not surprising that the empirical evidence simultaneously supports many differing theories of acquisitions (Bartley and Boardman, 1990). Therefore, examination of the maximum number of potentially relevant variables is considered appropriate given the absence of theoretical support for a particular set of variables (Barnes, 1990).

In a study of the characteristics of targets of banks mergers during the 1980s and early 1990s in the US, Wheelock and Wilson (2000) include several financial ratios designed to mirror various aspects of bank condition that bank regulators and banks' credit analysts evaluate in their examinations of bank safety and soundness: Capital, Asset Quality, Management, Earnings and Liquidity (CAMEL). In the present study, all the 36 pre-calculated ratios from Bankscope were initially considered. These 36 ratios correspond to asset quality, capital strength, cost and profit efficiency and liquidity. In addition to these ratios, 4 more variables were taken into account: total assets, total assets annual change, loans market share and deposits market share. The first one corresponds to size, the second to growth, and the third and fourth to market power. Thus, a total set of 40 financial variables was initially considered in the study.

Table 4.5 - Financial variables considered in study after excluding those with more than 5% missing values

Category		Description
Capital strength	g1	Equity/Total assets
	g2	Equity / Net loans
	g3	Equity / Customer & short term funding
	g4	Equity / liabilities
	g5	Capital funds / liabilities
Operations (profitability & cost efficiency)	g6	Net interest margin
	g7	Net interest revenue / Average assets
	g8	Other operating income / Average assets
	g9	Non interest expenses / Average assets
	g10	Return on average assets (ROAA)
	g11	Return on average equity (ROAE)
	g12	Cost to income ratio
Liquidity	g13	Net loans / Total assets
	g14	Net loans/Customers & short term funding
	g15	Liquid assets / Customers & short term funding
Growth	g16	Total assets annual change
Size	g17	Total assets
Market power	g18	Loans market share
	g19	Deposits market share

Following the suggestion of Tabachnick and Fidell (2001), those variables with missing values of more than 5% were excluded, reducing the number of candidate financial variables to 19, shown in Table 4.5. A more detailed discussion of the 19 financial variables considered in the study as well as the motivation for their inclusion in the analysis is given below.

Capital Ratios

Capital ratios measure capital strength, the extent of a bank's ability to absorb any shocks that it might experience and have long been a valuable tool for bank regulators and supervisors, as well as for bank analysts in general. Wheelock and Wilson (2000) in their study of the U.S. banking system found that the lower a bank's capitalization, the greater the probability that it would be acquired and argued that this is consistent with the acquisition of failing banks prior to insolvency as well as with the purchase of banks with skillful managers who are able to operate successfully with high leverage.

The importance of capital for banks has been emphasised and put into regulatory forefront by the Basel Committee in the form of capital requirement ratios. The capital adequacy requirements imposed by the 1988 Accord as well as the new capital framework[7] (Basell II) imply, that the total capital ratio (Tier 1 and Tier 2), calculated using the definition of regulatory capital and risk-weighted assets must be at least 8%. Although it was not possible to use such risk-weighted ratios due to data availability, a number of alternative measures were considered. After all, Estrella et al. (2000) in a study of bank default prediction,

---

[7] Recently the new capital framework was released (Basel II). The Basel Committee on Banking Supervision issued its first proposal for the new capital adequacy framework on June 1999. The Committee subsequently released additional proposals for consultation in January 2001 and April 2003 and furthermore conducted three quantitative impact studies related to its proposals. The final document for the new capital adequacy framework was released on June 2004 under the title "International Convergence of Capital Measurement and Capital Standards: a Revised Framework". The Committee intends the Framework to be available for implementation as of year-end 2006. However, it feels that one further year of impact studies or parallel calculations will be needed for the most advanced approaches, and these therefore will be available for implementation as of year-end 2007.

illustrate that simple leverage ratios, predict as well as much more complex risk-weighted ratios over one or two year horizons

The first ratio of this category is equity to assets (g1). This is considered one of the basic ratios for capital strength whose use dates back to the early 1990s (Golin, 2001) and its importance is highlighted by the fact that it is still being used by Moody's in its "RiskCalc Model For Privately-Held U.S. Banks" (Kocagil et al., 2002). It measures the amount of protection afforded to the bank by the equity they invested in it and the higher this ratio the more protected the bank is.

The ratio equity to net loans (g2) measures the equity available to absorb losses on the bank's loan portfolio. Golin (2001) argues that this measure represents an improvement over the equity to assets ratio. The rationale of using equity to net loans ratio is that since loans are the riskiest assets banks generally hold, it is the proportion of capital to these assets that is relevant. Therefore, the ratio of equity to loans above is the simple form of risk assets measure.

The third ratio (g3), calculated as equity divided by customer & short term funding provides a measure of the amount of permanent funding (equity) relative to short term potentially volatile funding (customer and short term funding). This ratio is quite similar to the ratio equity to deposits, which is considered along with the equity to assets ratios among the most basic ratios for measuring capital strength. In the US, a ratio of one part capital to each ten of deposits became a rule of thumb of reasonable bank capitalization at the beginning of the century, although it was neglected after the Second World War (Golin, 2001).

The equity to liabilities ratio (g4) is an alternative measure, or simply another way of looking at the equity funding of the balance sheet. The fifth capital ratio considered in the present study (g5, capital funds divided by liabilities) adds hybrid capital and subordinated debt to shareholders' equity in the numerator (while the denominator is the same as in g4), thereby providing a slightly different picture of banks' capital strength.

Management Performance

A major hypothesis is that acquisitions serve to drive out bad management. There are many financial measures for management performance, but probably the mot commonly used one is profitability. Golin (2001) characterizes profits as the lifeblood of any commercial firm, and continues: *"By making adequate earnings, a bank, like any other firm, will be able-barring exceptional circumstances-to maintain solvency, survive, and, in a suitable environment, grow and prosper"* (p.107).
Another factor that has a significant effect on the performance of banks is the efficiency in expenses management. This study employs the following 7 variables as proxies for bank and managerial performance that measure both profit and cost efficiency:

(g6)   Net interest margin (NIM)
(g7)   Net interest revenue / Average assets
(g8)   Other operating income / Average assets
(g9)   Non-interest expenses / Average assets
(g10)   Return on average assets (ROAA)
(g11)   Return on average equity (ROAE)
(g12)   Cost / Income

Variables g9 and g12 are measures of cost efficiency while the remaining are measures of profitability. These are discussed more detailed in the following sections.

Profit Efficiency

Net interest margin (NIM) (g6) is the net interest income (calculated by subtracting interest expense – the interest the bank must pay to its depositors and creditors from whom it has borrowed funds - from interest income – i.e. income from loans and securities) expressed as a percentage of average earning assets[8] (the sum of the bank's assets that

---

[8] Average assets are used to capture any differences that occurred in assets during the fiscal year.

earn interest such as loans and investments in fixed-income securities). It can alternatively be defined as total assets less fixed assets and non-interest earning assets. Hence, NIM reflects the profitability of the bank's interest-earning business and can vary according to the bank's strategy. In attempting to gain market share (by growing its loan portfolio or attracting additional deposits), an aggressive bank might cut lending rates or raise borrowing rates above those of its competitors.

Variable g7, the ratio of Net interest revenue to average total assets, is actually the same as NIM, but expressed as percentage of average total assets rather than earning assets.

Usually the majority of a commercial bank's earnings will be earned from interest-generating activities (i.e. loans, fixed-income securities). However, diversification between interest income and non-interest income (i.e. fees, commissions, trading, sales of assets) is desired, since the latter can supplement the earlier during periods when demand for loans is constrained. Compared to the above ratios, g8 (other operating income / average assets) indicates to what extent non-interest income represents a greater percentage of operating income (net interest income + non-interest income) of the bank. While some of the sources of non-interest income are quite stable (i.e. fees and commissions), others may be more volatile (i.e. trading). So the less volatile the sources of non-interest income, the lower the risk of this form of income, and the more stable this ratio (g8) will be.

g9 (Net interest expenses / Average assets) is one of the cost efficiency variables discussed below. ROAA (g10) is calculated as net profit divided by average total assets and is used to measure the overall profitability of a bank. This ratio measures bank's ability to efficiently fund and service its assets in order to generate appropriate profits. It defines the bank's earnings power and the strength of its business model and it is probably the most important single ratio in comparing the efficiency and operating performance of banks. Golin (2001) has referred to ROAA as the "key measure of profitability".

ROAE (g11), calculated as net profit divided by average shareholders equity, measures the return on shareholders' investment. It is therefore considered as management's report card to its shareholders, although it can have implications for the bank's creditors too. If the bank has not met its return targets, it will be under pressure to amend its corporate governance policies, possible undertaking additional operating and financial risks. Thus, lower ROAE could signify a warning to creditors that a deterioration of other ratios is imminent.

Cost Efficiency

The ratios non-interest expenses to average assets (g9) and cost to income (g12) are considered two primary cost efficiency indicators. The first measures overheads[9] plus loan loss provisions as a proportion of total assets, hence providing information on the efficiency of the bank's management performance regarding expenses relative to the owned assets. A variation of this ratio is to exclude loan loss provisions from the nominator and use income as the denominator, hence measuring overheads as a proportion of operating income. Cost efficiency, in other words, indicates the extent of expenses in terms of revenue or assets. Thus, a bank that makes efficient use of inputs (i.e. non-interest expenses) will have an efficiency indicator that is a low ratio, while a bank with poor cost efficiency will exhibit a high ratio.

Liquidity Ratios

Another important decision that the managers of commercial banks must take refers to liquidity management and more specifically to the process of managing assets and cash flow to maintain the ability to meet current liabilities as they come due. Without the required liquidity to meet obligations, a bank may fail, or at least will become technically insolvent, unless external support is provided. It can be argued that the liquidity position of a bank may influence the probability of acquisition. However, it is difficult to determine a priori what the direction of the influence will be. On one hand, some banks may be acquired precisely because of their good liquidity position (i.e. the size of their liquid assets attracts acquirers). On the other hand, it is possible that some illiquid

---

[9] Overheads are the costs of running business, such as staff salaries and benefits, rent expenses, equipments expenses and other administrative expenses.

banks will be quite willing to be acquired, because they will find it difficult to resolve their illiquidity without acquisition.

In the present study, three ratios are considered as measures of a bank's liquidity position. The first ratio is calculated as net loans divided by total assets (g13) and indicates the percentage of bank assets that are tied up in loans. Hence, the higher this ratio, the less liquid is the bank. The ratio of net loans to customers & short term funding (g14) is another measure of liquidity that shows the relationship between comparatively illiquid assets (i.e. loans) and moderately stable funding sources (i.e. deposits & other short term funding). In other words, it shows to what extent the bank has lent its deposits; therefore lower figures indicate higher liquidity. The last liquidity ratio is defined as liquid assets to customers & short term funding (g15); here liquid assets replace net loans as the numerator in g14. All these are generally short-term assets that can be easily converted into cash, such as cash itself, deposits with the central bank, treasury bills, other government securities and interbank deposits, among others.

Growth

Kocagil et al. (2002) refer to previous empirical evidence suggesting that some banks whose growth rates where relatively high have experienced problems because their management and/or structure were not able to deal with and sustain exceptional growth. It is therefore possible that a firm, which is constrained in this way, could be an attractive acquisition for a firm with surplus resources or management available to help (Barnes, 1999). In the present study, Growth (g16) is measured using bank's total assets change during the fiscal year computed as: (Bank's Total Assets in year 1 / Bank's Total Assets in Year 0) minus 1.

Size

Bank's size will have a negative influence on its chance of being acquired for various reasons. Firstly, large companies are more expensive to be acquired. Secondly, larger companies have greater resources to fight an acquisition. Thirdly, once acquired these banks are also more difficult to absorb in the existing organisation of the acquiring company. Several studies have found that target firms are on average smaller than acquirers (e.g. Franks et al., 1988) or non-targets (e.g. Palepu, 1986; Ambrose and Megginson, 1992). Wheelock and Wilson (2000) document that smaller banks are more likely to be acquired than larger banks. Bank's total assets (g17) is the most commonly used measure of bank's size and is the one employed in the present study too[10].

Market Share

Market power, interpreted as an increase in market share, was found to be among the most important motivating factors in the study of Group of Ten (2001). The market share of a bank is related to its size and the size of its competitors. If the needs of deficit economic units (either individuals or firms) for loans and the ability of surplus economic units for savings in a specific period are taken as given, then, if a bank transforms more deposits into loans relative to its competitors, the marker share, interest margin, and profit of that bank will be higher. The market share of the bank in terms of loans (deposits) is defined by dividing its loans (deposits) with the total loans (deposits) of the banking industry in which it operates (variables g18 and g19, where deposits replace loans).

4.5 Financial Variables and Country (Industry) Adjustment

As the study of the Group of Ten (2001) points out, it is possible that the nature of acquisition activity and the dominant motivations for acquisitions differ between countries. For example, it can be argued that the motives and/or the opportunities for acquisitions, and hence the characteristics of the acquired banks, are likely to be different in, say, a

---

[10] In the case of raw ratios, the logarithmic transformation of total assets is used to reduce the outlier bias, making extremely large or small banks less influential. In the case of country-adjusted ratios (see section 4.5), a transformation was accomplished by dividing the assets of the bank with the average assets of the national banking industry. Thus it was not considered necessary to use the logarithmic transformation too.

country where there have already occurred a number of acquisitions than in one whether there has been little acquisition activity in the recent past, or in a country populated by small banks than in one dominated by larger banks. Barnes (1990) argues that the best and easiest way to adjust for industry specific differences in a general prediction model for acquisitions is to use industry-adjusted ratios, as Platt and Platt (1990) illustrated in bankruptcy prediction. In this case, the industry-adjusted ratio is defined to be the ratio of a firm's financial ratio relative to the average value for that ratio in the firm's industry with each country at a point in time, as expressed by:

Firm's Industry-adjusted Ratio $_{year\ 0}$ = Firm's k ratio $_{year\ 0}$ / Average value of k ratio in corresponding Industry $_{year\ 0}$

In the present study since all banks operate in the commercial banking sector, industry average for a ratio g refers to the average value for that ratio for all commercial banks operating in a specific country Y^{11}. Henceforth, we will refer to the adjusted variables as country-adjusted. The following example illustrates such an adjustment for a hypothetical bank "*XYZ*" operating in Greece. Let us assume that the return on assets (ROA) of the bank in 1998 was 1.6 and that the average ROA of the Greek commercial banking industry over the same year was 2. Then the country-adjusted ROA for "*XYZ*" will be calculated as follows:

Country-adjusted ROA for bank "XYZ" in 1998 = ROA value for "XYZ" in 1998 / Average value of ROA in the Greek commercial banking industry in 1998 = 1.6 / 2 = 0.8

Standardising by country (or industry) averages deflates raw values and expresses the variables in terms of proportions to enhance comparability. Also, because values of the ratios were computed over different years, standardising also controls for the mean shift in the ratios

---

[11] For the purposes of the present study, country average values were calculated from Bankscope database for each one of the 15-EU commercial banking industries for each year over the period 1996-2001.

from year to year. Platt and Platt (1990) argue that the adjustment results in: (a) more stable financial ratios, (b) more stable coefficient estimates over time, and (c) less disparity between ex ante and ex post forecast results.

Table 4.6 Summary of training and testing samples by form of variables (i.e raw or country-adjusted)

Sample	Year of Acquisition	Acquired Banks	Non-acquired banks	Variables
Training sample A1*	1998-2000	109	109	Raw
Training sample A2*	1998-2000	109	109	Country-adjusted
Training sample B1 *	1998-2000	109	218	Raw
Training sample B2 *	1998-2000	109	218	Country adjusted
Testing sample A1**	2001-2002	59	59	Raw
Testing sample A2**	2001-2002	59	59	Country-adjusted
Testing sample B1**	2001-2002	59	348	Raw
Testing sample B2**	2001-2002	59	348	Country-adjusted

Notes: * The same acquired banks were used in both training samples A1, A2, B1, B2. The non-acquired banks in training samples B1 and B2 sum up to 218 by adding another 109 non-acquired banks to the 109 non-acquired banks of training samples A1 and A2. ** The same acquired banks were used in both testing samples A1, A2, B1, B2. The 348 non-acquired banks of testing samples B1 and B2 are calculated as 566 (initial set) minus 218 (used for development purposes). The 59 non-acquired banks of testing samples A1 and A2 were randomly chosen from the 348 non-acquired banks of testing samples B1 and B2.

With this adjustment it has been possible to use both adjusted and unadjusted (raw) data, resulting in the following samples (see Table 4.6):

a. Training sample A1: Equal matched – Raw financial variables
b. Training sample A2: Equal matched – Country-adjusted financial variables
c. Training sample B1: Double matched – Raw financial variables
d. Training sample B2: Double matched – Country-adjusted financial variables
e. Testing Sample A1: Equal matched – Raw financial variables
f. Testing sample A2: Equal matched – Country-adjusted financial variables
g. Testing Sample B1: Unequal matched – Raw financial variables

h. Testing sample B2: Unequal matched – Country-adjusted financial variables

4.6 Variables Reduction Process

It was discussed in section 3.3 that in order to avoid multicollinearity problems and increase the applicability of the model, it is necessary to reduce the number of input variables. We have also mentioned that the three most commonly used techniques are: logical screening, dimension reduction and statistical screening. In the present study, we rely on the latter approach (i.e. statistical screening through a Kruskal-Wallis test[12] of means' differences). As discussed in section 3.3.2, the rule of thumb is keeping the set of variables small and not including a variable unless its discriminating power is statistically demonstrated on a univariate basis (Kocagil et al., 2002). To ensure that the development of the model would not be biased towards equal or double matching procedure or towards raw or country-adjusted financial variables, the Kruskal-Wallis test was applied in all training samples.

4.6.1 Descriptive statistics

Since the characteristics of the acquired and non-acquired banks are compared in terms of a relatively large number of candidate variables (g1-g19), and as there are different variants of the sample (i.e.

---

[12] The objective of the Kruskal-Wallis test is to examine if K random samples could have come from K populations with the same mean. The results of the K samples are combined and arranged in order of increasing size and given a rank number. In cases where equal results occur the mean of the available rank numbers is used. The rank sum for each of the K samples is calculated. Let R_j be the rank sum of the jth sample, n_j be the size of the jth sample, and N be the size of the combined sample. The test statistic is $H = \{[12 / (N/(N+1))] * (\Sigma R_j^2 / n_j)\} - 3 \ (N+1)$. This follows a χ^2 distribution with (K-1) degrees of freedom. The hull hypothesis of equal means is rejected when H exceeds the critical value (Kanji, 1993). The Kruskal-Wallis test was preferred over a parametric test (e.g. t-test) based on the results of a Kolmogorov-Smirnov (K-S) test which reveals that the majority of the variables in the study do not follow a normal distribution (see section 3.3.2 for a discussion on the usefulness of K-S test in determining whether a parametric or non-parametric test should be preferred and Table 4.9 for the results in the present study).

equal/double matched and raw/country-adjusted) it is proposed first to review in a very general way the nature of the differences that exist between the two groups of banks. This is accomplished through the calculation of basic descriptive statistics for the whole set of 19 variables. Tables 4.7 and 4.8 present the mean and standard deviation for each variable using raw and country-adjusted data respectively[13], summarizing the characteristics of the acquired and the non-acquired banks over the period 1998-2000 (training samples). Thus, in other words, these tables provide just a simple comparison of the relative characteristics of the two groups of banks; with respect to a particular characteristic, say the liquidity variables g13-g15, the statistics would reveal how liquid the average acquired bank is relative to the average non-acquired bank.

The main results in Table 4.7 can be summarized as follows:

Non-acquired banks were better capitalized, on average, over the period 1998-2000, with higher values for all 5 capital ratios. This is probably a first indication in support of the previously mentioned argument, that banks, which are close to insolvency, or banks with skillful managers who are able to operate successfully with high leverage, are the ones that are likely to be acquired.

The acquired firms seem to be under-performers with respect to both cost and profit efficiency. Concerning profitability, the highest difference is observed in the ROAA (g10) that is almost 16 times larger for non-acquired banks (just over 13 in the double matched sample), followed by ROAE (g11) which is nearly 3 times higher. Turning to cost efficiency, similar characteristics are observed with both cost to income (g12) and non-interest expenses to average assets (g7) ratios being lower for the non-acquired banks, indicating a more efficient management of costs. These differences in performance measures are probably a first indication in favor of the argument that shareholders, who do not earn

---

[13] The summary statistics shown in Tables 4.7 and 4.8 do not use the Kruskal-Wallis statistical test, which is employed below (Table 4.10).

the required return, perceive acquisitions as a way to replace inefficient management.

Table 4.7 Mean and Standard Deviation of raw financial variables of the acquired and non-acquired banks in training sample (period 1998-2000)

| | Non-Acquired | | | | Acquired | |
| | 1:1 Match (N =109) | | 1:2 Match (N = 218) | | (N = 109) | |
Financial Variables	Average	St.Dev	Average	St.Dev	Average	St.Dev
g1	10.25	10.86	9.05	8.37	7.73	9.35
g2	43.28	92.33	40.78	84.66	39.20	92.80
g3	17.14	32.56	14.04	23.98	12.47	21.75
g4	14.72	27.73	11.82	20.21	9.63	12.74
g5	15.95	28.26	13.24	20.62	10.73	12.34
g6	3.12	3.41	2.98	2.86	2.65	1.68
g7	2.86	2.90	2.76	2.51	2.45	1.54
g8	2.23	4.35	2.05	3.55	1.66	3.05
g9	3.62	4.21	3.53	3.61	3.85	3.93
g10	1.14	2.05	0.96	1.54	0.07	2.70
g11	11.86	9.85	11.44	9.35	3.23	23.62
g12	61.63	24.97	64.42	28.38	78.23	29.31
g13	40.17	25.21	47.42	26.38	47.93	26.16
g14	61.37	37.01	62.03	40.85	65.01	42.60
g15	40.17	38.32	38.63	34.48	40.52	60.82
g16	10.08	26.31	12.84	35.61	7.70	30.80
g17	3.05	0.82	3.08	0.77	3.10	0.87
g18	1.14	5.15	0.94	4.22	1.20	3.11
g19	1.23	5.94	1.03	4.97	1.34	3.48

In terms of liquidity, the differences between the two groups are small for all three ratios, nevertheless some difference is observed in the ratio net loans to customers and short-term funding (g14).

The figures for size and market shares suggest that on average there are no differences between the two groups of banks.

Finally, non-acquired banks experienced a higher growth in terms of total assets, contrary to prior expectations that the opposite would hold.

Average growth for non-acquired banks was 10.08% (equally matched sample) and 12.84% (double matched sample) compared to 7.70% for acquired banks, over the period 1998 to 2000.

Table 4.8 Mean and Standard Deviation of country-adjusted financial variables of the acquired and non-acquired banks in training sample (period 1998-2000)

| Financial Variables | Non-Acquired | | | | Acquired | |
| | 1:1 Match (N =109) | | 1:2 Match (N = 218) | | (N = 109) | |
	Average	St.Dev	Average	St.Dev	Average	St.Dev
g1	10.25	10.86	9.05	8.37	7.73	9.35
g2	43.28	92.33	40.78	84.66	39.20	92.80
g3	17.14	32.56	14.04	23.98	12.47	21.75
g4	14.72	27.73	11.82	20.21	9.63	12.74
g5	15.95	28.26	13.24	20.62	10.73	12.34
g6	3.12	3.41	2.98	2.86	2.65	1.68
g7	2.86	2.90	2.76	2.51	2.45	1.54
g8	2.23	4.35	2.05	3.55	1.66	3.05
g9	3.62	4.21	3.53	3.61	3.85	3.93
g10	1.14	2.05	0.96	1.54	0.07	2.70
g11	11.86	9.85	11.44	9.35	3.23	23.62
g12	61.63	24.97	64.42	28.38	78.23	29.31
g13	40.17	25.21	47.42	26.38	47.93	26.16
g14	61.37	37.01	62.03	40.85	65.01	42.60
g15	40.17	38.32	38.63	34.48	40.52	60.82
g16	10.08	26.31	12.84	35.61	7.70	30.80
g17	3.05	0.82	3.08	0.77	3.10	0.87
g18	1.14	5.15	0.94	4.22	1.20	3.11
g19	1.23	5.94	1.03	4.97	1.34	3.48

We now turn to the differences between the two groups, when the variables are adjusted by country[14] (Table 4.8). In general the results are quite similar as it concerns which group has higher (lower) ratios on

---

[14] The figures in Table 4.8 appear lower because they have been divided with the average of the country where the bank operates. The variables g18 and g19 are unchanged because as market shares they are already expressed relatively to the values of the industry.

average and therefore only cases where differences in comparison to the raw financial variables are observed are discussed below.

The ratio non – interest expenses to average assets (g7) in the equally matched sample is now slightly higher for the non-acquired banks, although it remains lower in the double matched sample. However, the differences in both cases are quite small.

Among the performance measures, the largest differences are observed again in ROAA and ROAE but differences are now slightly larger in the case of ROAE. The figures for net loans to total assets (g13) are now higher for the non-acquired banks, while the relationship also changes in the case of liquid assets to customers and short term funding (g15). Nevertheless, the differences are rather small for both ratios.

It must be emphasised at this point that these general impressions do no more than provide a general picture of the kind of differences that exist between the two groups. A question therefore arises whether it is possible to say anything more about the extent of the differences between the average characteristics of the two groups of banks. In order to arrive at more reliable conclusions about the nature of these differences, it is necessary to study the comparative group characteristics in much greater detail, using a statistical test of the two group mean differences.

4.6.2 Univariate test of two groups mean differences

Eisenbeis (1977) points out that the deviation from the normal distribution in many economics and finance applications appear more likely to be the rule rather than the exception. Therefore, in this section we employ a Kolmogorov-Smirnov (K-S) test to decide whether a parametric or a non-parametric test should be used to compare the means of the two groups.

Table 4.9 presents the results of the K-S test for the four training samples. The low p-values indicate that we can reject the null hypothesis that the sample has been drawn from a normal distribution for the majority of the variables, the only exceptions being the variables g13 (net loans to total assets) for training samples A2, B1 and B2 and g14 (net loans/ customers & short term funding) for training samples A1 and A2.

Application of Quantitative Techniques

Table 4.9 Kolmogorov-Smirnov Test for normality

Financial ratios	Training Sample A1		Training Sample A2		Training Sample B1		Training Sample B2	
	KS-Z	p-value	KS-Z	p-value	KS-Z	p-value	KS-Z	p-value
g1	3.281	0.000	3.384	0.000	3.700	0.000	3.858	0.000
g2	4.728	0.000	4.751	0.000	5.759	0.000	5.841	0.000
g3	4.898	0.000	5.125	0.000	5.524	0.000	5.706	0.000
g4	4.631	0.000	4.632	0.000	5.250	0.000	5.332	0.000
g5	4.628	0.000	4.521	0.000	5.023	0.000	5.218	0.000
g6	2.204	0.000	2.803	0.000	2.451	0.000	3.380	0.000
g7	2.147	0.000	2.901	0.000	2.362	0.000	3.511	0.000
g8	4.066	0.000	4.087	0.000	4.579	0.000	4.374	0.000
g9	3.161	0.000	2.816	0.000	3.456	0.000	3.380	0.000
g10	4.856	0.000	5.685	0.000	5.571	0.000	6.672	0.000
g11	4.104	0.000	4.359	0.000	4.261	0.000	4.565	0.000
g12	1.757	0.004	1.802	0.003	2.153	0.000	2.143	0.000
g13	1.240	0.093	0.774	0.603	1.035	0.235	0.896	0.399
g14	1.156	0.138	1.104	0.186	1.411	0.037	1.620	0.011
g15	3.147	0.000	3.244	0.000	3.457	0.000	3.590	0.000
g16	2.147	0.000	6.207	0.000	3.030	0.000	7.314	0.000
g17	1.352	0.052	5.516	0.000	1.540	0.017	6.868	0.000
g18	5.773	0.000	5.773	0.000	7.160	0.000	7.160	0.000
g19	5.840	0.000	5.840	0.000	7.255	0.000	7.255	0.000

The above results indicate that a non-parametric test, rather a parametric one (e.g. Student's t-test) should be employed to test the differences in the means of the variables between the two groups. Thus, Table 4.10 shows the results of the Kruskal-Wallis non-parametric test employed to examine the differences between acquired and non-acquired banks.

The first remark is that only the capital and performance (both profit and cost) ratios (variables g1-g5 and g10-12) appear to show some degree of significance in discriminating (on a univariate basis) between the acquired and the non-acquired banks over the period 1998-2000. In particular, these 8 ratios exhibit mean differences between the acquired and non-acquired banks at the 10% level in at least one training sample. From these 8 ratios, 3 measure managerial performance (g10-g11) whose means were found to be statistically significant different between the two groups at the 1% level in all training samples (i.e. irrespective of whether raw or country-adjusted, or equal or double matching samples was used). These are: g10 (return on average assets), g11 (return on average equity), and g12 (cost to income). As mentioned previously, the first two (g10 and g11) measure bank's profit efficiency while the last (g12) measures bank's cost efficiency. Turning to the capital ratios (g1-g5), the results are not invariant to country adjustment.

Table 4.10 The Kruskal – Wallis Test for mean differences between acquired and non-acquired groups of banks

Financial Variables	Training Sample A1	Training Sample A2	Training Sample B1	Training Sample B2
g1	2.612	7.609***	2.452	8.109***
g2	0.845	2.250	1.337	3.222*
g3	0.913	2.992*	0.878	3.386*
g4	2.745*	7.486**	2.693	8.035***
g5	3.519*	6.265**	3.949**	7.718***
g6	0.194	1.994	0.033	1.126
g7	0.236	2.070	0.076	1.329
g8	0.397	1.759	0.918	2.538
g9	1.094	0.012	1.239	0.009
g10	17.773***	20.349***	19.220***	23.587***
g11	16.284***	11.689***	18.353***	14.459***
g12	21.408***	20.097***	21.072***	20.851***
g13	0.033	0.098	0.078	0.000
g14	0.151	0.296	0.397	0.871
g15	1.565	1.522	1.183	1.191
g16	0.162	0.103	0.998	1.068
g17	0.013	0.007	0.079	0.035
g18	0.056	0.056	0.326	0.326
g19	0.071	0.071	0.369	0.369

* Statistically significant at the 10% level
** Statistically significant at the 5% level
*** Statistically significant at the 1% level

In particular, ratios g1 and g3 are statistically significant only when country-adjusted ratios were considered (training samples A2 and B2). The ratio g4 (equity / liabilities) is only statistically significant in training samples A2 (at the 10% level), B1 and B2 (at 1% level). The capital funds to liabilities ratio (g5) is the only variable measuring capital strength that is statistically significant across all the training samples.

Finally, the ratio equity to net loans (g2) is significant only for the double matched country-adjusted training sample B2.

4.6.3 Correlation analysis

The outcome of the Kruskal-Wallis test shows that further attention needs to focus mainly on the g1-g5 and g10-g12, as the other variables are unlikely to discriminate between the two groups of banks. The next step in the analysis, therefore, was to examine the correlations among these variables. Table 4.11 shows the correlations among the selected variables for the four training sample[15]. The results indicate that the capital ratios (g1-g5) are highly correlated amongst themselves (except g2 in sample B2), but comparatively not much correlation exists amongst the performance ratios (g10-g12). In particular, g4 and g5 are found to be highly correlated (0.997) in training sample A1, while all four capital ratios are highly correlated with each other in training sample A2 (with correlation coefficient higher than 0.88).

The last step was to exclude those variables with correlation in excess of 0.65 to avoid possible multicollinearity problems (Barnes, 2000). Thus, among the capital ratios, capital funds to liabilities (g5) was selected as this ratio was found to be significant in all cases and was appeared less correlated with the performance ratios than the other three ratios.

Ultimately, the above selection procedure incorporating the Kruskal-Wallis non-parametric test and correlation analysis leads to the choice of 4 input variables for the training samples A1, A2 and B1, together with an additional variable (g2: equity / net loans) for training sample B2, as presented in Table 4.12. A robust outcome of this analysis seems to be the uniformity among final set of input variables irrespective of the sample. That is, whether we use the equal or double matched training samples, or raw or country-adjusted financial variables, variable g5, g10-g12 remain robustly significant.

---

[15] Only the significant variables from each sample are considered further for correlation analysis.

Table 4.11 Correlation coefficients in training samples

Training sample A1	g4	g5	g10	g11	g12		
g4	1						
g5	0.997	1					
g10	0.344	0.317	1				
g11	0.040	0.040	0.383	1			
g12	-0.088	-0.068	-0.359	-0.527	1		
Training sample A2	g1	g3	g4	g5	g10	g11	g12
g1	1						
g3	0.883	1					
g4	0.906	0.955	1				
g5	0.886	0.951	0.995	1			
g10	0.542	0.306	0.297	0.269	1		
g11	0.070	0.036	0.037	0.043	0.213	1	
g12	-0.115	-0.060	-0.067	-0.057	-0.219	-0.433	1
Training sample B1	g5	g10	g11	g12			
g5	1						
g10	0.311	1					
g11	0.017	0.401	1				
g12	-0.057	-0.321	-0.466	1			
Training sample B2	g1	g2	g3	g4	g5	g10	g11	g12
g1	1							
g2	0.417	1						
g3	0.875	0.425	1					
g4	0.905	0.478	0.947	1				
g5	0.883	0.460	0.947	0.991	1			
g10	0.52	0.096	0.296	0.288	0.261	1		
g11	0.041	-0.010	0.016	0.015	0.020	0.241	1	
g12	-0.096	0.012	-0.059	-0.055	-0.052	-0.208	-0.397	1

Table 4.12 - Summary of input variables according to Kruskal-Wallis and correlation analysis by training sample

Training sample A1	Training sample A2	Training sample B1	Training sample B2
			Equity to Net Loans (g2)
Capital Funds to Liabilities (g5)	Capital Funds to Liabilities (g5)	Capital Funds to Liabilities (g5)	Capital Funds to Liabilities (g5)
Return on average assets (g10)	Return on average assets (g10)	Return on average assets (g10)	Return on average assets (g10)
Return on average equity (g11)	Return on average equity (g11)	Return on average equity (g11)	Return on average equity (g11)
Cost to income (g12)	Cost to income (g12)	Cost to income (g12)	Cost to income (g12)

The only exception to this finding is variable g2 (equity to net loans) that has been selected for the training sample B2 because of its low correlation with g5. On the other hand, variables g1, g3 and g4, albeit significant in some cases, could have been potential candidates but were eliminated due to their correlation with g5.

4.7 Conclusion

This chapter began with a discussion of the data sources and issues relating to sample selection. The sample consisted of 168 commercial banks acquired between 1998 and 2002, and 566 non-acquired as of the end of 2002, that was split into training and testing sub-samples to ensure the proper evaluation of the models. Based on data availability, 19 financial variables were initially considered, most of which are unique to the banking industry, measuring capital strength, profit and cost efficiency, liquidity, growth, size and market power. Both raw and country-adjusted variables (i.e. raw variables divided by the average of the baking sector for the corresponding country) were considered. To avoid potential overfitting or multicollinearity problems we selected, for inclusion in the models, only those variables that demonstrated high discriminatory power on univariate tests and low correlation with other variables in the training sample. This resulted in a total of 4 or 5 input variables to be included in the models, represented in the form of raw or country-adjusted ratios.

Chapter 5

Development of Acquisitions Prediction Models

5.1 Introduction

The main purpose of this chapter is to develop classification models that would discriminate the two groups of banks, acquired and non-acquired, on the basis of the samples designed in the previous chapter. Chapter 4 explained the procedure used to obtain a sample of acquired and non-acquired banks, and determined the choice of variables that are to be used further in distinguishing the two groups of banks. We have seen that, on the basis of univariate statistical analyses, acquired and non-acquired banks have similar financial profiles, and there are significant differences among only a few variables.

The final step in this process, discussed in the present chapter, is to employ a classification method in order to analyse the dataset in a multivariate context and develop the prediction model. In principle, it is possible that, even if none of the variables is a very good discriminator individually, the whole set of variables taken together may achieve a high degree of discrimination. The present study employs 7 classification methods representing a variety of disciplines such as statistics, econometrics, operational research, machine learning. These are: (1) Discriminant Analysis, (2) Logit Analysis, (3) UTilités Additives DIScriminantes (UTADIS), (4) Multi-group Hierarchical DIScrimination (MHDIS), (5) Classification And Regression Trees (CART), (6) k-Nearest Neighbors (k-NN), and (7) Support Vector Machines (SVMs).

Methods 1-5 have been applied in previous studies, while 6 and 7 are applied for the first time in the present study. For each one of the 7 classification techniques, 4 prediction models are developed. The prediction ability of these models is then examined using different testing samples (i.e. equal and unequal, as to the proportion of acquired and-non acquired banks), resulting in a total of 6 combinations, as shown in Table 5.1.

Table 5.1 Summary of combinations for models development and testing

Combination	Model	Variables	Matching in training sample	Matching in testing sample
1	1	Raw	Equal	Equal
2	1	Raw	Equal	Unequal
3	2	Country-adjusted	Equal	Equal
4	2	Country-adjusted	Equal	Unequal
5	3	Raw	Double	Unequal
6	4	Country-adjusted	Double	Unequal

For each classification method, the first model is developed using a 1:1 matched training sample (i.e. equal number of acquired and non-acquired banks) and unadjusted country data (i.e. raw financial variables). This model is then tested for predictive accuracy using (i) a 1:1 testing sample and (ii) an unequal testing sample[1] (resulting in combinations 1 and 2). Similarly, a second model is developed using a 1:1 matched training sample, but with country-adjusted financial variables, and its performance is examined using the testing samples as for Model 1 (resulting in combinations 3 and 4). Finally, Models 3 and 4 are developed to replicate the procedures as in Models 1 and 2 respectively, but with a double matched training sample (i.e. each acquired bank is matched with 2 non-acquired banks), and their prediction ability is examined using unequal testing samples (thus resulting in combinations 5 and 6). With 4 prediction models per each of the seven classification techniques, a total of 28 prediction models are entertained in this chapter. The development of discriminant and logit

---

[1] See Table 4.4 for the proportions of acquired and non-acquired banks in the unequal validation sample (i.e. testing sample B).

models is relatively straightforward, applying standard statistical methods. However, the construction of models using the techniques 3-7 involves more complex procedures, including finding an appropriate combination of a number of parameters such as the upper and lower bounds and minimal distance in MHDIS, similarly the upper bound and the kernel parameter in SVMs, the number of nearest neighbors in k-NN, the value of the sub-intervals in UTADIS, and so on. Improper selection of these parameters could result in over-fitting or under-fitting of the models. The selection of these parameters is usually done using a holdout technique within the training sample. With this approach, the training sample has to be split into two parts, one used for estimation and the remainder for validation. Alternatively, a cross-validation in the training sample can be employed (e.g. Espahbodi and Espahbodi, 2003; Doumpos and Pasiouras, 2004). In the present study, a 10-fold cross-validation is used. More specifically, the 218 banks of the training sample (327 in the case of double matched training sample) are randomly divided into 10 almost equal datasets, each one having a similar distribution for the dependent variable. The model is developed using 9 data sets, the 10th being used to obtain initial estimates of the error rates. The process is repeated ten times, each time using a different set for validation. Finally, the results of the 10 iterations are then averaged to calculate the error rate (for a more detailed discussion of the cross validation technique, see section 3.2.2.2). The performance of the model in the validation set is used to access its generalization ability.

It should be emphasised at this point that we assumed equal costs of two types of error and equal group probabilities during the development of all models. The issue of the cost of these two types of errors was discussed in section 3.5.2, where it was mentioned that the cost attributed to each type of error may be subject to the use of the model and therefore different users will have different cost preferences. Consequently, most of the previous studies (including the present study) have assumed that costs are equal to avoid an arbitrary selection. As Bartley and Boardman (1990) mention, when the acquired and non-acquired groups are unequal in number, the use of actual prior probabilities will result in a large percentage of the sample companies being classified as nontargets irrespective of the statistical fit of the model. They point out that the solution to this problem is to compare classification accuracy using equal prior probabilities, as was suggested by Morrison (1969) and Pinches (1980). Such an approach is followed in the present study. In the case of the double matched samples a weighting of the cases of the two groups was performed[2].

5.2 Summary of Results of Model Comparisons

As mentioned above, a total of 28 prediction models were developed using 7 different classification methods. A detailed discussion of the results for each model, and the issues involved in the process of evaluating the predictive accuracy of the models is discussed at greater length in Section 5.3, where the outcome of each classification method is discussed in turn. Given the extensive set of results that are presented in Section 5.3, it is convenient to summarize the evaluative performance of the models in this section.

All results on classification accuracy presented in Tables 5.2-5.4 are for the holdout samples and refer to the post-sample prediction ability of the models[3]. In other words, the prediction ability of the models was tested over a "future" period using banks that were not included in the training sample, thus resulting in an out-of-sample evaluation of the models, ensuring that the modelling approach captures changes in population drift. As a benchmark the performance of the models is also compared with chance predictions (Barnes, 2000).[4]

---

[2] Preliminary results that were conducted without weighting confirmed the argument of Bartley and Boardman (1990) as the performance of the models relatively to the acquired banks was very poor irrespective of the method used.

[3] For the classification accuracies based on the training samples that refer to the same banks that were used to develop the models, see section 5.3.

[4] As mentioned in section 3.5.1, if we have a sample with equal number of acquired and non-acquired banks, it would be reasonable to expect that by using the flip of a coin to decide group membership we could classify about 50% of the firms correctly. Thus, the critical question would be, if by using a classification model, we could classify correct more than 50% of the banks. For samples with unequal numbers of acquired and non-acquired banks the Cohen's Kappa and PABAK can be used to measure the reduction in error generated by a classification model, compared with the errors a completely random classification would generate.

Before moving on to the discussion of the results presented in Tables 5.2-5.4 it should be noted that for discriminant and logit models we present the results obtained using (a) a cut-off point equal to 0.5, an approach that is commonly used, and (b) an "optimum" cut-off point that is empirically estimated based on the suggestion of Palepu (1986). Under the 0.5 cut-off rule, banks with estimated probability higher than 0.5 are classified as acquired, and lower than 0.5 as non-acquired. Using Palepu's method, the cut-off point is determined where the conditional marginal probability densities for the acquired and non-acquired banks are equal and is equivalent to minimising the total error probabilities.[5]

Table 5.2 shows the accuracy results for all 7 classification methods referring to the model developed with an equal matched training sample and raw data (i.e. Model 1). The results indicate that all the models have performed better than chance, as confirmed by the Cohen's Kappa and PABAK measures, discussed in Chapter 3. Panel A shows the prediction accuracies of models tested on a common holdout sample of an equal number of acquired and non-acquired banks, while Panel B results are for the same models tested on a common but unequal holdout sample (i.e. 59 acquired banks and 348 non-acquired ones).[6] For both testing samples, the UTADIS model performs best in terms of overall classification accuracy. However, its overall performance reflects mainly its ability to classify most accurately the holdout group of non-acquired banks, as it does a poor job in classifying the acquired banks. On the other hand, the CART model performs best in classifying most accurately the holdout group of acquired banks, but at the cost of misclassifying approximately 60% of the non-acquired banks. Models developed through discriminant, logit and SVMs are capable of achieving a balance between the two types of error by performing relatively well in terms of classifying both groups of banks. The results do not change significantly between the two holdout samples, at least in

---

[5] See Sections 5.3.1 (Discriminant analysis) and 5.3.2 (Logit analysis) for a more detailed discussion of these classification rules, where we also examine how Palepu's optimum cut-off point is estimated.

[6] See Table 4.4 and the discussion in Chapter 4 of the two testing samples A and B. In terms of Table 5.1, this amounts to combinations 1 and 2 pertaining to Model 1 based on raw data.

terms of the relative performance of the classification methods, the only difference being that the SVMs model ranks first on average classification accuracy and Cohen's Kappa for the unequal holdout sample, offsetting UTADIS. However, it is interesting to note that the overall and average classification accuracies (as well as PABAK) are generally higher on the unequal holdout sample, partly due to the ability of the models to classify correctly a higher proportion of the non-acquired banks. This appears to contradict the argument of Palepu (1986) that testing on an equal matched sample overstates the prediction ability of the model.

Table 5.2 Summary of evaluation performance based on equal matched training samples and raw data (i.e. model 1)

Evaluation measures (%)						
Model 1	Acquired	Non-scquired	Overall	Average	Cohen's Kappa	PABAK
Panel A: Equal Holdout sample						
Discriminant						
Cut-off = 0.5	54.2%	64.4%	59.3%	59.3%	18.6%	18.6%
Estimated cut-off	52.5%	64.4%	58.5%	58.5%	16.9%	16.9%
Logit						
Cut-off = 0.5	50.8%	61.0%	55.9%	55.9%	11.9%	11.9%
Estimated cut-off	32.2%	71.2%	51.7%	51.7%	3.4%	3.4%
UTADIS	39.0%	83.1%	61.0%	61.0%	22.0%	22.0%
MHDIS	49.2%	61.0%	55.1%	55.1%	10.2%	10.2%
CART	61.0%	40.7%	50.8%	50.8%	1.7%	1.7%
k-NN	45.8%	62.7%	54.2%	54.2%	8.5%	8.5%
SVMs	55.9%	64.4%	60.2%	60.2%	20.3%	20.3%
Panel B: Unequal Holdout Sample						
Discriminant						
Cut-off = 0.5	54.2%	65.8%	64.1%	60.0%	12.2%	28.3%
Estimated cut-off	52.5%	68.1%	65.8%	60.3%	13.0%	31.7%
Logit						
Cut-off = 0.5	50.8%	65.8%	63.6%	58.3%	10.2%	27.3%
Estimated cut-off	32.2%	73.9%	67.8%	53.0%	4.5%	35.6%
UTADIS	39.0%	77.9%	72.2%	58.4%	13.1%	44.5%
MHDIS	49.2%	64.4%	62.2%	56.8%	8.1%	24.3%
CART	61.0%	48.0%	49.9%	54.5%	4.3%	-0.2%
k-NN	45.8%	65.8%	62.9%	55.8%	7.2%	25.8%
SVMs	55.9%	66.7%	65.1%	61.3%	13.8%	30.2%

Table 5.3 shows the accuracy results of the same models developed with an equal matched training sample but using country-adjusted data (i.e. Model 2)[7]. Interestingly, the UTADIS model now performs best in classifying accurately the holdout group of acquired banks, for both testing samples. By contrast, the discriminant model performs best in classifying the non-acquired banks, and so achieves the highest overall (and average) classification accuracy, showing also the highest level of improvement over chance (18.6% and 38.6% respectively) as indicated by the Kappa measure. Furthermore, the performance of CART and k-NN models turn out to be inferior to chance assignment for the equal holdout sample (Panel A), while the other models achieved improvements over chance between 8.5% (SVMs) and 15.3% (UTADIS). Comparing the results with Table 5.2 we observe fairly significant differences between country-adjusted and unadjusted (i.e. raw) data, given that the same set of financial variables were used in developing the models. However, as with Table 5.2, the performance results are generally higher for the unequal holdout sample, although the difference observed here is not as great.

Table 5.4 presents the results obtained by models developed with an unequal (double matched) training sample (i.e. 109 acquired banks and 218 non-acquired ones), Model 3 (Panel A) using raw data and Model 4 (Panel B) using country-adjusted data, both tested on the common unequal holdout sample. Panel A shows that, as with Model 1 based on raw data, UTADIS is the best performing one in terms of overall classification Panel A accuracy (as well as average accuracy and PABAK measures), and relatively worse compared to others in predicting the holdout sample of acquired banks. Panel B reveals a slightly different picture when compared with the results of Model 2 (Table 5.3, Panel B), with the discriminant model losing out to the CART model on overall classification accuracy, although the former is now the best performing in terms of predicting the acquired banks. CART's highest accuracy in predicting non-acquired banks makes it the best performing in terms of overall and average accuracy, with an improvement over chance of 32.7% according to PABAK. This

---

[7] With regard to Table 5.1, this amounts to combinations 3 and 4.

difference between the results could be attributed partly to the inclusion of an additional ratio (i.e. Equity/Net Loans) in Model 4 that was found to be statistically significant in the univariate environment (see Table 4.11). It turns out, in the case of Model 4, that all methods achieve classification accuracies above 50% for both holdout groups, acquired and non-acquired.

Table 5.3 Summary evaluation performance based on equal matched training samples and country adjusted data (i.e. model 2)

Evaluation measures (%)						
Model 2	Acquired	Non-scquired	Overall	Average	Cohen's Kappa	PABAK
Panel A: Equal Holdout sample						
Discriminant						
Cut-off = 0.5	55.9%	62.7%	59.3%	59.3%	18.6%	18.6%
Estimated cut-off	50.8%	67.8%	59.3%	59.3%	18.6%	18.6%
Logit						
Cut-off = 0.5	59.3%	52.5%	55.9%	55.9%	11.9%	11.9%
Estimated cut-off	45.8%	67.8%	56.8%	56.8%	13.6%	13.6%
UTADIS	61.0%	54.2%	57.6%	57.6%	15.3%	15.3%
MHDIS	55.9%	55.9%	55.9%	55.9%	11.9%	11.9%
CART	44.1%	54.2%	49.2%	49.2%	-1.7%	-1.7%
k-NN	44.1%	52.5%	48.3%	48.3%	-3.4%	-3.4%
SVMs	55.9%	52.5%	54.2%	54.2%	8.5%	8.5%
Panel B: Unequal Holdout Sample						
Discriminant						
Cut-off = 0.5	55.9%	66.1%	64.6%	61.0%	13.4%	29.2%
Estimated cut-off	50.8%	72.4%	69.3%	61.6%	15.8%	38.6%
Logit						
Cut-off = 0.5	59.3%	58.9%	59.0%	59.1%	9.9%	17.9%
Estimated cut-off	45.8%	72.1%	68.3%	58.9%	12.3%	36.6%
UTADIS	61.0%	60.9%	60.9%	61.0%	12.2%	21.9%
MHDIS	55.9%	61.2%	60.4%	58.6%	9.7%	20.9%
CART	44.1%	61.8%	59.2%	52.9%	3.4%	18.4%
k-NN	44.1%	54.3%	52.8%	49.2%	-0.9%	5.7%
SVMs	55.9%	60.1%	59.5%	58.0%	8.9%	18.9%

To summarize, the optimal selection of a "best" model is a difficult task. More specifically, model selection will vary according to the evaluation measure used. If we assume that we have no preference over the correct classification of acquired or non-acquired banks, then the overall performance and PABAK are the more appropriate measures. In this context, the UTADIS model is the "best" between the ones developed with unadjusted country data (i.e. raw financial variables).

Table 5.4 Summary of evaluation performance of models based on unequal (double matched) training sample and unequal holdout testing sample (i.e. Models 3 & 4)

Evaluation measures (%)	Acquired	Non-acquired	Overall	Average	Cohen's Kappa	PABAK
Panel A: Model 3 (raw data)						
Discriminant						
Cut-off = 0.5	44.1%	70.4%	66.6%	57.2%	9.7%	33.2%
Estimated cut-off	52.5%	66.7%	64.6%	59.6%	11.9%	29.2%
Logit						
Cut-off = 0.5	45.8%	65.8%	62.9%	55.8%	7.2%	25.8%
Estimated cut-off	47.5%	64.1%	61.7%	55.8%	6.9%	23.3%
UTADIS	42.4%	77.9%	72.7%	60.1%	15.5%	45.5%
MHDIS	40.7%	65.2%	61.7%	53.0%	3.7%	23.3%
CART	45.8%	55.2%	53.8%	50.5%	0.5%	7.6%
k-NN	44.1%	63.8%	60.9%	53.9%	4.8%	21.9%
SVMs	44.1%	69.8%	66.1%	56.9%	9.2%	32.2%
Panel B: Model 4 (country-adjusted data)						
Discriminant						
Cut-off = 0.5	54.2%	68.1%	66.1%	61.2%	14.0%	32.2%
Estimated cut-off	59.3%	60.6%	60.4%	60.0%	11.1%	20.9%
Logit						
Cut-off = 0.5	55.9%	60.6%	60.0%	58.3%	9.3%	19.9%
Estimated cut-off	52.5%	66.4%	64.4%	59.5%	11.6%	28.7%
UTADIS	50.8%	66.4%	64.1%	58.5%	10.6%	28.3%
MHDIS	57.6%	54.0%	54.5%	55.8%	6.0%	9.1%
CART	52.5%	68.7%	66.3%	60.6%	13.5%	32.7%
k-NN	52.5%	67.5%	65.4%	60.0%	12.6%	30.7%
SVMs	50.8%	67.0%	64.6%	58.9%	11.1%	29.2%

When country-adjusted variables are used, Discriminant and CART are the two "best" depending on the matching procedure used for training. Assuming a preference on classifying correct acquired banks (non-acquired banks), then CART (UTADIS) is the best under model 1, UTADIS (Discriminant & Logit) under model 2, Discriminant under models 3 (UTADIS) and 4 (CART). Finally, if we are interesting in achieving a balance between the two types of error, implying that the model performs relatively well in classifying banks from both groups, then discriminant analysis and SMVs are the "best", depending on whether equal or unequal samples are used for training and testing when the models are developed with raw data. On the other hand, discriminant analysis and UTADIS are the "best" when country-adjusted financial ratios are used. Turning to the Kappa measures, we observe that the methods that achieve higher classification accuracies also perform well in terms of Cohen's Kappa, while those that perform well in terms of overall classification accuracy also perform well in terms of PABAK.

Finally, to compare our results with other studies, we present in Table 5.5 the results of previous studies that employed a similar approach to evaluate their models. These include performance results that used holdout samples not from the same period as the training sample, but holdout based on out-of-time and out-of-sample period. It should be borne in mind that the results of the present study cannot be suitably compared with the results of Table 5.5, as the latter include studies that have examined other countries, industries or time periods[8]. However, the table shows that there is fair amount of misclassification of the acquired firms in most other studies, highlighting the difficulties in predicting acquisition targets especially when the models are evaluated in a future period.

5.3 Development and Evaluation of Prediction Models

In this section we discuss in detail the results obtained under each classification method, taken in turn, and in doing so we also explain the procedures used to develop the four different models under each method and evaluate their predictive ability.

---

[8] Kocagil et al. (2002) as well as Gupton and Stein (2002) among others point out that the comparison of the performance of various models should be done on the same dataset, as only this allows for a true comparison of model power alone.

Table 5.5　Summary of results of previous studies testing predictive accuracy in out-of-time and out-of-samples, Part A

Study		Acquired	Non-Acquired	Overall	Average	Cohen's	PABAK
Palepu (1986)	Logit	80.0%	44.7%	45.7%	62.4%	2.3%	-8.7%
Walter (1994)	Historical cost data Logit Model	60.0%	74.1%	72.5%	67.0%	19.5%	45.1%
	Current cost data Logit Model	40.0%	69.1%	65.9%	54.6%	5.0%	31.9%
Barnes (1998)	Logit						
	Non-share price models						
	Weighted average cut-off general model	0.0%	99.8%	98.5%	49.9%	-0.3%	97.0%
	Weighted average cut-off specific model	0.0%	99.4%	98.0%	49.7%	-0.8%	95.9%
	Min. of errors cut-off general model	0.0%	99.0%	97.6%	49.5%	-1.2%	95.3%
	Min. of errors cut-off specific model	0.0%	92.4%	91.1%	46.2%	-2.5%	82.2%
	Max. of returns cut-off general model	0.0%	99.8%	98.5%	49.9%	-0.3%	97.0%
	Max. of returns cut-off specific model	0.0%	98.9%	97.4%	49.4%	-1.3%	94.8%
	Share price models						
	Weighted average cut-off general model	0.0%	99.9%	98.6%	50.0%	-0.2%	97.1%
	Weighted average cut-off specific model	0.0%	99.5%	98.1%	49.8%	-0.7%	96.2%
	Min. of errors cut-off general model	0.0%	99.1%	97.7%	49.5%	-1.1%	95.4%
	Min. of errors cut-off specific model	0.0%	92.2%	90.9%	46.1%	-2.5%	81.7%
	Max. of returns cut-off general model	0.0%	99.8%	98.5%	49.9%	-0.3%	97.0%
	Max. of returns cut-off specific model	0.0%	99.2%	97.7%	49.6%	-1.0%	95.5%

Table 5.5 Summary of results of previous studies testing predictive accuracy in out-of-time and out-of-samples, Part B

Study		Acquired	Non-Acquired	Overall	Average	Cohen's	PABAK
Barnes (2000)	Discriminant						
	Weighted average cut-off general model	0.0%	99.5%	98.1%	49.7%	-0.7%	96.3%
	Weighted average cut-off specific model	7.7%	99.4%	98.1%	53.6%	9.7%	96.2%
	Max. of returns general model	0.0%	99.1%	97.8%	49.6%	-1.0%	95.6%
	Max. of returns specific model	7.7%	99.1%	97.7%	53.4%	8.0%	95.5%
	Logit						
	Logit Model 1 (Unadjusted)	61.5%	62.0%	61.9%	61.7%	3.2%	23.9%
Cudd & Dougal (2000)	Logit Model 2 (Adjusted for industry distrib. Charact.)	38.5%	58.3%	57.7%	48.4%	-0.4%	15.4%
	Logit Model 3 (adj. For indu. Distr. & month spec. charact.)	7.1%	78.0%	75.9%	42.6%	-3.7%	51.9%
Powell (2001)	Max. of proportion of target firms cut-off	24.1%	78.5%	76.9%	51.3%	0.6%	53.8%
	Min. of absolute number of misclassifications cut-off	6.9%	90.3%	87.9%	48.6%	-1.3%	75.8%
Espahbodi & Espahbdoi (2003)	Discriminant	52.6%	51.0%	51.3%	51.8%	2.0%	2.5%
	Logit	55.3%	51.5%	52.1%	53.4%	3.7%	4.2%
	Probit	55.3%	51.5%	52.1%	53.4%	3.7%	4.2%
	Recursive Partitioning (CART)	65.8%	66.0%	66.0%	65.9%	20.0%	31.9%

Notes: 1. min and max in Barnes (1998 and 2000) denote minimization and maximization; 2. The Logit model in Barnes (2000) correspond to the weighted average cut-ff and maximization of returns non-share-price models from Barnes (1998) and are reported in the study for comparison reasons; 3. Cohen's Kappa and PABAK are not reported in the original studies but were calculated from the reported data for comparisons reasons with the present study. The same applies for some cases for the average or overall accuracy as most studies report only one of the two.

5.3.1 Discriminant analysis

Table 5.6 presents the coefficients (both unstandardized and standardized) of the four discriminant models. As the results of Chapter 4 showed, on a strictly univariate basis, the capital strength and profitability variables had lower values for the acquired banks, while the opposite was observed for the cost to income ratio. Consequently, as expected, the discriminant coefficients for variables Equity to Net Loans (g2), Capital Funds to Liabilities (g5), Return on Average Assets (g10), and Return on Average Equity (g11), display negative signs while that of Cost to Income (g12) a positive sign in all models.

The values in parentheses are the standardized coefficients that are useful in determining the relative contribution of each variable to the total discriminating power of the functions. Standardizing the variables ensures that scale differences between the variables are eliminated. Consequently, absolute values (i.e. ignore the sign) can be used to rank variables in terms of their discriminating power, the largest value being associated with the most powerful discriminating variable. Variables with large values are those that contribute most to differentiating the groups. The results in Table 5.6 indicate that the largest contributor to group separation of the discriminant function is g12 (Cost to income), followed by g11 (ROAE).

The statistical significance of the discriminatory power of the 4 models is evaluated using the Wilk's Lambda statistic. The results indicate that with a Wilk's Lambda that ranges between 0.890 (raw equal developed model) and 0.920 (raw double developed) all models are statistically significant at the 1% level.

We now turn to the evaluation of the models in terms of their classification ability. As mentioned earlier this is the most important aspect of a prediction model. It was discussed in Chapter 3 that the classification of firms into one of the two groups is usually made on the basis of some classification rule. Once the values of the discriminant coefficients are estimated, it is possible to calculate discriminant scores for each bank in the sample and classify it on the basis of its D score and a cut-off point (usually zero on the case of equal groups), or according to the probability of group membership and a cut-off probability.

Table 5.6   Discriminant models classification function coefficients

	Unstandardized (Adjusted) Coefficients			
Variable	Model 1	Model 2	Model 3	Model 4
G2	---	---	---	-0.017
				(-0.147)
G5	-0.011	-0.082	-0.007	-0.037
	(-0.235)	(-0.273)	(-0.114)	(-0.096)
G10	-0.112	-0.030	-0.165	-0.037
	(-0.269)	(-0.265)	(-0.362)	(-0.322)
G11	-0.015	-0.155	-0.023	-0.211
	(-0.266)	(-0.293)	(-0.414)	(-0.399)
G12	0.024	1.615	0.017	1.385
	(0.648)	(0.686)	(0.488)	(0.596)
Constant	- 1.343	-1.384	-0.872	-1.165
Wilk's Lambda	0.890	0.888	0.920	0.913
Chi-square	24.849***	25.368***	26.768***	19.185 ***

Note: values in parentheses correspond to standardized coefficients
*** Statistically significant at the 1% level

Palepu (1986) criticized previous studies for applying classification rules derived from equal groups to unequal groups. Therefore, to avoid such criticisms as well as to examine how the change of the classification rule will affect the results, we follow two approaches to evaluate the models. In the first case, the classification is performed using the probabilities of group membership and a cut-off probability equal to 0.5, an approach that is commonly used. In the second case, we use an optimum cut-off point that is calculated based on the suggestions of Palepu (1986)[9].

---

[9] As mentioned in Chapter 3, other classification rules also exist. For example, Barnes (1998) proposed the use of a maximization of returns cut-off or a weighted cut-off point based on historical data. We rely only on the above-mentioned rules for two reasons. First, the results of Barnes do not indicate any superiority of these alternative classification rules when compared to the one of Palepu. Second, the 0.5 cut-off point and Palepu's optimum cut-off point are the two most commonly used cut-off points.

(i) Cut-off probability equal to 0.5

The discriminating ability of the models is tested in two ways. First, the classification ability of the model is examined for the training sample. The values of the independent variables are computed for each one of the 218 banks that were used for the development of the model, to examine what percent of them are classified correctly as acquired or non-acquired. Then the models are tested on holdout samples from a future period.

Table 5.7 presents the re-classification of the banks that were used for the development of the models. The overall correct classification for the model ranges between 63.3% (model 2) and 66.1% (models 3 and 4). Thus, the double matched models achieve slightly higher overall classification accuracy in the training sample. Nevertheless, a closer look at the other measures (average, individual groups classification, Cohen's and PABAK) indicates that this can be attributed to the increased ability of these models to classify correct the non-acquired banks. Since, the classification accuracies in the training sample are not so important they will not be discussed further. The reason is that since the discriminant coefficients and the group distributions are derived from this sample at this point the model is actually explanatory, hence is subject to an upward bias in the model's classification accuracy (Altman, 1993). An alternative, more valid, approach is to test the model's predictive ability on observations not used for its development, typically from a time period after its development. Consequently, the holdout testing samples were employed to test the prediction ability of the models.

Table 5.7 Discriminant in-sample (training) classification results (Cut-off equal to 0.5)

	Acquired	Non-acquired	Overall	Average	Cohen's Kappa	PABAK
Model 1	63.3%	67.0%	65.1%	65.1%	30.3%	30.3%
Model 2	58.7%	67.9%	63.3%	63.3%	26.6%	26.6%
Model 3	61.5%	68.3%	66.1%	64.9%	28.1%	32.1%
Model 4	58.7%	69.7%	66.1%	64.2%	27.1%	32.1%

Panel A in Table 5.8 presents the classification results when models 1 and 2 were tested using the equal holdout samples. The overall classification accuracy of both models is 59.3%, which shows that they can predict better than chance (i.e. 50% in an equal sample). The Kappa tests indicate that the prediction accuracy of the two models represents an improvement over chance that amounts to 18.6%. It is interesting to note that although use of country-adjusted ratios (model 2) does not improve the overall classification ability of the model, it contributes to slightly less misclassification of the acquired banks and consequently achieves a slightly better balance between type I and II errors.

Table 5.8 Discriminant models holdout (testing) sample prediction results (cut-off equal to 0.5)

	Acquired	Non- acquired	Overall	Average	Cohen's Kappa	PABAK
Panel A: Equal Holdout Testing						
Model 1	54.2%	64.4%	59.3%	59.3%	18.6%	18.6%
Model 2	55.9%	62.7%	59.3%	59.3%	18.6%	18.6%
Panel B: Unequal Holdout Testing						
Model 1	54.2%	65.8%	64.1%	60.0%	12.2%	28.3%
Model 2	55.9%	66.1%	64.6%	61.0%	13.4%	29.2%
Model 3	44.1%	70.4%	66.6%	57.2%	9.7%	33.5%
Model 4	54.2%	68.1%	66.1%	61.2%	14.0%	32.2%

When the models are tested in the unequal samples (Panel B) we observe a slight increase in both the overall and the average correct classification rates for Models 1 and 2. The reason is that the prediction accuracy of the models for non-acquired banks increases by 1.4% for Model 1 and 3.4% for Model 2 in the unequal testing sample, while the classification accuracy for acquired banks remains constant. This adversely affects both Kappa tests, lowering Cohen's and raising PABAK. However, both Kappa tests indicate that all the models can predict better than chance. Model 3 achieves the higher overall classification accuracy (66.6%), but at the same time it misclassifies the highest percentage of acquired banks. This is the reason why its average classification accuracy and Cohen's kappa are inferior to those of the other three models. Obviously, Model 4 achieves a slightly better performance, as it has the ability to obtain relatively high classification accuracies in both groups with balanced type I and II errors resulting in higher average classification accuracy and Cohen's Kappa.

(ii) Cut-off point two - Acquisition probabilities distribution and Minimization of errors

In this case, a given bank is classified into the acquired group if the posterior probability of acquisition for that bank is greater than an optimum cut-off point. Palepu (1986) argues that an optimal classification rule should require that the conditional marginal probability densities of classifying a firm as acquired, if it is actually acquired (f_1), should equal or exceed the corresponding marginal probability of classifying the firm as acquired, if it is actually a non-acquired firm (f_2). The optimum cut-off probability that attempts to balance the probability of committing Type I and Type II errors is the value where the two conditional marginal densities are equal.

Following Palepu's (1986) procedure, the optimum cut-off point is determined as follows:

1. The probability of acquisition is computed for each bank in the training sample.

2. The estimated takeover probabilities for the acquired and non-acquired banks are divided into 10 equal intervals. The number of acquired and non-acquired banks falling within each one of the 10 intervals is expressed as a percentage of the total of acquired and non-acquired banks in the training sample, respectively.

3. The optimum cut-off probability is the value at which the estimated probability distributions for acquired (target) and non-acquired (non-target) banks intersect. Below this point, the probability of a bank being classified as acquired is less than the probability of being classified as non-acquired (see Figure 5.1 below for an illustration).

Table 5.9 presents the number and percentages of acquired and non-acquired banks following in each interval according to their corresponding acquisition probability. It is obvious that the empirical distributions of acquisition probabilities for the acquired and non-acquired banks are quite similar. This is consistent, with the studies that developed models for non-financial firms, showing the difficulty in predicting acquisition targets (e.g Palepu, 1986; Barnes, 2000; Espahbodi and Epahbodi, 2003). The numbers in columns f_1 (p) and f_2 (p) are calculated by dividing the number of acquired and non-acquired banks in each interval by the total of acquired and non-acquired banks in the sample (i.e. 109 or 218) and expressing the results as a percentage.

In Figure 5.1 the midpoint of each probability interval for the acquired banks is plotted against the percentage of acquired banks in the interval. A similar plot is formed for the non-acquired banks. The graph shows that the two distributions intersect at a probability value equal to 0.5050 for model 1, 0.5232 for model 2, 0.4885 for model 3 and 0.4849 for model 4[10].

Table 5.9 Acquisition Probability distributions (discriminant models), Part A

Estimated probability		Acquired banks		Non-acquired banks		
Range	Mid value	No.	f_1(p) (%)	No.	f_1(p) (%)	f_1(p)/ f_2(p)
Model 1						
0.000 – 0.099	0.05	0	0.0	2	1.8	0
0.100 – 0.199	0.15	0	0.0	2	1.8	0
0.200 – 0.299	0.25	4	3.7	5	4.6	0.8
0.300 – 0.399	0.35	7	6.4	19	17.4	0.368
0.400 – 0.499	0.45	29	26.6	45	41.3	0.644
0.500 – 0.599	0.55	40	36.7	31	28.4	1.290
0.600 – 0.699	0.65	18	16.5	4	3.7	4.500
0.700 – 0.799	0.75	3	2.8	0	0.0	---
0.800 – 0.899	0.85	6	5.5	1	0.9	6.000
0.900 – 0.999	0.95	2	1.8	0	0.0	---
Total		109		109		

---

[10] The point of intersection of the two distributions can also be estimated through interpolation. For example, for model 1, a value of 1 for f_1 (p) / f_2 (p) falls between the 5th and 6th interval. Hence, using the midpoints of the second and third classification intervals and their corresponding f_1 (p)/f_2 (p) values, the cut-off point is approximated as follows: 0.45 + ((1-0.644) / (1.290 – 0.644)) * (0.55-0.45) = 0.5050. The cut-off points for the other three models are calculated on a similar manner.

Table 5.9 Acquisition Probability distributions (discriminant models), Part B

Estimated probability		Acquired banks		Non-acquired banks		
Range	Mid value	No.	$f_1(p)$ (%)	No.	$f_1(p)$ (%)	$f_1(p)/f_2(p)$
Model 2						
0.000 – 0.099	0.05	0	0.0	2	1.8	0.000
0.100 – 0.199	0.15	0	0.0	4	3.7	0.000
0.200 – 0.299	0.25	2	1.8	2	1.8	1.000
0.300 – 0.399	0.35	11	10.1	22	20.2	0.500
0.400 – 0.499	0.45	32	29.4	44	40.4	0.727
0.500 – 0.599	0.55	33	30.3	30	27.5	1.100
0.600 – 0.699	0.65	20	18.3	4	3.7	5.000
0.700 – 0.799	0.75	4	3.7	1	0.9	4.000
0.800 – 0.899	0.85	4	3.7	0	0.0	---
0.900 – 0.999	0.95	3	2.8	0	0.0	---
Total		109		109		
Model 3						
0.000 – 0.099	0.05	0	0	1	0.5	0
0.100 – 0.199	0.15	0	0	2	0.9	0
0.200 – 0.299	0.25	2	1.8	6	2.8	0.667
0.300 – 0.399	0.35	7	6.4	37	17.0	0.378
0.400 – 0.499	0.45	33	30.3	103	47.2	0.641
0.500 – 0.599	0.55	48	44.0	61	28.0	1.574
0.600 – 0.699	0.65	10	9.2	6	2.8	3.333
0.700 – 0.799	0.75	2	1.8	1	0.5	4
0.800 – 0.899	0.85	4	3.7	0	0.0	---
0.900 – 0.999	0.95	3	2.8	1	0.5	6
Total		109		218		
Model 4						
0.000 – 0.099	0.05	0	0.0	1	0.5	0.000
0.100 – 0.199	0.15	0	0.0	2	0.9	0.000
0.200 – 0.299	0.25	2	1.8	8	3.7	0.500
0.300 – 0.399	0.35	8	7.3	46	21.1	0.348
0.400 – 0.499	0.45	35	32.1	95	43.6	0.737
0.500 – 0.599	0.55	41	37.6	55	25.2	1.491
0.600 – 0.699	0.65	13	11.9	9	4.1	2.889
0.700 – 0.799	0.75	3	2.8	1	0.5	6.000
0.800 – 0.899	0.85	4	3.7	0	0.0	---
0.900 – 0.999	0.95	3	2.8	1	0.5	6.000
Total		109		218		

It should be mentioned at this point that as Figure 5.1 shows, in the case of model 2 the two distributions overlap more than once. Thus, there are two potential cut-off points: 0.250 and 0.523. However, only the second one will be further considered as the first one does not minimize errors as its classification accuracy is 50.5%, while the second has a classification accuracy of 64.7%. Hence, the previously mentioned cut-off probabilities are used to access the classification and prediction ability of the models, by applying the following classification rules:

Model 1: classify a bank as acquired if its acquisition probability is greater than 0.5050 and as non-acquired if it is lower.

Model 2: classify a bank as acquired if its acquisition probability is greater than 0.5232 and as non-acquired if it is lower.

Model 3: classify a bank as acquired if its acquisition probability is greater than 0.4885 and as non-acquired if it is lower.

Model 4: classify a bank as acquired if its acquisition probability is greater than 0.4849 and as non-acquired if it is lower.

Table 5.10 shows the classification accuracies when the above cut-off rules are applied on the training samples. Two conclusions can be drawn: (a) All models achieve classification accuracies better than chance, and (b) The results concerning the performance of the models compared to the one achieved using 0.5 as a cut-off point are mixed, since some models achieve slightly better, and others worse, classification accuracies, while the increases or decreases on performance are subject to the evaluation measure used. Both rules, however, provide similar results in the training samples.

Table 5.10 Discriminant models in-sample (training) classification results (Palepu's optimum cut-off points)*

	Acquired	Non-acquired	Overall	Average	Cohen's Kappa	PABAK
Model 1	62.4%	69.7%	66.1%	66.1%	32.1%	32.1%
Model 2	51.4%	78.0%	64.7%	64.7%	29.4%	29.4%
Model 3	61.5%	68.3%	66.1%	64.9%	28.1%	32.1%
Model 4	52.5%	66.7%	64.6%	59.6%	11.9%	29.2%

Cut-off points: Model 1 = 0.5050, Model 2 = 0.5232 Model 3 = 0.4885, Model 4 = 0.4849

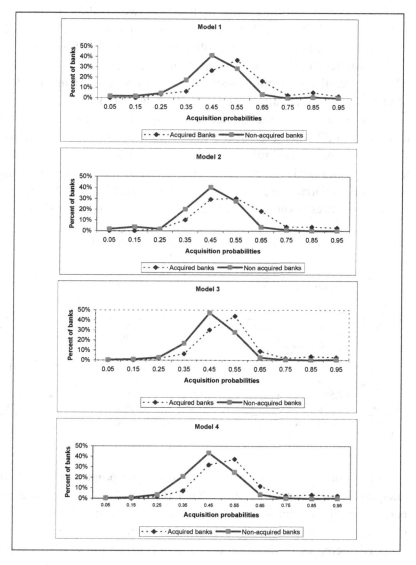

Figure 5.1 Distribution of acquisition probabilities (discriminant models)

We now turn to the testing of the first two models in the holdout samples (see Table 5.11). The overall classification accuracy of the models in the equal holdout sample (Panel A) is 58.5% (Model 1) and 59.3% (Model 2). Compared to the results presented in Table 5.7 (Panel A), the overall and average accuracies as well as the Kappa values of Model 2 remain unchanged; however, there is a trade-off between type I and type II errors as the model now misclassifies 29 acquired banks compared to 27 when the cut-off was set equal to 0.5. Turning to Model 1, the performance is similar compared to the classification rule of 0.5, in that the model achieves the same classification for non-acquired banks, but classifies correct one acquired bank less, resulting in a decrease in all overall measures (overall & average accuracy, Cohen and PABAK).

Table 5.11 Discriminant models holdout (testing) prediction results (Palepu's optimum cut-off points)*

	Acquired	Non-acquired	Overall	Average	Cohen's Kappa	PABAK
Panel A: Equal Holdout Testing						
Model 1	52.5%	64.4%	58.5%	58.5%	16.9%	16.9%
Model 2	50.8%	67.8%	59.3%	59.3%	18.6%	18.6%
Panel B: Unequal Holdout Testing						
Model 1	52.5%	68.1%	65.8%	60.3%	13.0%	31.7%
Model 2	50.8%	72.4%	69.3%	61.6%	15.8%	38.6%
Model 3	52.5%	66.7%	64.6%	59.6%	11.9%	29.2%
Model 4	59.3%	60.6%	60.4%	60.0%	11.1%	20.9%

*Cut-off points: Model 1 = 0.5050, Model 2 = 0.5232, Model 3 = 0.4885, Model 4 = 0.4849

When the models using the optimal cut-off points are tested in the unequal holdout testing sample (Panel B), the classification of acquired banks remains unchanged while that of non-acquired banks increases. Consequently, overall and average classification accuracy as well as PABAK increases for both Models 1 and 2, hence the results concerning the use of raw or country-adjusted financial variables are mixed. In the case of the equal matched trained models (models 1-2), the model with raw variables outperforms the one with country-adjusted variables in the prediction of acquired banks, but is inferior in the all other performance measures. However, in the case of the double matched trained models

(models 3-4), it is the model with raw variables that classifies correct a higher percentage of acquired banks and lower of non-acquired banks. Finally, the comparison of results based on the two classification rules (i.e. the two cut-off points) also reveals mixed results. In some cases the 0.5 cut-off rule provides better results than the optimal cut-off rule and in other cases the opposite occurs. The superiority of one of the two rules depends on the form of variables used (i.e. raw or country-adjusted), the matching procedure (i.e. equal or double) and the performance measure used to access the feasibility of the model.

5.3.2 Logit analysis

Table 5.12 presents maximum likelihood estimates of the logit coefficients as well as goodness of fit and other measures of the strength of association of our models. Obviously all the signs of the financial variables are as expected, i.e. Capital Funds to Liabilities (g5), Return on Average Assets (g10), Rerun on Average Equity (g11) for all models as well as Equity to Net Loans (g2) (model 4) are negatively related to the acquisition probability while Cost to Income (g12) is positively related. The Wald test indicates that the most powerful variables are: g12 that is significant in all models (significance ranges between 1% and 10% depending on the model), and g11 that is significant in three models in either the 5% or 10% level. However, the Wald test results should be treated with caution, as there are circumstances where they may lead to wrong interpretations[11].

Likelihood ratio test, Cox and Shell R^2, Nagelkerke R^2 and Hosmer & Lemeshow test are also employed to examine the goodness of fit and strength of association for all four models. First of all, Log-likelihood tests reject the null hypothesis that all coefficients are zero at the 1% level. The Hosmer & Lemeshow test is a test of the difference between

---

[11] Menard (1995) argues that when the absolute value of the regression coefficient is large, the estimated standard error tends to become too large, resulting in increased Type II error: making the test too conservative. A second disadvantage of the Wald test occurs when predictors have more than two levels (Tabachnick and Fidell, 2001). Nevertheless, despite its limitations the Walt test is often employed because it is easy to compute it and it is the standard outcome in all statistical/econometrical packages.

model-predicted values and observed values. A non-significant chi-square (Tabachnick and Fidell, 2001) and high p-values shown indicate there is no significant difference between the predicted and observed number of cases. Finally, Cox & Shell R^2 and Nagelkerke R^2 are similar to R^2 in ordinary linear regression (OLS). Although none of them has the same variance interpretation as R^2 for OLS, they both approximate it (Tabachnick and Fidell, 2001). The Nagelikerke[12] measure is an adjusted version of the Cox & Snell R^2, ranging between 0.137 (model 3) and 0.19 (model 2).

Table 5.12 Coefficient and goodness of fit of Logit models

Variable	Coefficients			
	Model 1	Model 2	Model 3	Model 4
g2	---	---	---	-0.014
				(0.688)
g5	-0.011	-0.07	-0.007	-0.028
	(1.591)	(1.386)	(0.756)	(0.222)
g10	-0.109	-0.073	-0.127	-0.061
	(0.517)	(0.563)	(1.105)	(0.79)
g11	-0.039	-0.271	-0.040	-0.327
	(3.047)*	(1.215)	(5.399)**	(3.185)*
g12	0.018	1.381	0.009	0.851
	(5.384)**	(6.632)***	(2.846)*	(5.037)**
Constant	-0.690	-0.967	-0.141	-0.445
	(1.135)	(2.146)	(0.091)	(0.845)
-2 Log likelihood	269.461	268.700	417.746	414.776
Likelihood ratio Chi-square	32.751***	33.512***	35.572***	38.543***
Hosmer & Lemeshow Test				
Chi-square	9.44	2.778	7.092	4.662
p-values	0.307	0.948	0.527	0.793
Cox & Snell R^2	0.139	0.142	0.103	0.111
Nagelkerke R^2	0.186	0.190	0.137	0.148

Notes: 1.Values in parentheses correspond to the Wald test; 2. *Significant at the 10% level; **Significant at the 5% level, ***Significant at the 1% level

---

[12] The Cox & Snell measure is based on the log-likelihood for the model compared with the log-likelihood for a baseline model, calculated as: Cox & Snell $R^2 = 1 - \exp[(-2/n)(LL(B) - LL(0)]$. Cox and Snell R^2, however, cannot achieve a maximum value of 1. An adjusted version of the Cox and Snell R^2 is the Nagelkerke measure that adjusts the scale of the statistic to cover the full range from 0 to 1. Nagelkerke R^2 = Cox & Snell R^2 / R^2_{MAX}, where $R^2_{MAX} = 1 - \exp[2(n^{-1}) LL(0)]$.

We now turn to the evaluation of the models in terms of their classification ability. Similar to the discriminant models, we apply two classification rules: (i) setting the cut-off equal to 0.5 by default and (ii) estimating optimally as Palepu (1986) suggested.

(i) Cut-off probability equal to 0.5

The in-sample (training) classification results for the four models based on a cut-off point equal to 0.5 are presented in Table 5.13, while those obtained for the holdout testing samples are presented in Table 5.14.

Table 5.13 Logit models in-sample (training) classification results (cut-off equal to 0.5)

	Acquired	Non-acquired	Overall	Average	Cohen's Kappa	PABAK
Model 1	65.1%	65.1%	65.1%	65.1%	30.3%	30.3%
Model 2	64.2%	60.6%	62.4%	62.4%	24.8%	24.8%
Model 3	62.4%	64.2%	63.6%	63.3%	24.5%	27.2%
Model 4	63.3%	62.4%	62.1%	61.5%	22.5%	24.2%

The results for the training samples are obviously better than chance classifications. The overall classification accuracy of the models is between 62.1% (model 4) and 65.1% (model 1), and the models achieve up to 30.3% improvement over allocation by chance. Concerning the matching procedure, we observe that both Cohen's and PABAK decrease when more non-acquired banks are included in the sample.

Table 5.14 Logit models holdout (testing) prediction results (cut-off equal to 0.5)

	Acquired	Non-acquired	Overall	Average	Cohen's Kappa	PABAK
Panel A: Equal Holdout Testing						
Model 1	50.8%	61.0%	55.9%	55.9%	11.9%	11.9%
Model 2	59.3%	52.5%	55.9%	55.9%	11.9%	11.9%
Panel B: Unequal Holdout Testing						
Model 1	50.8%	65.8%	63.6%	58.3%	10.2%	27.3%
Model 2	59.3%	58.9%	59.0%	59.1%	9.9%	17.9%
Model 3	45.8%	65.8%	62.9%	55.8%	7.2%	25.8%
Model 4	55.9%	60.6%	60.0%	58.3%	9.3%	19.9%

The results of Table 5.14 (Panel A) show the prediction ability of models 1 and 2 tested on the equal holdout samples, indicating that both models retain their ability to outperform chance. As with the corresponding discriminant models, these two logit models do not show much difference in terms of overall evaluation measures (overall, average and Kappa) but they differ substantially in terms of individual groups classification accuracies. Model 1 performs better with respect of the non-acquired banks, classifying correct 36 banks (but performs worse in terms of classification accuracies for acquired banks), while the opposite is the case with model 2, classifying correct 31 non-acquired banks.

Turning to the predictions based on the unequal holdout testing samples (Table 5.14, Panel B), we observe that both models 1 and 2 achieve higher average and overall classification accuracies, as a result of the increase in the percentage of non-acquired banks correctly classified. The performance relative to chance depends on the Kappa measure employed. As expected Cohen's Kappa declines while PABAK increases. Models 3 and 4 also predict better than chance with Cohen's Kappa 7.2% (model 3) and 9.3% (model 4), and PABAK equal 25.8% (model 3) and 19.9% (model 4). Finally, while the use of country-adjusted financial variables contributes to the correct classification of acquired banks, it leads at the same time to the misclassification of more non-acquired banks. Therefore the evaluation performance of the models varies with the form of variables and nature of data, although models 3 and 4 show lower differences than models 1 and 2.

(ii) Cut-off point two - Acquisition probabilities distribution and Minimization of errors

We now turn to the second classification rule. We follow the same procedure as in discriminant analysis to find the cut-off probability that corresponds to the value at which the estimated probability distributions for acquired and non-acquired banks intersect. Table 5.15 presents the number and percentages of acquired and non-acquired banks falling in each interval according to their corresponding acquisition probability.

We can see that the empirical distributions of acquisition probabilities for the acquired and non-acquired banks are again quite similar.

Table 5.15 Logit Acquisition Probability distributions, Part A

Estimated probability		Acquired banks		Non-acquired banks		
Range	Mid value	No.	$f_1(p)$ (%)	No.	$f_1(p)$ (%)	$f_1(p)/ f_2(p)$
Model 1						
0.000 – 0.099	0.05	1	0.9	5	4.6	0.200
0.100 – 0.199	0.15	2	1.8	4	3.7	0.500
0.200 – 0.299	0.25	6	5.5	13	11.9	0.462
0.300 – 0.399	0.35	9	8.3	14	12.8	0.643
0.400 – 0.499	0.45	20	18.3	35	32.1	0.571
0.500 – 0.599	0.55	26	23.9	29	26.6	0.897
0.600 – 0.699	0.65	26	23.9	8	7.3	3.250
0.700 – 0.799	0.75	8	7.3	0	0.0	---
0.800 – 0.899	0.85	4	3.7	1	0.9	4.000
0.900 – 0.999	0.95	7	6.4	0	0.0	---
Total		109		109		
Model 2						
0.000 – 0.099	0.05	0	0.0	4	3.7	0.000
0.100 – 0.199	0.15	2	1.8	4	3.7	0.500
0.200 – 0.299	0.25	4	3.7	12	11.0	0.333
0.300 – 0.399	0.35	15	13.8	22	20.2	0.682
0.400 – 0.499	0.45	18	16.5	24	22.0	0.750
0.500 – 0.599	0.55	26	23.9	32	29.4	0.813
0.600 – 0.699	0.65	22	20.2	6	5.5	3.667
0.700 – 0.799	0.75	11	10.1	4	3.9	2.750
0.800 – 0.899	0.85	4	3.7	1	0.9	---
0.900 – 0.999	0.95	7	6.4	0	0.0	---
Total		109		109		
Model 3						
0.000 – 0.099	0.05	0	0.0	2	0.9	0.000
0.100 – 0.199	0.15	2	1.8	7	3.2	0.571
0.200 – 0.299	0.25	4	3.7	16	7.3	0.500
0.300 – 0.399	0.35	7	6.4	42	19.3	0.333
0.400 – 0.499	0.45	28	25.7	73	33.5	0.767
0.500 – 0.599	0.55	36	33.0	57	26.1	1.263
0.600 – 0.699	0.65	18	16.5	16	7.3	2.250
0.700 – 0.799	0.75	4	3.7	4	1.8	2.000
0.800 – 0.899	0.85	5	4.6	0	0.0	---
0.900 – 0.999	0.95	5	4.6	1	0.5	10.000
Total		109		218		

Table 5.15 Logit Acquisition Probability distributions, Part B

Estimated probability		Acquired banks		Non-acquired banks		
Range	Mid value	No.	$f_1(p)$ (%)	No.	$f_1(p)$ (%)	$f_1(p)/f_2(p)$
Model 4						
0.000 – 0.099	0.05	0	0.0	2	0.9	0.000
0.100 – 0.199	0.15	2	1.8	9	4.1	0.444
0.200 – 0.299	0.25	2	1.8	24	11.0	0.167
0.300 – 0.399	0.35	12	11.0	33	15.1	0.727
0.400 – 0.499	0.45	24	22.0	66	30.3	0.727
0.500 – 0.599	0.55	35	32.1	61	28.0	1.148
0.600 – 0.699	0.65	18	16.5	19	8.7	1.895
0.700 – 0.799	0.75	7	6.4	3	1.4	4.667
0.800 – 0.899	0.85	3	2.8	0	0.0	---
0.900 – 0.999	0.95	6	5.5	1	0.5	12.000
Total		109		218		

In Figure 5.2 the midpoint of each probability interval for the acquired banks (non-acquired banks) is plotted against the percentage of acquired banks (non-acquired banks) in the interval. The graph shows that the two distributions intersect at a probability value equal to 0.5544 for model 1, 0.5566 for model 2, 0.4970 for model 3 and 0.5149 for model 4.

Not surprisingly, models 1, 2 and 4, where the cut-off point has been adjusted upwards, correctly classify more non-acquired banks (and less acquired banks) in the training sample, while an opposite picture is observed for model 3, where the cut-off is adjusted downwards (Table 5.16).

Table 5.16 Logit models in-sample (training) classification results (Palepu's cut-off points)*

	Acquired	Non-acquired	Overall	Average	Cohen's Kappa	PABAK
Model 1	53.2%	82.6%	67.9%	67.9%	35.8%	35.8%
Model 2	48.6%	80.7%	64.7%	64.7%	29.4%	29.4%
Model 3	64.2%	62.4%	63.0%	63.0%	24.2%	26.0%
Model 4	58.7%	68.3%	65.1%	63.5%	11.6%	28.7%

*Cut-off points: Model 1 = 0.5544, Model 2 = 0.5566, Model 3 = 0.4970, Model 4 = 0.5149

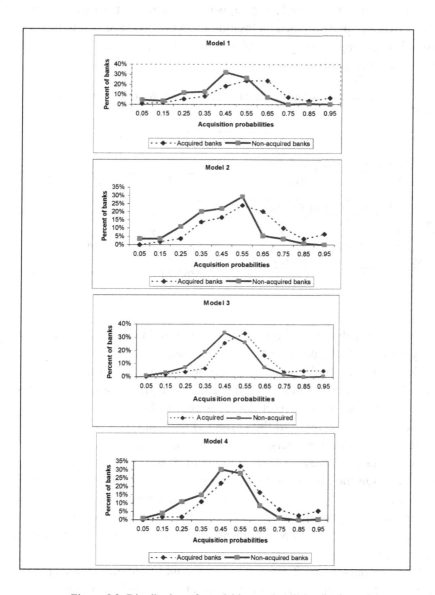

Figure 5.2 Distribution of acquisition probabilities (logit models)

Consequently, the models with upwards-adjusted cut-off demonstrate higher overall performance. Obviously, with average classification accuracies ranging between 63.0% (model 3) and 67.9% (model 1) all models outperform chance assignment.

Table 5.17 Logit models holdout (testing) prediction results (Palepu's optimum cut-off points)*

	Acquired	Non-acquired	Overall	Average	Cohen's Kappa	PABAK
Panel A: Equal Holdout Testing						
Model 1	32.2%	71.2%	51.7%	51.7%	3.4%	3.4%
Model 2	45.8%	67.8%	56.8%	56.8%	13.6%	13.6%
Panel B: Unequal Holdout Testing						
Model 1	32.2%	73.9%	67.8%	53.0%	4.5%	35.6%
Model 2	45.8%	72.1%	68.3%	58.9%	12.3%	36.6%
Model 3	47.5%	64.1%	61.7%	55.8%	6.9%	23.3%
Model 4	52.5%	66.4%	64.4%	59.5%	11.6%	28.7%

*Cut-off points: Model 1 = 0.5544, Model 2 = 0.5566, Model 3 = 0.4970, Model 4 = 0.5149

Panel A in Table 5.17 shows a similar picture in terms of the models' ability to classify banks into the two groups, on equal holdout-testing samples. That is, both models are inferior (compared to the results in Panel A of Table 5.14) in classifying correct acquired banks while they are better in classifying correct non-acquired banks. However, it should be noted that the decrease in the correct classification of acquired banks is quite large for both models, with model 1 now predicting correct only 32.2% and model 2 only 45.8%. In terms of overall measures, the results are mixed. On the one hand, model 1 with an average accuracy equal to 51.7% and a kappa index as low as 3.4% is, not surprisingly, inferior to the corresponding one in Table 5.15. On the other hand, model 2, with an average accuracy of 56.8% and Kappa index equal to 13.6% performs slightly better.

When models 1 and 2 are tested on unequal holdout samples (Panel B), however, their ability to classify correct non-acquired banks leads to an increase in the overall evaluation performance. Model 1 is now better than the corresponding one in Panel B of Table 5.14 in terms of overall classification accuracy (67.8%) and PABAK (35.6%), although due to the large differences between Type I and Type II errors, remains inferior in terms of the other two measures (i.e. average accuracy and Cohen's Kappa). Model 2, on the other hand, is better in three (i.e. overall accuracy, Cohen's, PABAK) of the four measures. However, the difference in average classification accuracy is very small and amounts to only 0.2%. Turning to the double matched models (i.e. models 3 and 4), we observe that they can both predict acquired banks better than the equal matched samples (i.e. models 1 and 2). Compared to the corresponding models in Table 5.14, model 3 achieves a higher performance in terms of acquired banks correct classification but is inferior in the other measures, while the opposite occurs for model 4.

5.3.3 UTADIS

The development of the UTADIS model is affected by the technical parameters involved in the solution process (i.e. the user defined constants, δ, s, and z), as well as by the way in which the piece-wise linear form of the marginal utility functions is considered (i.e. the way in which each criterion's range is divided into subintervals). However, after extensive simulation based on an experimental design, Doumpos and Zopounidis (2004) found that neither the value of δ nor the value of z has any significant impact on the error rates of the UTADIS models. On the other hand, the way in which the subintervals are specified was found to be a significant factor affecting both the error rates as well as the stability of the models.

On the basis of the above findings, in most financial applications of UTADIS the user-defined constants δ, s and z, are set equal to 0.01, 0.1 and 0.01 respectively, by default, and we follow the same approach in the present study. Thus, we only have to find the optimal value of sub-intervals. Doumpos and Zopounidis (2004) argue that although the selection of a higher number of subintervals would seem to provide the ability to perform a better approximation of the actual marginal utility function, this is rarely the case. More precisely, the selection of an arbitrarily high number of subintervals increases the degrees of freedom of the additive utility function, resulting in over-fitting of the model on the training sample. Therefore, unless the number of subintervals is properly defined, there can be cases where the linear program will have redundant incremental variables, which is likely to affect the evaluative performance of the model and the form of the marginal utility functions.

Since there is no general guidance to determine the number of subintervals, we compare the classification performance of UTADIS with respect to different values of the subinterval. As previously mentioned, the performance is measured on the validation data set during the estimation, obtained through a 10-fold cross validation in the training sample[13]. After some experimentation the results were obtained based on sub-intervals set equal to 1.12 (Model 1), 1.25 (Model 2), 1.00 (Model 3), and 1.4 (Model 4).

After choosing the sub-intervals we then re-estimated the models using the whole training sample (i.e. 218 observations for models 1 & 2 and 327 for models 3 & 4). Table 5.18 shows the percentage weightings on the variables to develop the models, and Tables 5.19-5.20 present the classification accuracies for the training and holdout testing samples, respectively.

Table 5.18 UTADIS models variables weights

Variable	Weights			
	Model 1	Model 2	Model 3	Model 4
g2	---	---	---	20.84%
g5	21.70%	21.55%	40.51%	16.57%
g10	19.08%	19.08%	21.68%	21.13%
g11	19.08%	38.47%	19.47%	26.38%
g12	40.15%	20.90%	18.34%	15.11%

We can see in Table 5.18 that although the variable weightings for each model vary, in general a balance exists between the relative contributions of the variables. In models 1, 2 and 3, at most one variable

---

[13] Previous studies that applied UTADIS and MHDIS (discussed in section 3.4) have not employed a ten fold cross validation to estimate the parameters and relied on the results in the training sample (as a whole) as these techniques do not tend to over-fit to a high degree. In the present study, we preferred to rely on a ten-fold cross validation, in order to follow a common approach with the remaining techniques were parameters had to be estimated (i.e. classification and regression trees, nearest neighbours, and support vector machines)

accounts for about 40% while the other three variables account for approximately 20% each. The weights in model 4 are more balanced, with the minimum weight being 15.11% (g12) and the maximum 26.38% (g11).

Table 5.19 UTADIS in-sample (training) classification results

	Acquired	Non-acquired	Overall	Average	Cohen's Kappa	PABAK
Model 1	55.0%	80.7%	67.9%	67.9%	35.8%	35.8%
Model 2	61.5%	76.2%	68.8%	68.8%	37.6%	37.6%
Model 3	56.0%	76.1%	69.4%	66.1%	31.8%	31.8%
Model 4	58.7%	79.8%	72.8%	69.3%	38.6%	45.6%

The in-sample (training) classification results, presented in Table 5.19, reveal that all the models assign banks to their actual group better than chance, and achieve an improvement that exceeds 30% in all cases. In addition, using country-adjusted financial variables contributes to the correct classification of acquired banks and improves the overall measures of performance. Finally, the double matching procedure also contributes to the increase of performance in terms of overall measures although the results with respect of the individual groups are mixed.

Table 5.20 UTADIS models holdout (testing) prediction results

	Acquired	Non-acquired	Overall	Average	Cohen's Kappa	PABAK
Panel A: Equal Holdout Testing						
Model 1	39.0%	83.1%	61.0%	61.0%	22.0%	22.0%
Model 2	61.0%	54.2%	57.6%	57.6%	15.3%	15.3%
Panel B: Unequal Holdout Testing						
Model 1	39.0%	77.9%	72.2%	58.4%	13.1%	44.5%
Model 2	61.0%	60.9%	60.9%	61.0%	12.2%	21.9%
Model 3	42.4%	77.9%	72.7%	60.1%	15.5%	45.5%
Model 4	50.8%	66.4%	64.1%	58.6%	10.6%	28.3%

Turning to the evaluation of the models in the equal holdout testing samples (Table 5.20, Panel A), we observe that while both models 1 and 2 perform better than chance, large differences exist in terms of their ability to classify correct banks from the two groups. On the one hand, model 1 correctly predicts 83.1% of the non-acquired, while model 2 predicts only 54.2%. On the other hand, model 2, outperforms model 1 by classifying correct 61.0% of the acquired banks as opposed to only 39% for model 1. In terms of overall accuracy and other measures, model 1 outperforms model 2. A similar picture emerges when the performance of models 1 and 2 is tested on the unequal holdout samples (Panel B). Although the ability of model 2 to classify correct non-acquired banks increases up to 60.9% it remains inferior to model 1 in terms of most of the general performance measures, while the latter clearly outperforms the former in terms of predicting the acquired banks.

Models 3 and 4 both predict better than chance, with Cohen's Kappa (PABAK) being 15.5% (45.5%) and 10.6% (28.3%) respectively. Although model 3 performs better than model 4 in all general evaluation measures, the latter is the only model that predicts correct more than half of the acquired banks (i.e. 50.8%).

5.3.4 MHDIS

Since the sample involves only two groups of banks, the MHDIS method described in chapter 3 involves only one stage, during which two additive utility functions are developed. From the discussion of Chapter 3 we note, that the additive utility models require setting of the lower and upper bounds as well as the minimum difference. By default, we set the minimum difference to 0.001 and attempt to determine the optimum levels of the bounds. In general, the lower bound should be set at a small positive number (e.g. 0.00001) to avoid an inappropriate solution in the mathematical programming. Similarly the upped bound should not be set too low and should obviously be set higher than the lower bound. Since there is not a general guidance for determining the optimal combination, we experimented with 20 combinations choosing lower bound values of 0.00001, 0.00002, 0.00003, 0.00004 and 0.00005 and upped bound values of 0.05, 0.1, 0.2, and 0.3, and compared the classification performance of the models on the validation dataset.

For model 1, the best performance (both in terms of higher average classification accuracy and the balance between the two groups) in the validation set was achieved with lower bound 0.00002 and upper bound 0.1. The model formed through this combination classifies correct 67.9% of the acquired banks and 72.0% of the non-acquired banks, resulting in an average of 69.9%. In the case of model 2, the optimum combination is 0.00002 (lower bound) and 0.3 (upper bound), resulting in the classification accuracies: 64.5% (acquired), 73.3% (non-acquired) and 68.9% (average). The classification accuracies for the double matched trained models 3 and 4 are lower than those achieved with the equal matched trained models 1 and 2. For model 3, the average classification accuracy is between 55.2% and 62.8%, achieved through the combination of 0.00005 (lower bound) and 0.1 (upper bound). The best performance for model 4 is achieved with combination 0.00001 (lower bound) and 0.05 (upper bound), classifying correct 60.0% of the acquired banks and 69.2% for the non-acquired, thus 64.6% on average.

As with UTADIS, after choosing these parameter values we re-estimated the models using the whole training sample (218 observations for models 1 & 2, and 327 for models 3 & 4). Table 5.21 presents the variable weights of two additive utility functions developed for each model, U_1 representing the non-acquired banks, and $U_{\sim 1}$ the acquired banks.

Table 5.21 Weights (in %) of the financial variables in the MHDIS models

Variable	Model 1		Model 2		Model 3		Model 4	
	U_1	$U_{\sim 1}$	U_1	$U_{\sim 1}$	U_1	$U_{\sim 1}$	U_1	$U_{\sim 1}$
g2	---	---	---	---	---	---	28.76%	27.55%
g5	46.95%	47.42%	50.90%	47.95%	54.18%	36.56%	21.92%	25.46%
g10	10.27%	5.03%	10.40%	18.68%	1.37%	18.47%	14.29%	17.58%
g11	20.44%	4.70%	12.80%	3.05%	10.64%	11.03%	9.38%	7.44%
g12	22.35%	42.86%	25.90%	30.32%	33.82%	33.94%	25.65%	31.88%

It turns out that, for all models, variables g5 and g12 are quite significant in discriminating between the two groups, since their weights always exceeds 20%. In addition, g2 also appears to be important discriminatory variable in model 4, ranking first among the weights for the non-acquired group, and second for the acquired group. Inclusion of this variable also reduces the significance of g5, and of g10 and g11 to some extent. The significance of g10 and g11 varies according to the model under examination and the group of interest (i.e. acquired / non-acquired). Finally, we observe that the variable weightings tend to be more balanced for U_1 in models 1 and 2, but not so much for models 3 and 4.

The classification results obtained from the 4 MHDIS models on the relevant training samples are presented in Table 5.22. All models classify banks better than chance with Cohen's Kappa taking values between 29.5% (models 3 &4) and 33.9% (model 2). While models 3 and 4 perform exactly the same in terms of percentage of banks correctly classified, we observe slight differences between models 1 and 2, with the latter being slightly better in terms of overall performance measures (overall, average accuracy and kappa). Finally, the results illustrate that both equal matched models (1&2) achieve slightly better performance than the double matched ones (3&4) in terms of average accuracy and Cohen's Kappa.

Table 5.22 MHDIS in-sample (training) classification results

	Acquired	Non-acquired	Overall	Average	Cohen's Kappa	PABAK
Model 1	67.0%	65.1%	66.1%	66.1%	32.1%	32.1%
Model 2	64.2%	69.7%	67.0%	67.0%	33.9%	33.9%
Model 3	64.2%	67.4%	66.4%	65.8%	29.5%	32.7%
Model 4	64.2%	67.4%	66.4%	65.8%	29.5%	32.7%

Turning to the testing of models 1 and 2 in the equal holdout samples (Table 5.23, Panel A), we observe that model 2 slightly outperforms model 1 in terms of balance of errors and prediction of acquired banks, while the latter is better in predicting non-acquired banks. Thus, adjusting the variables by country helps improve the prediction of acquired banks, but looses efficiency in predicting the non-acquired banks. Furthermore, although both models predict better than chance (with Kappa measures 10.2 for model 1 and 11.9% for model 2), the raw variables model 1 correctly predict only 49.2% of the acquired banks.

Table 5.23 MHDIS holdout (testing) prediction results

	Acquired	Non-acquired	Overall	Average	Cohen's Kappa	PABAK
Panel A: Equal Holdout Testing						
Model 1	49.2%	61.0%	55.1%	55.1%	10.2%	10.2%
Model 2	55.9%	55.9%	55.9%	55.9%	11.9%	11.9%
Panel B: Unequal Holdout Testing						
Model 1	49.2%	64.4%	62.2%	56.8%	8.1%	24.3%
Model 2	55.9%	61.2%	60.4%	58.6%	9.7%	20.9%
Model 3	40.7%	65.2%	61.7%	53.0%	3.7%	23.3%
Model 4	57.6%	54.0%	54.5%	55.8%	6.0%	9.1%

In Panel B (Table 5.23), we present the results of the 4 MHDIS models tested on the unequal holdout samples. Both models 1 and 2 achieve higher classification accuracies for the non-acquired banks compared to the equal testing samples. Model 1 now classifies correct 64.4% of the non-acquired banks (compared to 61.0% in the equal holdout testing sample). Similarly, model 2 classifies correct 61.2% of the non-acquired banks (compared to 55.9% correct classification in the equal holdout testing sample). Consequently, 3 of the 4 overall measures of performance increase, while Cohen's Kappa decreases due to its tendency to penalise unbalanced performance in terms of Type I and Type II errors. Obviously, the country-adjusted model (model 2) offers a more satisfactory performance compared to the raw model (model 1). Although its overall correct classification accuracy and PABAK are lower than those of model 1, it achieves satisfactory accuracies for both groups (i.e. acquired and non-acquired) as opposed to model 1, that predicts less than half of the acquired banks. As a result, model 2 achieves higher Cohen's Kappa and average classification accuracy. Turning to the double matched models (models 3 & 4), both perform worse than the equal matched ones (models 1 & 2), in terms of all overall performance measures. For example, using Cohen's Kappa to access improvement over chance allocation, model 3 achieves only a 3.7% improvement while model 4 achieves 6.0%.

5.3.5 CART

The development of the CART model, as described in Chapter 3, requires the specification of: (1) the split criterion, (2) whether pruning will be performed or not, (3) a number n such that impure nodes must have n or more observations to be split, (4) the prior probabilities of group membership, and (5) the misclassification costs. As mentioned in Section 5.1 we assumed equal costs of two types of error and equal group probabilities during the development of all models and, therefore, we only have to decide upon the first three requirements. Preliminary results have shown that the best split is defined by the Gini criterion[14], which is consistent with Espahbodi and Espahbodi (2003). Consequently, we rely on this criterion for the development of the final models. We experimented with 11 values for n starting from 10 (used as default in MATLAB) and moving up to 20. For each one of these values we developed the model both with and without pruning. Consequently, we developed 22 versions for each one of the 4 CART models. As with UTADIS and MHDIS, we used the 10-fold cross validation approach as our criterion for automatically stopping the splitting (tree-building) process. This method of pruning a tree (i.e. of selecting a smaller tree or a sequence of smaller trees), is considered very powerful, particularly for small data sets.

The average classification accuracies we obtained using the cross validation approach during the validation of the models are in the range: 55.3% - 65.3% for model 1, 52.0% - 63.2% for model 2, 55.4% - 60.4% for model 3, and 45.6% - 58.5% for model 4. Although the models developed with pruning achieve higher average classification accuracies, their ability to correctly classify acquired banks were found to be inferior to those achieved without pruning, as can be observed from Figure 5.3. Furthermore, models developed with pruning resulted in a decision tree with just one node, which may be considered as insufficient (see Figure

---

[14] MATLAB offers two more criteria for splitting, the twoing rule and the maximum deviance. We did some preliminary tests with the 10-fold cross validation, but the results with these criteria were inferior to the ones achieved with the Gini criterion.

5.4). We therefore decided to develop our CART models without pruning. On the basis of the results obtained through the cross-validation approach, we set n equal to 20, 14, 20 and 16 for models 1, 2, 3 and 4 respectively. Figures 5.5 –5.8 show the final CART models that were developed using all the observations in the training sample.

The interpretation of the trees is straightforward. All banks are finally classified at a group based on a series of yes/no answers on questions regarding the values of the financial variables. For each brand node, the left child node corresponds to the points that satisfy the conditions (yes answer), and the right child node corresponds to the points that do not satisfy the condition (no answer). Obviously numerous rules are formed from each tree. For example, we can see from Figure 5.6 that when using model 1, a bank with g12 lower than 77.525 and g10 lower than 0.11 is classified as acquired. A bank is also classified as acquired if g12 is lower than 77.525, g10 is higher than 1.155, and g5 is lower than 6.85. On the other hand, when using country-adjusted variables (model 2), a bank could be classified as acquired if it had g12 lower than 1.211 and g5 lower than 1.123 and g10 lower than 1.396 and g12 lower than 0.4.

We now turn to the classification results achieved from the CART models. All models achieve very high classification accuracies in the training sample (Table 5.24) with average accuracy ranging between 80.5% (model 3) and 83.5% (model 2). However, achieving such accuracies in the training sample is not surprising for CART as this method obviously adapts very well to the data from which it is formed, and we will therefore not discuss these results any further.

Table 5.24 CART in-sample (training) classification results

	Acquired	Non-acquired	Overall	Average	Cohen's Kappa	PABAK
Model 1	881.%	78.0%	83.0%	83.0%	66.1%	66.1%
Model 2	76.1%	90.8%	83.5%	83.5%	67.0%	67.0%
Model 3	87.2%	73.9%	78.3%	80.5%	55.5%	56.5%
Model 4	84.4%	81.7%	82.6%	83.0%	62.7%	65.1%

When models 1 and 2 are evaluated on the equal holdout sample (Table 5.25, Panel A) we observe a substantial decrease in accuracies compared to the corresponding results of the training sample, with average accuracies now being 50.8% and 49.2% respectively.

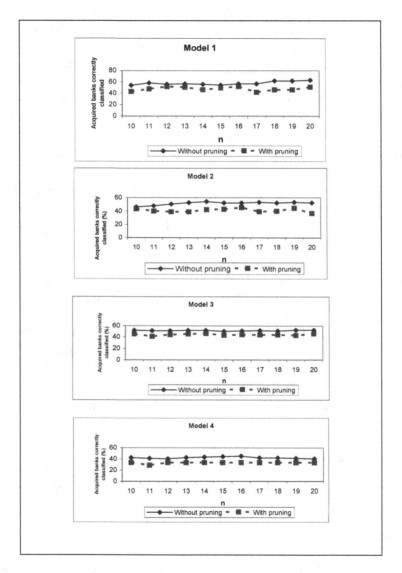

Figure 5.3 CART models classification accuracies of acquired banks with and without pruning

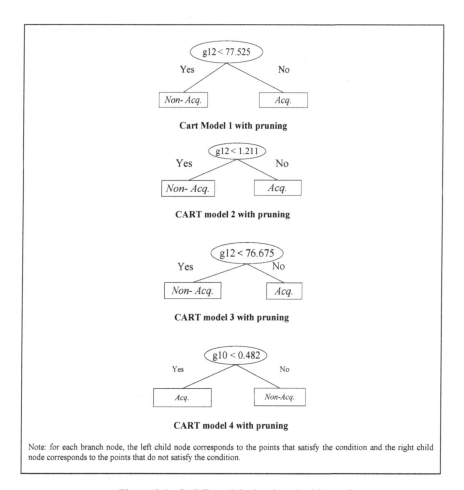

Figure 5.4 CART models developed with pruning

Model 1 performs well in predicting the acquired banks (61.0%) but it manages to correctly predict only 40.7% of the non-acquired banks. Consequently, model 1 outperforms chance by only 1.7% on the overall/average classification accuracy. Model 2, with a Kappa index of −1.7%, cannot even outperform chance, owing to its poor ability to correctly predict both groups of banks.

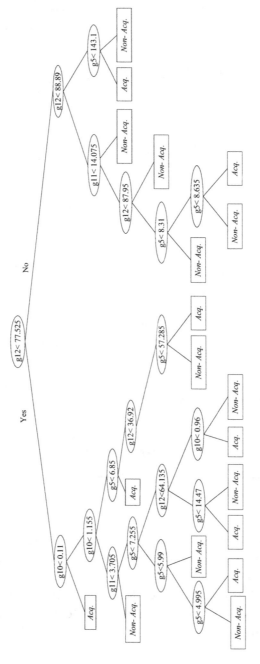

Figure 5.5 CART Model 1 (without pruning)

Note: for each branch node, the left child node corresponds to the points that satisfy the condition and the right child node corresponds to the points that do not satisfy the condition.

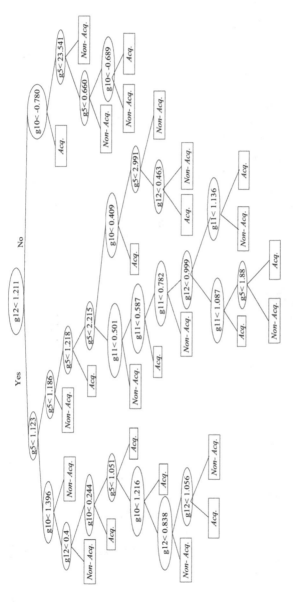

Figure 5.6 CART Model 2 (without pruning)

Note: for each branch node, the left child node corresponds to the points that satisfy the condition and the right child node corresponds to the points that do not satisfy the condition.

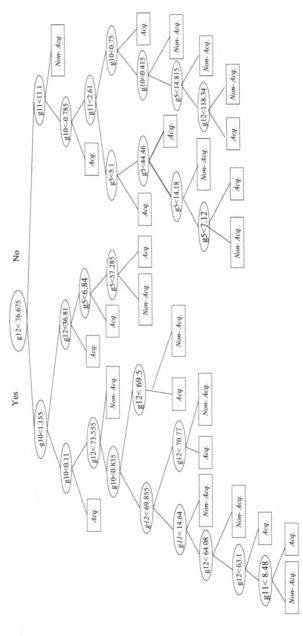

Figure 5.7 CART Model 3 (without pruning)

Note: For each node, the left child node corresponds to the points that satisfy the condition and the right child node corresponds to the points that do not satisfy the condition.

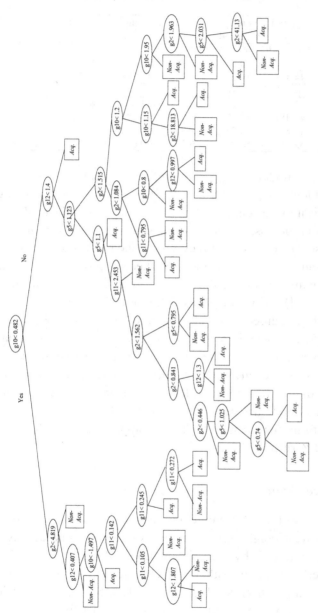

Figure 5.8 CART Model 4 (without pruning)

Note: For each node, the left child node corresponds to the points that satisfy the condition and the right child node corresponds to the points that do not satisfy the condition

Table 5.25 CART models holdout (testing) sample prediction results

	Acquired	Non-acquired	Overall	Average	Cohen's Kappa	PABAK
Panel A: Equal Holdout Testing						
Model 1	61.0%	40.7%	50.8%	50.8%	1.7%	1.7%
Model 2	44.1%	54.2%	49.2%	49.2%	-1.7%	-1.7%
Panel B: Unequal Holdout Testing						
Model 1	61.0%	48.0%	49.9%	54.5%	4.3%	-0.2%
Model 2	44.1%	61.8%	59.2%	52.9%	3.4%	18.4%
Model 3	45.8%	55.2%	53.8%	50.5%	0.5%	7.6%
Model 4	52.5%	68.7%	66.3%	60.6%	13.5%	32.7%

The results for models 1 and 2 look marginally better when tested on the unequal holdout samples (Table 5.25, Panel B). Both achieve slightly higher classification accuracy for the non-acquired banks, thus contributing to an increase in all the evaluation measures for model 2, as well as increase in average accuracy and Cohen's Kappa for model 1. The improvement over chance is more marked for model 2, as for model 1 PABAK remains negative (-0.2%). Turning to the double matched models (i.e. 3 and 4), the results show that model 4 is clearly better of the two, and in fact outperforms all the four models. With correct predictions of 52.5% (acquired banks) and 68.7% (non-acquired banks), model 4 achieves a Cohen's Kappa of 13.5% and PABAK of 32.7%, clearly outperforming chance. The results of model 3 are more similar with the ones of the first two models. With an average accuracy of 50.5% and an overall accuracy equal to 53.8% the model can only slightly outperform chance with Cohen's Kappa and PABAK measures of 0.5% and 7.6% respectively.

5.3.6 Nearest neighbours

The development of the k-NN model requires specification of a number k of so-called nearest neighbours. We follow previous studies (e.g. Liu, 2002) in determining k by experimentation, whereby the number is adjusted and performance is evaluated each time. We experimented with 18 values of k, ranging between 1 and 35 ($k = 1, 3, 5, ..., 35$), and selected the number that provided a satisfactory performance both in terms of average classification accuracy and balance between Type I and Type II errors in the validation sub-sample. The ranges of the average classification in the validation sub-sample were as follows: 58.3% - 68.0% for model 1, 56.2% - 63.9% for model 2, 56.2% - 63.4% for model 3, 52.4% - 60.8% for model 4. We set *k* equal to 7 for model 1, because it provided relatively high average classification accuracy (66.1%) (59.7% for acquired and 72.4% for non-acquired banks). Similarly, observing the average classification measure, we selected: k =1 for model 2, k =17 for model 3, and k=11 for model 4.

Table 5.26 k-NN in-sample (training) classification results

	Acquired	Non-acquired	Overall	Average	Cohen's Kappa	PABAK
Model 1	66.1%	78.0%	72.0%	72.0%	44.0%	44.0%
Model 2	100.0%	100.0%	100.0%	100.0%	100.%	100.0%
Model 3	65.1%	65.6%	65.4%	65.4%	28.3%	30.9%
Model 4	52.3%	74.3%	67.0%	63.3%	26.4%	33.9%

We then re-estimated the models using the entire training sample, obtaining the classification accuracies shown in Table 5.26. Not surprisingly, the results are quite similar to the ones obtained in the estimation sub-sample during the 10-fold cross validation. We can see that k-NN achieves high classification accuracies on the training sample (even 100% for model 2). Thus, as with CART, we will limit our evaluation to the holdout testing samples, but observe here that k-NN models developed on equal matched sample (models 1 and 2) provide higher classification accuracies than those developed on unequal samples (models 3 and 4).

Table 5.27 shows classification accuracies for the holdout testing samples. As before, we first consider the equal holdout-testing sample (Panel A). The first conclusion is that both models achieve accuracies below 50% for the acquired group. Second, model 1 achieves better accuracy for the non-acquired group (62.7%) than model 2 (52.5%), which cannot outperform chance. It is possible that the relatively small sample size used for our study contributes to high classification accuracies on the training sample but poor results on the holdout sample. By comparison, Liu (2002) developed a credit model using 26,430 alternatives while Galindo and Tamayo (2000) found that approximately

22,000 observations would be necessary to develop a powerful k-NN model in their case.

Table 5.27 k-NN models holdout (testing) sample prediction results

	Acquired	Non-acquired	Overall	Average	Cohen's Kappa	PABAK
Panel A: Equal Holdout Testing						
Model 1	45.8%	62.7%	54.2%	54.2%	8.5%	8.5%
Model 2	44.1%	52.5%	48.3%	48.3%	-3.4%	-3.4%
Panel B: Unequal Holdout Testing						
Model 1	45.8%	65.8%	62.9%	55.8%	7.2%	25.8%
Model 2	44.1%	54.3%	52.8%	49.2%	-0.9%	5.7%
Model 3	44.1%	63.8%	60.9%	53.9%	4.8%	21.9%
Model 4	52.5%	67.5%	65.4%	60.0%	12.6%	30.7%

Turning to the evaluation of the models in the unequal holdout-testing sample (Panel B), the models achieve better overall classification accuracy, as a result of slightly higher accuracies predicted for the non-acquired banks. However, the models show hardly any improvement in the classification of the acquired banks. The results for Cohen's Kappa are mixed, remaining negative for model 2. However, between models 1 and 2, the first one still outperforms the second in all cases. Concerning models 3 and 4, the picture is somewhat different than in the training sample. Model 3, with an average and overall accuracies of 53.9% and 50.9%, does better than model 2 although shows similar performance results as model 1. It is Model 4 that achieves higher accuracy for both the acquired and non-acquired banks, with overall and average accuracies of 60% and 65.4% respectively, outperforming the others and showing an improvement over chance of 12.6% by Cohen's Kappa and 30.7% by PABAK.

5.3.7 SVMs

Based on the findings of previous studies, we rely on the Gaussian function as the kernel function for the development of the SVMs models. First of all, preliminary results of previous empirical studies suggest that the Gaussian kernel outperforms the polynomial kernel (Tay and Cao,

2001, Kim, 2003). In addition, Gaussian kernels tend to give good performance under general smoothness assumptions and, as Tay and Cao (2002) suggest, they should be therefore considered if no additional knowledge of the data is available. Furthermore, the polynomial kernel takes a longer time in the training of SVMs (Tay and Cao, 2001; Kim, 2003).

Again, without general guidance on determining the upper bound C and the kernel parameter, we experimented with various values to select the optimal values to achieve the best prediction performance[15]. More specifically, we set C equal to 0.5, 1, 10, 50, 75, 100 and the kernel parameter equal to 0.1, 1, 25, 50, 75, 100, resulting in a total of 36 combinations. As with other classification methods, we follow the 10-fold cross-validation procedure within the training sample and evaluate the performance of the models on the validation sub-samples. The following ranges of the average classification were obtained on the validation sub-sample: 61.0% - 67.6% for model 1, 54.6% - 65.0% for model 2, 56.6% - 66.5% for model 3, 49.8% - 64.0% for model 4. We finally set C equal to 0.5 and δ^2 equal to 0.1 for Model 1, while the corresponding values for the other three models are: $C = 50$ and $\delta^2 = 0.1$ for Model 2, $C = 50$ and $\delta^2 = 0.1$ for Model 3, and $C = 10$ and $\delta^2 = 1$ for Model 4.

Based on the above parameter combinations, 4 SVMs models were re-estimated on the relevant training samples, and their performance tested using the holdout-testing samples.

We first present the performance results of the SVMs models on the training samples (Table 5.28). As with k-NN, the classification accuracies are similar to the ones achieved in the estimation sub-samples in the 10-fold cross-validation procedure, and all models perform better than chance predictions. Among models 1 and 2, the one with the country-adjusted variables (Model 2) is slightly inferior in terms of the 5 out of the 6 evaluation measures, due to the fact that it misclassifies two more acquired banks than does model 1, which results in a difference of

---

[15] The same approach has been followed in previous studies in the filed of finance such as bankruptcy prediction (Shin et al., 2004) and financial time series forecasting (Kim, 2003).

1.8% in the classification accuracy for that group. Turning to the double matched models, the one with raw financial variables (Model 3) is clearly better, since it outperforms model 4 in all evaluation measures. Model 3 is also the best performer of the 4 SVMs.

Table 5.28 SVMs in-sample (training) classification results

	Acquired	Non-acquired	Overall	Average	Cohen's Kappa	PABAK
Model 1	63.3%	64.2%	63.8%	63.8%	27.5%	27.5%
Model 2	63.3%	60.6%	61.9%	61.9%	23.9%	23.9%
Model 3	65.1%	68.3%	67.3%	66.7%	31.3%	34.6%
Model 4	58.7%	67.0%	63.9%	62.8%	23.7%	27.8%

Turning to the results on the equal holdout testing samples (Table 5.29, Panel A), model 1 retains its superiority by achieving better results than model 2, by virtue of achieving a higher classification accuracy for the non-acquired banks. More specifically, both models achieve a prediction accuracy of 55.9% for acquired banks, but model 1 correctly predicts 64.4% of the non-acquired banks while model 2 only 52.5%. Consequently, model 2 achieves an 8.5% improvement over chance, while model 1 is much higher at 20.3%. It may be noted that, on the training sample, model 1 was also superior to model 2, but by virtue of achieving a higher classification accuracy for the acquired group of banks.

Table 5.29 SMVs models holdout (testing) prediction results

	Acquired	Non-acquired	Overall	Average	Cohen's Kappa	PABAK
Panel A: Equal Holdout Testing						
Model 1	55.9%	64.4%	60.2%	60.2%	20.3%	20.3%
Model 2	55.9%	52.5%	54.2%	54.2%	8.5%	8.5%
Panel B: Unequal Holdout Testing						
Model 1	55.9%	66.7%	65.1%	61.3%	13.8%	30.2%
Model 2	55.9%	60.1%	59.5%	58.0%	8.9%	18.9%
Model 3	44.1%	69.8%	66.1%	56.9%	9.2%	32.2%
Model 4	50.8%	67.0%	64.6%	58.9%	11.1%	29.2%

We finally examine the prediction ability of the models on the unequal holdout-testing samples (Table 5.29, Panel B). All models outperform chance with Cohen's Kappa being between 8.9% (model 2) and 13.8% (model 1). As with most of the previously examined classification methods, the double matched models 3 and 4 are capable of predicting correct more of the non-acquired banks, and less of the acquired banks, compared to the equal matched models 1 and 2.

The best model appears to be model 1 (developed with equal number of acquired and non-acquired training sample and raw financial variables), achieving the highest average classification accuracy (61.3%) and Cohen's Kappa (13.8%). Model 3 (also developed with raw data), achieves the best performance in terms of overall accuracy (66.1%) and PABAK (32.2%) but it can predict correct only 44.1% of the acquired banks. Model 4 achieves a better balance better Type I and Type II errors than model 3 (hence achieving a higher Cohen's Kappa), but is beaten here by model 1.

5.4 Conclusions

This chapter has evaluated 7 different classification methodologies, using a total of 28 models (4 per classification method) developed on equal and double matched training samples. The evaluation process and analysis of results is largely based on the holdout testing samples, as well as the use of country-adjusted and unadjusted data for the choice of up to five discriminating financial variables. The results show that there is a fair amount of misclassification, which is hard to avoid given the nature of the problem. This is consistent with previous studies concluding that prediction of acquisitions is quite difficult. However, as Liu (2002) points out by referring to credit modeling "...for various reasons, a perfect model with zero prediction error rates does not exist in practical applications". This is obviously the case and perhaps more so in the prediction of acquisitions. As Barnes (1999) mentions business failure prediction essentially involves identifying significant signs of under or abnormal performance that implies that failing firms have some general and basic characteristics during the period leading up to collapse.

However, in the case of acquisitions prediction, there are several reasons for which a firm could be acquired, and probably not all the acquired firms have a common set of financial characteristics. Overall, across all models evaluated on equal or unequal holdout samples, we find that the discriminant analysis and SVMs perform reasonably well in terms of achieving balanced classification accuracies of above 50% for both groups of banks, with discriminant being the best performing method for Model 2. The performance of discriminant analysis is also robust under both 0.5 and Palepu's optimal cut-off rules. It must be argued that, for the same set of financial variables used, country-adjusted or not, only discriminant analysis remains relatively robust in achieving classification accuracies above 50% for both categories of banks. However, we also find that in the case of Model 4 (which includes an additional variable: Equity/Net Loans), all classification methods achieve accuracies above 50% for both holdout groups, acquired and non-acquired, suggesting that the outcome of which method performs best is dependent on the choice of discriminating variables. It also turns out, across all models, that while some methods (e.g. UTADIS) achieve very high accuracies in classifying non-acquired banks, this normally comes at the cost of relatively poor accuracy performance in predicting the acquired group of banks. Thus, there appears to be a trade-off in achieving high classification accuracy, and therefore the question of what method does best depends very much on the classification accuracy and evaluation criteria used.

Concerning the use of country-adjusted ratios as opposed to raw variables, we conclude that the results are generally mixed. Depending on the method or measure of performance the use of country-adjusted financial variables may result in a decrease or increase relatively to the one achieved with the raw financial variables. Thus we do not conclude as to whether it is better to use raw or country-adjusted variables. The results in the literature are also mixed. For example, the results of Cudd and Duggal (2000) highly depend on the definition of a dummy industry disturbance variable, while Asterbo and Winter (2001) found that models with industry-adjusted variables performed worse than those with non-adjusted variables.

Concerning the matching procedure and the proportion of banks in the training sample, the classification accuracy for acquired banks decreases when more non-acquired firms are included into the training sample. In the case of the raw financial variables, most of the models developed with double matched sample are inferior to the ones developed with equal matched sample. Comparing the results of the models developed with country-adjusted ratios (i.e. model 2 and model 4) we observe that in most cases model 4 achieves higher classification accuracies, and we find that under most methods the additional variable g2 (Equity/Net Loans) has contributed to an increase in classification accuracy.

Turning to the proportion of acquired and non-acquired firms in the testing sample, Palepu (1986) suggests that the use of equal sized samples tend to overstate the prediction ability of the models. However, in our case, the overall classification accuracy (that is the measure used by Palepu) increases rather than decreases in unequal holdout samples, as a result of the ability of the models to classify correct more of the non-acquired banks.

Comparing the two methodologies (SVMs and k-NN) not previously used for the development of acquisition targets prediction models, we find that SVM has performed better and achieved more satisfactory results compared to k-NN, showing improvement over chance that amounts by up to 20.3% according to Cohen's Kappa or 32.2% according to PABAK. Probably the poor results of k-NN could be attributed to the relatively small sample we have used, compared to other studies as mentioned in section 5.3.6.

Chapter 6

Integration of Prediction Models

6.1 Introduction

The results of the previous chapter have shown that there is no perfect method for the prediction of acquisition targets. Some methods are more accurate in classifying non-acquired banks while others appear to classify more accurately acquired banks. It was also found that the proportion of acquired and non-acquired in the training samples, and the use of country-adjusted or raw ratios, affect differently the classification ability of the various methods. In the present chapter, we employ two integration techniques, namely majority voting and stacked generalization, in order to examine whether integration of different methods can lead to better classification results.

The combination of multiple classifiers has recently received increased attention from the pattern recognition community and numerous studies have found that such an approach yields improved performance (e.g. Xu et al., 1992; Suen et al., 1993; Ho et al., 1994; Huang and Suen, 1995). Promising results were also obtained in a few applications in finance such as credit scoring (Doumpos, 2002; Lee et al., 2002), bankruptcy prediction (McKee and Lensberg, 2002) and acquisitions prediction (Tartari et al., 2003).

Tartari et al. (2003) combined discriminant analysis, probabilistic neural networks, rough sets and UTADIS multicriteria decision aid using a stacked generalization approach. While applying stacked generalization, we distinguish our study from Tartari et al. (2003) in four ways. First, we combine 7 different classification methods while Tartari *et al.* employ 5, of which only the discriminant and UTADIS are common between the two studies. This allows us to combine the output from 7 different methods and, in doing so, we therefore develop 7 different stacked models. Second, while Tartari et al. (2003) examined the UK non-financial sector, the focus of our study is the EU banking industry. Third, we extend our study by examining the stability of the model through time, not undertaken by Tartari et al. (2003). Finally, we also compare the predictive ability of the stacked generalization model with a model developed using the majority-voting rule.

The remainder of the present chapter is organised as follows. Section 6.2 provides a short introduction to multiple classifiers and outlines the two integration techniques (i.e. majority voting and stacked generalization). Majority voting was selected because it is one of the simplest combining methods that has been found to be comparable with more advanced combiners, while stacked generalization has been found to perform well in recent applications in finance (Doumpos, 2002; Tartari et al., 2003). In Section 6.3, we employ these techniques to combine the individual prediction models developed in Chapter 5, and compare the prediction ability of the two integration techniques and the individual classifiers. In evaluating these techniques we restrict our attention to developing models using equal matched samples and unequal holdout samples for testing, which is the most commonly used approach in recent studies. We also compare the prediction performance of the integration methods against the results of individual classification methods discussed in Chapter 5.

6.2 Integrated (Multi-Classifiers) Models

Techniques for combining classification methods have received increased attention recently in an attempt to overcome the limitations of individual classifier methods and consequently achieve better classification accuracy. As a result contributions have been made in a variety of pattern recognition fields, such as handwritten word recognition (Gunter and Bunke, 2004), face-based identity verification

(Czyz et al., 2004), natural language call routing systems (Zitouni et al., 2003), and speaker recognition (Farell and Mammone, 1995).

Lam and Moy (2002) point out three possible benefits of using a combined method:
1. Lowering the risk of choosing a wrong classification method.
2. Obtaining a more stable prediction performance, since combining different methods can offset certain biases inherited from particular methods.
3. Producing a better prediction of the classification of new observations, since the combined method provides additional information from different sources.

Multi-classifiers (that is the term commonly used for integrated models) seek to combine the predictions of individual classifiers, and these can be performed using various methods such as the Majority Voting (MV) rule, the Borda count, the Behavior-Knowledge Space (BKS) (Huang and Suen, 1993), Stacked Generalization (Wolpert, 1992), Bagging (Breiman, 1996) and Boosting (Freund and Schapire, 1997), among others.

Depending on how the output (e.g. score, probability or prediction) from the single classifiers is fed into the multi-classifier, the latter can in general fall within two categories of combination (Kim et al., 2002): (i) serial combination that arranges classifiers sequentially and the result from the prior classifier is fed to the next classifier, or (ii) parallel combination that arranges classifiers in parallel. When an input is given, multiple classifiers classify it concurrently, and then a combining algorithm integrates the individual classification results. The structures of both serial and parallel forms of combination are shown in Figures 6.1 and 6.2 respectively. Obviously in serial combination, the order of arrangement is crucial for the classification performance of the system while in parallel combination system, performance depends on the combination algorithm.

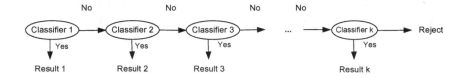

Figure 6.1 A schematic representation of a serial combination

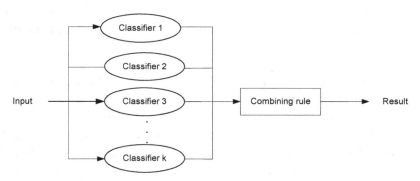

Figure 6.2 A schematic representation of a parallel combination

Since the outputs of individual classifiers are used as inputs to the integrated classifiers, it is also important to examine what kinds of output information classifiers can support (Kim et al., 2002). Xu et al. (1992) have categorized multiple classifiers according to the output information they can support in abstract level methods (e.g. majority voting), rank level methods (e.g. borda count), and measurement level methods (e.g. stacked approach). At the abstract level, the output of the classifier is a unique class "label" for each input observation (e.g. acquired/non-acquired). At the rank level, the classifier outputs correspond to rankings of a subset of candidate classes from the highest to the lowest "likelihood". Finally, at the measurement level, classifiers assign each class a measurement value (score) to indicate the possibility that the input observation belongs to the class.

When a single classifier is considered, the assignment of the alternative (e.g. firm) in one of the groups (e.g. acquired/non-acquired) is obviously the most important output. However, using only this abstract level method for combining multiple classifier outputs may lead to a loss of valuable information that could be helpful to improve performance (Saranli and Demirekler, 2001). Nevertheless, abstract level multi-classifiers (e.g. majority voting) have advantages as well. For example, the most important advantage of majority voting is that it is very simple and needs no extra memory. Therefore, it can be applied in situations where using other more advanced combination would lead to intractability. In addition, it can be employed with any kind of classifier since it is always possible to express their outputs in the form of a binary representation. At the same time, despite its simplicity, majority voting has in some cases turned out to be comparable with more advanced combiners (Cho and Kim, 1995). By contrast, rank level methods, such as the Borda Count (which is the main method for combining classifiers at this level), are not supported by theoretical underpinnings and strongly depend on the rank definition. Measurement level classifiers (e.g. stacked approach), on the other hand, work in an "enriched" feature space (Roli, 2002).

6.2.1 Majority voting

MV is one of the simplest combining methods operating on binary classification outputs (e.g. acquired/non-acquired, bankrupt/non-bankrupt). The MV method goes with the decision where there is a consensus that at least more than half of the classifiers agree on it. Let us assume there is a system of M classifiers: $L = \{L_1, ..., L_M\}$, and $y_j(x_i)$ i = 1, ..., N and j = 1,..., M denote the output of the jth classifier for the ith multidimensional input sample x_i. Given the binary outputs from the M classifiers for a single input sample, the decision of the MV classifier can be represented as follows:

$$y_i^{MV} = 0 \text{ if } \sum_{j=1}^{M} y_j(x_i) \leq (M/2) \text{ and } y_i^{MV} = 1 \text{ if } \sum_{j=1}^{M} y_j(x_i) \succ (M/2)$$

A more detailed discussion of MV, including the rejection rule in the case the number of classifiers is even, can be found in Lam and Suen (1997). However, in our case, since the number of classifiers is odd, we will not go into further details.

Figure 6.3 presents an example, where the MV is applied to combine the output of three classifiers. Classifiers 1 and 2 assign the firm under consideration in the group of acquired, while classifier 3 assigns it to the group of non-acquired. Consequently, under the majority voting rule, the firm is classified as acquired.

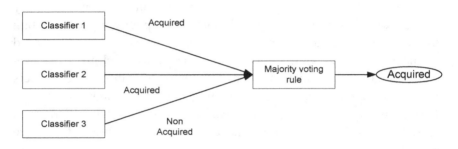

Figure 6.3 An example of majority voting rule in the case of acquisitions prediction

By way of an illustrative example, Table 6.1 presents the outcome of the application of the majority voting rule on 5 banks from the holdout sample. With seven classification methods used in our study, at least four classifiers should agree for a bank to be classified into one of the two groups, 1 (acquired) or 2 (non-acquired). The first two columns in Panel A show, respectively, the name of the banks and the actual group where the bank belongs. Columns 3-9 show the outcome assigned by the individual classifiers. The final column show, the outcome of the integrated model using the majority-voting rule. Panel B presents the evaluation measures (i.e. classification accuracies and Kappa tests) for the seven individual models as well as the integrated one. In this hypothetical example, the MV method incorrectly classifies one of the two acquired banks (implying 50% classification accuracy for the acquired) and correctly classifies all three of the non-acquired banks (implying 100% non-acquired accuracy).

Table 6.1 An illustrative example of the majority voting for 5 banks in the holdout sample

Panel A: Classification decisions									
Banks	Actual Group	DA**	LA**	UTADIS	MHDIS	SVMs	CART	k-NN	MV model
B1	1	1	1	2	1	1	1	2	1
B2	1	2	2	2	2	2	2	1	2
B3	2	2	2	2	1	2	1	2	2
B4	2	2	2	2	2	2	2	2	2
B5	2	2	2	2	2	2	1	1	2

Panel B: Evaluation measures						
	Acquired	Non-acquired	Overall	Average	Cohen's Kappa	PABAK
DA	50.0%	100%	80.0%	75.0%	54.5%	60.0%
LA	50.0%	100%	80.0%	75.0%	54.5%	60.0%
UTADIS	0.0%	100%	60.0%	50.0%	0.0%	20.0%
MHDIS	50.0%	66.7%	60.0%	58.3%	16.7%	20.0%
SVMs	50.0%	100%	80.0%	75.0%	54.5%	60.0%
CART	50.0%	33.3%	40.0%	41.7%	-15.4%	-20.0%
KNN	50.0%	66.7%	60.0%	58.3%	16.7%	20.0%
MV model	50.0%	100%	80.0%	75.0%	54.5%	60.0%

*Group 1 Acquired banks; Group 2: Non-acquired banks
** DA: Discriminant Analysis; LA: Logit Analysis. For both DA & LA the classifications were assigned using 0.5 as the cut-off point.

Thus, in this case, the model achieves an overall classification accuracy of 80% (4 out of 5 banks correctly classified), while the average classification accuracy is 75% (being the average of 50% and 100%). For this example, the calculated percentages for Cohen and PABAK tests are 54.5% and 60% respectively. The illustrative example clearly suggests that the MV integration method performs better in classifying the non-acquired banks, and this outcome reflects the fact that the majority of the individual classifiers (all except CART) appear to show a higher classification accuracy rate for non-acquired banks. In terms of overall performance, the MV model outperforms 4 of the individual models and achieves equal accuracies with the remaining 3 ones.

6.2.2 Stacked generalization approach

The stacked generalization method (Wolpert, 1992) is an approach for combining classification models (i.e. base models), in which the latter are designed to be part of a meta-level classifier (i.e. stacked model) that receives the output predicted by the base models as an input. The meta-model can be developed by any one of the initially considered classification methods. In general, there are four steps that should be followed for the development and validation of a stacked classification model:

Step 1: A resampling technique is initially used to split the training sample T into p partitions and form sub-samples T_{s1} and T_{s2} ($s = 1,2,...p$). Wolpert (1992) proposed the use of leave-one-out fold cross-validation technique, but Doumpos (2002) suggests other resampling techniques such as bootstrapping or k-fold cross-validation can also be used.

Step 2: For each partition $s = 1,2,...p$, the sub-sample T_{s1} is used to develop a classification model f_{ls} (base model) using method l ($l = 1,2,...m$). Each base model is then used to assign an output (e.g. score, distance measure, probability, group assignment) for each alternative (i.e. firms, banks, etc.) in validation sub-sample T_{s2} and decide for its classification.

Step 3: When the re-sampling method has been completed and all p partitions have been considered, the assignments for the alternatives in every validation sub-sample T_{s2} are used to create a new training sample for the development of the stacked generalization (meta) model, thus integrating the results of all individual models. At this point, normalization to the range [0, 1] is usually required when combining the outputs of classifiers with different outputs ranges and different output types.

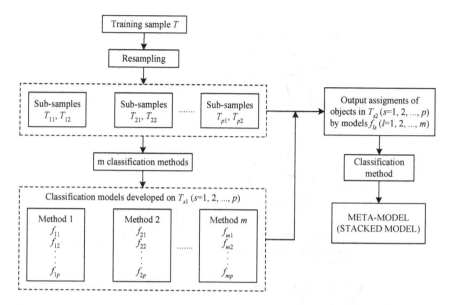

Figure 6.4 General schematic representation of a stacked generalization model combining multiple methods (source: Doumpos, 2002)

<u>Step 4</u>: When the stacked model has been developed through steps 1-3 (Figure 6.4), it can be used to classify any new objects (i.e. firms) (Figure 6.5). Thus, all the methods that are integrated in the stacked generalization model are used to assign an output for the object. Specifically, the assignment by method l is obtained by model F_l using the initial training sample T. The m different output assignments c_l ($l = 1,2,...,m$), determined by the models $F_1, F_2..., F_m$ developed by all the m methods, are then combined by the developed stacked (meta) model to obtain a final classification decision.

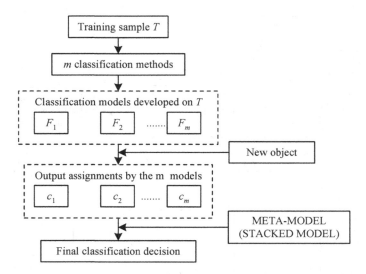

Figure 6.5 Employment of stacked generalization model for the classification of new objects (Source: Doumpos, 2000)

6.3 Development and Evaluation of Integration Models

In this section we apply the procedures explained above to develop 16 prediction models, of which 2 are MV integrated models and 14 are stacked models. Since our investigation in focused on (i) which integrated model delivers better classification accuracy, and (ii) whether the integrated models achieve higher accuracies than the individual ones, we restrict our attention to using equal matched samples for development of models and unequal holdout samples for evaluation purposes, that is the most commonly followed approach in recent studies[1]. However, we utilize the results of individual classification models based on raw as well as country-adjusted data, so that the corresponding integrated model

---

[1] Obviously we could also develop the models using a double matching for training or an equal matched sample for testing, in addition the approach followed here, as in Chapter 5. However given the purposes of the present Chapter, we believe that the results are unlikely to be significantly different, in terms of the comparisons mentioned in (i) and (ii). We therefore focus only on the most commonly used sampling approach in recent studies.

is developed for each set of data.[2] Thus, for example, we have 2 integrated models developed using the MV method, one based on raw data and the other on country-adjusted data. Similarly, of the 14 prediction models using the stacked generalization method, 7 are developed on raw data and 7 on country-adjusted data. Each of these 7 pairs of models is "stacked" using a separate classification method to examine how effectively each method combines the output of the 7 classification methods discussed in chapter 5[3].

6.3.1 Application of the majority voting rule

Table 6.2 presents a summary of the results when the MV was applied to the models developed using raw and country-adjusted financial ratios respectively[4]. As the illustrative example in Table 6.1 shows, the results reflect the outcome of the majority decision rule on the holdout sample of banks, based on the outcome of each classification method, and the percentages reflect the accuracy rates of the actual versus predicted, for both acquired and non-acquired banks, as well as the overall and average classification accuracy rates.

The results for the two integrated models are similar, suggesting that classification accuracy does not seem to be greatly affected by the adjustment of raw data into country-adjusted ones. Although the integrated model developed with country-adjusted data achieves higher classification accuracy (by 3.4%) for the group of acquired banks, its overall accuracy rate and PABAK are lower, confirming that there is no clear winner here.

---

[2] In the context of Table 5.1, the training and testing samples correspond to combinations 2 and 4.
[3] See Figure 6.6 and discussion below for more details.
[4] For discriminant and logit the outputs of the 0.5 cut-off point were used.

Table 6.2 Evaluation measures for majority voting rule and comparison with individual model

	Evaluation measures (%)					
Panel A: Models developed with unadjusted raw ratios						
	Acquired	Non-Acquired	Overall	Average	Cohen's Kappa	PABAK
Discriminant	54.2%	65.8%	64.1%	60.0%	12.2%	28.3%
Logit	50.8%	65.8%	63.6%	58.3%	10.2%	27.3%
UTADIS	39.0%	77.9%	72.2%	58.4%	13.1%	44.5%
MHDIS	49.2%	64.4%	62.2%	56.8%	8.1%	24.3%
CART	61.0%	48.0%	49.9%	54.5%	4.3%	-0.2%
k-NN	45.8%	65.8%	62.9%	55.8%	7.2%	25.8%
SVMs	55.9%	66.7%	65.1%	61.3%	13.8%	30.2%
MV	52.5%	66.7%	64.6%	59.6%	11.2%	29.2%
Panel B: Models developed with country-adjusted ratios						
Discriminant	55.9%	66.1%	64.6%	61.0%	13.4%	29.2%
Logit	59.3%	58.9%	59.0%	59.1%	9.9%	17.9%
UTADIS	61.0%	60.9%	60.9%	61.0%	12.2%	21.9%
MHDIS	55.9%	51.2%	60.4%	58.6%	9.7%	20.9%
CART	44.1%	61.8%	59.2%	52.9%	3.4%	18.4%
k-NN	44.1%	54.3%	52.8%	49.2%	-0.9%	5.7%
SVMs	55.9%	60.1%	59.5%	58.0%	8.9%	18.9%
MV	55.9%	63.2%	62.2%	59.6%	11.1%	24.3%

However, appropriate basis for comparison of these results are the prediction accuracies of the individual models evaluated on the same (unequal) holdout sample also shown in the table[5]. Here, we observe that the results of both the integrated models perform relatively well, thus outperforming some of the individual models although not all of them. For example, in Panel A, CART achieves a higher accuracy whereas UTADIS performs poorly for the acquired group but does exceptionally well for the non-acquired group. In Panel B, UTADIS achieves higher accuracy but CART and k-NN perform poorly for the acquired group. Thus, despite achieving a higher accuracy, the integrated model based on raw data (64.6%) does not outperform all the individual classifiers, since its overall accuracy here is seemingly affected by the good performance

[5] To make comparison easier, the results for the individual classifiers are also shown here, drawn from the lower half of Table 5.2 for raw data, and similarly Table 5.3 for country-adjusted data.

of the UTADIS and the poor performance of the k-NN method. The MV rule has to balance higher accuracy rates obtained for some individual classifiers against lower accuracy rates obtained for others. However, the integrated model based on country-adjusted data (62.2%) appears to outperform all the individual classifiers, except from discriminant, in terms of overall accuracy.

6.3.2 Application of stacked generalization approach

The methodology for the development and validation of the stacked model was outlined in Section 6.2.2. Here it remains to explain the application of this process in our sample. First, we constructed the training dataset using the output of the individual models (i.e. scores or probabilities assigned to the banks by each method) in the validation sub-samples during the 10-fold cross-validation approach performed in chapter 5[6]. Then we performed the integration of the model following the same approach as in the case of the individual models[7]. Finally each stacked model is tested on the holdout dataset. The latter was constructed using the outputs of the individual classifiers (base models) assigned in the banks of the initial unequal holdout sample (combinations 2 and 4 of Table 6.1). Table 6.3 shows how the training and holdout samples were constructed while Figure 6.6 shows the development and testing process of the stacked models, indicating a total of 7 meta-models based on 7 classifier methods, each stacked model essentially requiring as input the output of all the 7 classifiers. Obviously the process followed is similar to the one employed in chapter 5 for the estimation and validation of the individual models. The difference is that the output of the individual

---

[6] Recall that, in Chapter 5, a 10-fold partitioning of the training sample and cross-validation was used to develop models based on the UTADIS, MHDIS, SVM, CART and k-NN methods. Consequently, at this stage we had to obtain similar outputs for the discriminant and logit methods.

[7] Similarly to the development of the individual models in Chapter 5, we employed a 10-fold cross validation within the training sample to estimate the parameters for UTADIS, MHDIS, SVM, CART, and k-NN. Once the optimal parameters were found (based on the results of the 10-fold cross validation), the model was re-estimated using all observations in the training sample. The estimation of the discriminant and logit models was obviously straightforward and cross validation was not necessary.

prediction models is used as the input variables, instead of the discriminating financial variables that were used for the development of the individual models.

Table 6.3 Input data matrix for the development and testing of a stacked model

Training dataset*	Actual Group	Output assigned by individual (base) models in validation sub-samples T_{S2} during 10-fold cross-validation for the development of base models
		DA LA UTADIS MHDIS SVM CART k-NN
Bank T1	Acquired	
...	...	
Bank T109	Acquired	
Bank T110	Non-Acquired	
...	...	
Bank T218	Non-acquired	
Holdout dataset*		Output assigned by individual (base) models in banks included in the unequal holdout during the testing of base models in chapter 5
Bank H1	Acquired	
Bank H59	Acquired	
Bank H60	Non-acquired	
...	...	
Bank H407	Non-acquired	

*Note: The "T" denotes that the bank belongs in the Training sample, while "H" denotes that the bank belongs in the Holdout sample.

Table 6.4 presents a summary of the results of the 14 stacked models. Models 1 to 7 correspond to the integration of the output of the base models developed using raw data, while models 8-14 correspond to those based on country-adjusted data. The combining method (in column 2) corresponds to the classification method that was used to perform the integration. The results clearly indicate that no method outperforms all others; although the UTADIS stacked model appears to do marginally better on the overall accuracy its performance is among the worst in classifying the acquired group of banks.

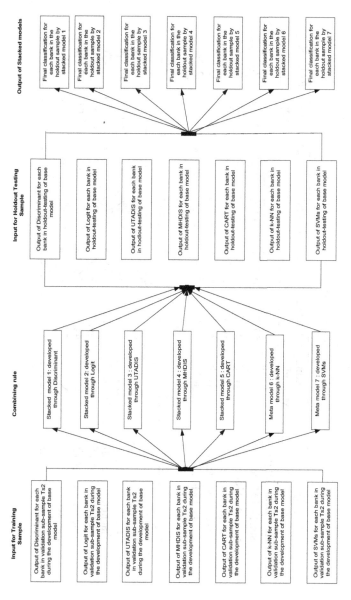

Figure 6.6   The development and testing process of the 7 stacked models

Table 6.4 Evaluation measures of stacked models

	Combining Method	Acquired	Non-Acquired	Overall	Average	Cohen's Kappa	PABAK
Raw financial ratios							
Stacked Model 1	DA	59.3%	53.7%	54.5%	56.5%	6.6%	9.1%
Stacked Model 2	LA	61.0%	52.0%	53.3%	56.5%	6.5%	6.6%
Stacked Model 3	UTADIS	30.5%	81.3%	74.0%	55.9%	10.1%	47.9%
Stacked Model 4	MHDIS	32.2%	72.7%	66.8%	52.5%	3.5%	33.7%
Stacked Model 5	CART	47.5%	48.3%	48.2%	47.9%	-2.1%	-3.7%
Stacked Model 6	KNN	49.2%	57.5%	56.3%	53.3%	3.6%	12.5%
Stacked Model 7	SVM	49.2%	58.9%	54.0%	57.5%	4.5%	15.0%
Country- adjusted financial ratios							
Stacked Model 8	DA	62.7%	56.9%	57.7%	59.8%	10.3%	15.5%
Stacked Model 9	LA	64.4%	56.0%	57.2%	60.2%	10.6%	14.5%
Stacked Model 10	UTADIS	47.5%	75.9%	71.7%	61.7%	17.0%	43.5%
Stacked Model 11	MHDIS	59.3%	62.1%	61.7%	60.7%	12.2%	23.3%
Stacked Model 12	CART	44.1%	76.1%	71.5%	60.1%	15.0%	43.0%
Stacked Model 13	KNN	52.5%	62.4%	60.9%	57.4%	8.6%	21.9%
Stacked Model 14	SVM	57.6%	55.5%	55.8%	56.5%	6.8%	11.5%

Comparing the models 1-7, we can see that the highest classification accuracy is achieved by logit for the acquired group (61.0%), and UTADIS for the non-acquired group (81.3%). As noted UTADIS also achieves the higher overall accuracy (74.0%), owing to its ability to correctly predict most of the non-acquired banks, and therefore also achieves the highest improvement over chance with Cohen's Kappa (10.1%) and PABAK (47.9%). However, if one is more interested in predicting correct at least 50% of the banks from each group, then only the discriminant and logit models would meet the requirement.

Turning to models 8-14, again logit achieves the highest accuracy for the acquired group (64.4%), while CART ranks first for the non-acquired banks. Overall, the UTADIS stacked model ranks first, by virtue of performing better for the non-acquired group as well as in terms of the remaining three measures (i.e. average accuracy, Cohen's Kappa and PABAK).

Comparing stacked models 1-7 with stacked models 8-14, like for like (i.e. model 1 versus model 8, model 2 versus model 9, etc), there appears to be some support for the use of raw data, in that the latter class of models perform broadly better in classifying the acquired group of banks, although the results are somewhat mixed for the classification of the non-acquired group. For example, stacked models 3 (UTADIS), and 4 (MHDIS) achieve higher (lower) overall (average) accuracies than corresponding stacked models 10 and 11 based on country-adjusted data. On most other cases, the latter class of models outperforms the former, unlike the case of the integrated models based on the majority voting rule where there was no clear difference in results between the two sets of data.

As previously mentioned, one of the purposes of the present Chapter is to examine whether integration of different methods can lead to better classification results than the ones achieved by the individual models. It is therefore more appropriate to compare the classification accuracies of the stacked models with those of the individual base model based on the same (unequal) holdout sample group. In this case, the results seem to indicate that there is no clear outright winner when considering all measures of performance and the data set used. For example, with country-adjusted data, the UTADIS stacked model achieves higher accuracies (as well as Cohen's and PABAK) than all the individual models, but it ranks 6th in the prediction of the acquired group of banks[8]. The results are more or less similar for models based on raw data, since no stacked model performs better than the best individual model in terms of average accuracy and Cohen's Kappa.

6.3.3 Comparison of majority voting and stacked models

The comparison of the stacked models with that of the MV rule also provides mixed results. Looking at the results for raw data, we could argue that the MV method performs relatively better as the integrated model achieves higher overall accuracy than 5 of the 7 stacked models (since UTADIS and MHDIS models do relatively better for the non-acquired firms, and discriminant and logit stacked models do relatively better for the acquired firms). On balance, the MV method achieves better accuracies for both groups of banks, as evidenced by the fact that it also achieves higher average accuracy and Cohen's Kappa.

Turning to the comparison of models based on country-adjusted data, the performance of the MV model is less clear cut relative to the staked models 8-14. For example, it ranks between 3rd and 5th in terms of classification accuracy, and Cohen's Kappa and PABAK measures. For example, the MHDIS stacked model achieves better performance, and so it may be argued that the MV model is favored by the use of country-adjusted data.

6.4 Conclusions

In this chapter we have examined whether combining the outcome of individual models into multi-classifiers (i.e. integrated models) leads to improved classification accuracy. Two well-known integration techniques, namely majority voting rule and stacked generalization have

---

[8] Of course, if prediction of acquired banks was the main criterion we would have selected the logit stacked model that predicts correctly 64.4% of the acquired banks, as opposed to 61.0% predicted by the best individual model (i.e. UTADIS). Note that we consider only two from the four discriminant and logit models, since the other two are actually the same models but with different cut-off points.

been applied to individual models developed in Chapter 5, resulting in a total of 16 integrated models, utilizing both raw and country-adjusted financial ratios. The results could be summarized as follows. First, the majority voting model performs relatively well and outperforms some of the individual models but not all of them. A similar conclusion is drawn from the comparison of the stacked models with the individual (base) ones. The comparison between the two integration methods provides somewhat mixed results. In general, it seems that the majority voting rule can perform better than most of the stacked models when using raw financial ratios, although the outcome is mixed for models developed with country-adjusted data.

In general, the results are quite mixed, suggesting that the integration techniques applied to the individual models have not led to increased prediction ability on account of all measures of classification accuracy, and to a degree that has been observed in previous studies. Integration of the variety of classification methods has revealed that the comparatively good performance of some individual classifiers has been counterbalanced by the relatively bad performance of others. Hence, not surprisingly, the integrated models have not outperformed all individual models, given the number of classification methods compared. However, it would appear from the results that the MV method, in view of its simplicity and ease of implementation, would be more attractive than the more sophisticated stacked generalization technique, and it would be challenging to find out if other sophisticated integration techniques (i.e. bagging, boosting) outperforming the MV combination method of integrating individual model results, leading to better predictive accuracy.

Chapter 7

Conclusions

7.1 Introduction

This study has been concerned with the development of models for the prediction of acquisition targets in the EU banking industry. In this concluding chapter, we first explain why we have sought to focus on the EU banking sector, and then summarize our main findings. Although the prediction models we develop show classification accuracies generally higher than chance assignment based on prior probabilities, there tends to be a fair amount of misclassification for some models and prediction accuracies also differ significantly across the range of methods considered. It is therefore appropriate to explain these results, and also seek to understand why classification accuracies differ across different methods, before finally offering some recommendations for further research.

7.2 Why Prediction Models for EU Banks

Over the last thirty years, there have been approximately 30 studies that have attempted to identify potential acquisition targets, all focused on non-financial sectors. None has considered banks (or other financial firms), and this lack of effort is due in part to the unusual structure of banks' financial statements and the differences in the environment in which banks operate. A prediction model developed specifically for the banking industry requires input variables that are specific to the banking sector. The use of the Bankscope database (and other databases on bank

M&As) together with the associated financial ratios permits the development of such a model.

We focus on the EU banking industry for three reasons. First, because of the large number of mergers and acquisitions that occurred in recent years. Second, despite structural reforms in the EU banking industry, most of the studies in banks M&As have focussed on the US and, consequently, the literature on EU banks' M&As is so far limited. There have been recent studies on other aspects of bank M&As, as noted in the introductory chapter, but none on the prediction of targets. Finally, all the studies on the prediction of acquisition targets have so far examined individual countries, with the majority of them focusing on the US or the UK. An explanation, based on Barnes (2000), could be that takeover targets within countries are comparable because they are not affected by cross-country institutional factors that arise from various stock exchanges or the corporate control market that is different across Europe. As Gual (1999) points out, the European banking industry has undergone a process of integration that reached its peak with the adoption of the single currency in 1999. In addition, the completion of the single market for banking has involved the implementation of directives aimed at opening domestic markets and partially harmonising banking markets across the EU. The single market in the EU therefore provides a fertile base for developing a prediction model using a sample of banks pooled across all the 15 EU member countries (as of 2002). Indeed, the present study is the first that has attempted the development of prediction models with a sample of commercial banks drawn from across 15 countries. We consider that prediction models of this nature can, with quantitative and analytic techniques, be converted into effective decision systems for the management of corporate risk across Europe.

7.3 Summary of the Findings

Although our empirical study is confined to commercial bank acquisitions in the EU, we compared and evaluated seven individual classification methodologies (Discriminant, Logit, UTADIS, MHDIS,

CART, k-NN and SVM). In addition, we evaluated two integrated methodologies (majority voting and stacked generalisation) for combining the predictions of individual classification methods. In order to allow for a proper comparative evaluation of these classification methods, we selected common subsets of our base sample of acquired and non-acquired banks and variables with high discriminatory power, dividing the sample period (1998-2002) into training sub-sample for model development (1998-2000), and holdout sub-sample for model evaluation (2001-2002), using both equal and unequal matched holdout samples.

The results showed that, on univariate Kruskal-Wallis tests of variables, acquired and non-acquired banks operating in the EU over the period 1998-2000 had similar financial profiles. Although acquired banks were less well capitalised and less profit and cost efficient, no statistically significant differences were observed in terms of liquidity, growth (measured by annual change of total assets), size (measured by total assets) and market power (measured by market shares in terms of loans or deposits).

Concerning the prediction of acquisitions, the results showed overall a fair amount of misclassification on holdout samples, which is hard to avoid given the nature of the problem. This is consistent with previous studies in non-financial sectors that found that prediction of acquisitions is quite difficult (e.g. Palepu, 1986; Espahbodi and Espahbodi, 2003). However, it is important to realise that no model could capture all possible motivations for acquisition activity that would enhance its prediction ability. Such "perfect" models have been hard to develop even in the bankruptcy prediction literature were failing firms have definitely inferior or abnormal performance characteristics compared to healthy firms. The problem with the prediction of acquisition targets is that are numerous reasons for acquisitions, not least that managers do not always act in a manner that maximizes shareholder returns (i.e. hubris, agency motives). It is therefore important to ensure, at minimum, that the models compare favourably with chance predictions (Barnes, 2000). Of the 28 models individual prediction developed in total, utilising all methodologies, 26 were capable of performing better than chance, as indicated by the Cohen's Kappa and PABAK tests.

With regard to the relative performance of the methodologies, this depends on the evaluation measure used for comparison. In general, some methods performed relatively well in classifying correct the acquired banks while others in classifying correct the non-acquired banks. For example, the UTADIS method achieved very high accuracies in classifying non-acquired banks, but normally at the cost of poor accuracy performance in predicting the acquired banks. This suggests a trade-off in achieving high classification accuracy, and therefore the question of what method does best depends very much on the group classification accuracy considered. Overall, Discriminant, Logit, UTADIS, CART and SVMs, all ranked relatively well, achieving high classification accuracies for at least one holdout sample, although, across all models evaluated on equal or unequal holdout samples, we found that discriminant and SVMs performed reasonably well in terms of achieving balanced classification accuracies of above 50% for both groups of banks. However, we also found that all classification methods achieved accuracies above 50% for both groups when the model included an additional discriminatory variable (Equity/Net Loans), suggesting that the outcome of which method performs best is also dependent on the choice of discriminating variables.

Concerning the use of equal or unequal holdout samples for testing, we find that the prediction ability of the models does not necessarily decrease with the use of unequal sized holdout samples, as Palepu claimed with regard to his re-calculation of the overall accuracy results of the study by Stevens (1973).

Concerning the use of country-adjusted or raw financial variables, we found no clear effect on the prediction ability of the models whatever the classification method used. Thus, in general, we cannot conclude as to whether it is better to use raw or country-adjusted financial variables.

As for the two methodologies we have applied for the first time to the prediction of acquisitions targets (SVMs and k-NN), we found that SVMs performed relatively well compared to other methods as well as to chance assignment. The results of k-NN were inferior, probably affected by the small number of banks in the training sample.

Finally, considering the use of two multi-classifier methodologies, we found that of the 16 integrated prediction models developed, 15 were capable of performing better than chance. With regard to the evaluation performance of the two integration techniques, the results are mixed. In general we found that the MV method performed relatively better than the stacked approach in the case of models developed with raw data, while the opposite was the case with country-adjusted data. The results of the integrated models have shown that relatively good performance of some individual models has been counterbalanced by the relatively poor performance of others. Hence, not surprisingly, none of the integrated models have out-performed all the individual prediction models. However, we find that the MV method, in view of its simplicity and ease of implementation, would be more appealing compared to the more sophisticated stacked generalization technique, although, given that the idea of integration in financial classification problems is relatively new, further research is needed before any generalization can be made.

7.4 Why Classification Results Differ Across Methods?

As we noted in Chapter 5, some methods are on average more accurate in classifying acquired banks, while others appear to classify more accurately non-acquired banks, and yet others achieve a balanced performance in classifying the acquired and the non-acquired banks. At the same time, we found that the use of raw or county-adjusted raw ratios also affected differently the classification ability of the methods. Although it is obvious that use of separate datasets can generate different results, it is also important to understand that different techniques process information in different ways and therefore can generate different classification results, even on the same dataset. In this section we attempt to offer some insight into how the application of quantitative methods we have used can produce varying classification accuracies across the same set of holdout samples.

Despite using the same information in terms of the dataset employed, each quantitative method processes the information differently, because of the differences in the implicit criteria for solving the problem. This is not surprising since these methods originate from different disciplines (e.g. statistics, econometrics, operational research, machine learning), and they utilise different objective functions or modelling forms (e.g. discriminant function, utility functions, decision trees), as well as employ different algorithms for model development.

For example, as noted in Chapter 3, discriminant analysis maximizes the ratio of among-groups to within-groups variance to determine a discriminant function on the basis of which the classification is performed, using a discriminant score for each bank and a cut-off point. By contrast, the logit method maximises a log-likelihood function to obtain the coefficient estimates that are used to estimate the group membership probabilities of all banks, on the basis of which the classification is performed using a cut-off point. Thus, classification accuracies in these two traditional methods are determined not just by the implicit objective criteria generating the coefficient estimators but also by the appropriate cut-off point, which may be pre-determined or optimally estimated using Palepu's (1986) method.

The two MCDA methods, UTADIS and MHDIS, employ mathematical programming techniques to estimate an additive utility function and a utility threshold (i.e. a cut-off point). Even between these two techniques, there are differences in the way the classification is performed. For example, UTADIS solves one linear programming formulation to minimize the sum of all misclassifications (section 3.4.3), while MHDIS solves three mathematical programming formulations, two linear and one mixed-integer, involving (1) minimisation of overall classification error, (2) minimization of the number of misclassifications, and (3) maximization of the minimum distance between the global utilities of the correctly classified banks (see Table 3.2). Furthermore, in UTADIS there is only the additive utility function that characterizes all the banks and not just the ones that belong to a specific group (i.e. acquired and non-acquired), as in the case of MHDIS. However, in general it might be the case that a specific variable is important in characterizing the banks belonging to one group but not the other. Hence the procedure followed under MHDIS leads to the specification of one utility function for each group that enables the modelling of such cases. Thus, these two multicriteria methods will generate different weights affecting the utility scores, and consequently the classification accuracies will differ.

The three machine learning methods, CART, k-NN and SVMs, also employ different algorithms to solve the respective decision making problem. In the case of CART, instead of a classification function, a binary decision tree is developed, while under k-NN a bank is classified to the group of its nearest neighbour using some kind of distance measure, such as the Euclidean. It is claimed that both these methods are data intensive, requiring large number of observations (typically thousands) to perform well. It is therefore not surprising that these methods have not performed well in our relatively small sample. SVMs, by contrast, works efficiently with large as well as small samples, in part because it relies only on the training points that are closest to the maximum margin hyperplane, known as support vectors, while all other training cases (i.e. banks) are irrelevant for determining the binary class boundaries. A distinguishing feature of SVMs is that it implements the structural risk minimisation principle, which minimizes the upper bound for the generalisation error rather than minimizing the training error as other techniques do, thus providing a robust set of results between training and testing datasets. CART and k-NN, on the other hand, seem to over-fit in the training samples, leading to poorer results in the testing samples.

To conclude, differences among the methods employed, such as the criteria for maximization or minimization or the searching pattern of the algorithm imply that the information is processed differently and therefore classification accuracies can vary over the same dataset. Of course, classification results will differ if the model is trained on a different data set, so that raw and country-adjusted data need not produce similar classification accuracies even for the same method, as the information dataset is not the same.

7.5 Suggestions for Further Research

As the present study represents a first attempt to develop prediction models for the EU banking industry, future research would extend our study in several directions. This study has restricted itself to the use of financial variables, as have most previous studies, owing to data availability. It is hoped that future research will take account of non-financial factors, such as concentration of firm ownership, although as we noted above this would be a difficult but challenging task. On the methodological side, an extension to current research would be the employment of rough sets and neural networks and their comparison with the methodologies used in the present study, as well as other methods for combining the output of individual models, such as bagging and boosting. On the sampling side, prediction models could possibly be developed distinguishing domestic and foreign banks on the basis of performance characteristics. In our case, however, although Bankscope provides information for the ownership of non-acquired banks, such information was not available for the acquired banks. Thus, it was not possible to separate between foreign and domestic based on the proportion of ownership that foreigners hold, but this information could be obtained from other sources. Another potential extension could be the development of separate models for each of the 15 EU banking sectors, allowing comparison with other within country models, similar to what Barnes (2000) did for each industrial UK sector. However, this was not possible in the present study due to the relatively small number of acquired banks for each country. It is hoped that this extension would be possible if other types of banks (e.g. savings, cooperatives) are included in the sample. A sufficiently large sample size could also make possible the development of models for small and large banks, hopefully leading to better prediction models.

Bibliography

Abrahams, A. 2004, *Evaluating Models*, Lecture 12, OPIM 410/672 Decision Support Systems, University of Cambridge Computer Laboratory & The Wharton School.

Abreu, M., Mendes, V. 2001, "Commercial bank interest margins and profitability: evidence from some EU countries", *Paper presented at the Pan-European Conference Jointly organised by the IEFS-UK & University of Macedonia Economic & Social Sciences*, Thessaloniki, Greece, May 17-20.

Adkisson, J., Fraser, D. 1990, "The ineluctable lure of softly leverage", *Journal of Retail Banking*, vol. 12, no. 3, pp. 25-30.

Agarwal, N.C. 1981, "Determinants of executive compensation", *Industrial Relations*, vol. 20, no. 1, pp. 36–58.

Akhavein, J.D., Berger, A.N., Humphrey, D.B. 1997, "The effects of megamergers on efficiency and prices: Evidence from a bank profit function", *Review of Industrial Organization*, vol. 12, pp. 95-139.

Ali-Yrkko, J. 2002, *Mergers and acquisitions-reasons and results*, The Research Institute of the Finnish Economy, Discussion papers No. 792, ISSN 0781-6847.

Allen, L., Cebenoyan, A.S. 1991, "Bank Acquisitions and Ownership Structure: Theory and Evidence", *Journal of Banking and Finance*, vol. 15, no. 2, pp. 425-448.

Altman, E.I. 1968, "Financial ratios, discriminant analysis and the prediction of corporate bankruptcy", *The Journal of Finance*, vol. 23, pp. 589-609.

Altman, E.I. 1993, *Corporate financial distress: a complete guide to predicting, avoiding, and dealing with bankruptcy*, Wiley, New York

Altunbas, Y., Goddard, J., Molyneux, P. 1999, "Technical change in banking", *Economics Letters*, vol. 64, pp. 215-221.

Ambrose, B.W., Megginson, W.L. 1992, "The Role of Asset Structure, Ownership Structure and Takeover Defenses in Determining Acquisition Likelihood", *Journal of Financial and Quantitative Analysis*, vol. 27, no. 4, pp. 575-589.

Amel, D., Barnes, C., Panetta, F., Salleo, C. 2004, "Consolidation and efficiency in the financial sector: A review of the international evidence", *Journal of Banking & Finance*, vol. 28, no. 10, pp. 2493-2519.

Anderson, Ch.W., Becher, D.A., Campbell, T.L. 2004, "Bank mergers, the market for bank CEOs, and managerial incentives", *Journal of Financial Intermediation*, vol. 13, no. 1, pp. 6-27.

Arnold, G. 1998, *Corporate Financial Management*, 1st edition, Financial Times Prentice Hall.

Asterbo, T., Winter, J.K. 2001, "More than a Dummy: The Probability of Failure, Survival and Acquisition of Firms in Financial Distress", Working Paper, University of Waterloo.

Balcaen, S., Ooghe, H. 2004, "Alternative methodologies in studies of business failure: do they produce better results than the classical statistical methods?", Universiteit Gent, Faculteit Economie En Bedrijfskunde, Belgium, Working Paper 2004/249.

Banerjee, A., Cooperman E. 1998, "Returns to Targets and Acquirers: Evidence from Bank Mergers in the '90s". Unpublished working paper, University of Colorado, Denver.

Baradwaj, B.G., Dubofsky, D.A., Fraser, D.R 1992, "Bidder returns in interstate and intrastate bank acquisitions", *Journal of Financial Services Research*, vol. 5, no. 3, pp. 261–273.

Baradwaj, B.G., Fraser, D.R., Furtado, E.P-H. 1990, "Hostile Bank Takeover Offers: Analysis and Implications", *Journal of Banking and Finance*, vol. 14, pp. 1229-1242.

Barnes, P. 1987, "The Analysis and Use of Financial Ratios: A Review Article", *Journal of Business Finance and Accounting*, vol. 14, pp. 449-461

Barnes, P. 1990, "The prediction of takeover targets in the U.K. by means of multiple discriminant analysis", *Journal of Business Finance & Accounting*, vol. 17, no. 1 (Spring), pp. 73-84.

Barnes, P. 1998, "Can takeover targets be identified by statistical techniques?: Some UK evidence", *The Statistician*, vol. 47, no. 4, pp. 573-591.

Barnes, P. 1999, "Predicting UK Takeover Targets: Some Methodological Issues and an Empirical Study", *Review of Quantitative Finance and Accounting*, vol. 12, no. 3, pp. 283-301.

Barnes, P. 2000, "The identification of U.K. takeover targets using published historical cost accounting data. Some empirical evidence comparing logit with linear discriminant analysis and raw financial ratios with industry-relative ratios", *International Review of Financial Analysis*, vol. 9, no. 2, pp. 147-162.

Bartley, J.W., Boardman, C.M. 1986, "Replacement-Cost-Adjusted Valuation Ratio as a Discriminator Among Takeover Target and Nontarget Firms", *Journal of Economics and Business*, vol. 38, pp. 41-55.

Bartley, J.W., Boardman, C.M. 1990, "The relevance of inflation adjusted accounting data to the prediction of corporate takeovers", *Journal of Business Finance and Accounting*, vol. 17, no. 1, 53-72.

Bauer, W., Ryser, M., 2004, "Risk management strategies for banks", *Journal of Banking and Finance*, vol. 28, pp. 331-352.

Beatty, R.P., Santomero, A.M., Smirlock, M.L. 1987, *Bank Merger Premiums: Analysis and Evidence*, Salomon Brothers Center for the Study of Financial Institutions Monograph Series in Finance and Economics, Monograph 1987-3.

Becher, D.A. 2000, "The valuation effects of bank mergers", *Journal of Corporate Finance*, vol. 6, no. 2, pp. 189-214.

Beitel, P., Schiereck, D. 2001, "Value creation at the ongoing consolidation of the European banking market", *Presented at the X international conference on banking and finance,* Tor Vergata University Rome, December 5-7.

Beitel, P., Schiereck, D., Wahrenburg, M. 2002, "Explaining the M&A success in European bank mergers and acquisitions", Institute for Mergers and Acquisitions (IMA), Working Paper, January 25.

Belaisch, A., Kodres, L., Levy, J., Ubide, A. 2001, *Euro-Area Banking and the Crossroads*, IMF Working Paper, WP 01/28.

Belkaoui, A. 1978, "Financial ratios as predictors of Canadian takeovers", *Journal of Business Finance and Accounting*, vol. 5, no. 1, pp. 93-107.

Benston, G.J., Hunter, W.C., Wall, L.D. 1995, "Motivations for Bank Mergers and Acquisitions: Enhancing the Deposit Insurance Put Option versus Earning Diversification", *Journal of Money, Credit and Banking*, vol. 27, no. 3, pp. 777-788.

Berger, A.N. 1995, "The profit-structure relationship in banking-tests of market power and efficient structure hypothesis", *Journal of Money, Credit and Banking*, vol. 27, pp. 404-431.

Berger, A.N. 1998, "The efficiency effects of bank mergers and acquisitions: A preliminary look at the 1990s data". In *Bank Mergers and Acquisitions*, Amihud Y., Miller G., (eds), Kluwer Academic Publishers, Dordrecht, pp. 79-11.

Berger, A.N., Demsetz, R.S., Strahan, P.E. 1999, "The consolidation of the financial services industry, causes, consequences and implications for the future", *Journal of Banking and Finance*, vol. 23, no. 2-4, pp.135-194.

Berger, A.N., DeYoung, R., Genay, H., Udell, G.F. 2000, "The Globalization of Financial Institutions: Evidence from Cross-Border Banking Performance", Brookings-Wharton Papers on Financial Services 3.

Berger, A.N., Humphrey, D.B., 1992, "Megamergers in banking and the use of cost efficiency as an antitrust defense", *Antitrust Bulletin*, vol. 37, pp. 541-600.

Berger, A.N., Mester, L.J., 1997, "Inside the black box: What explains the differences in the efficiencies of financial institutions?", *Journal of Banking and Finance*, vol. 21, no. 7, pp. 895–947.

Berger, A.N., Saunders, A., Scalise, J.M., Udell, G.F. 1998, "The effects of bank mergers and acquisitions on small business lending", *Journal of Financial Economics*, vol. 50, no. 2, pp. 187-229.

Berkovitch, E., Narayanan, M.P. 1993, "Motives for Takeovers: An Empirical Investigation", *Journal of Financial and Quantitative Analysis*, vol. 28, no. 3, pp. 347-362.

Bliss, R.T., Rosen, R.J. 2001, "CEO compensation and bank mergers", *Journal of Financial Economics*, vol. 61, no. 1, pp. 107-138.

Bradley, M., Desai, A., Kim, E.H. 1983, "The Rationale Behind Interfirm Tender Offers: Information or Synergy?", *Journal of Financial Economics*, April, pp. 183-206.

Brealey, R.A., Myers, S.C., Marcus, A.J. 2001, *Fundamentals of Corporate Finance*, 3rd ed, International Edition , McGraw-Hill Comp. Inc.

Breiman, L. 1996, Bagging predictors, *Machine Learning*, vol. 26, pp. 123-140.

Breiman, L., Friedman, J.H., Olshen, R.A, Stone, C.J. 1984, Classification *and Regression Trees*, Pacific Glove, Wadsworth Inc.

Brewer, E.I., Jackson, W.E.I., Jagtiani, J.A., Nguyen, Th. 2000, "The price of bank mergers in the 1990s", *Federal Reserve Bank of Chicago Economic Perspectives*, First Quarter 2000, pp. 2-23.

Byrt, T., Bishop, J., Carlin, J.B. 1993, "Bias, prevalence and kappa", *Journal of Clinical Epidemiology*, vol. 46, pp. 423-429.

Cheh, J.J., Weinber, R.S., Yook, K.C. 1999, "An Application Of An Artificial Neural Network Investment System To Predict Takeover Targets", *The Journal of Applied Business Research*, vol. 15, no. 4, pp. 33-45.

Cheng, D.C., Gup, B.E., Wall, L.D. 1989, "Financial Determinants of Bank Takeovers: A Note", *Journal of Money, Credit and Banking*, vol. 21, no. 4, pp. 524-536.

Cho, SB., Kim, JH. 1995, Combining multiple neural networks by fuzzy integral or robust classification, *IEEE Transactions on Systems, Man and Cybernetics*, vol. 25, no. 2, pp. 380 384.

Ciscel, D., Carroll, T. 1980, "The Determinants of Executive Salaries: An Econometric Survey", *Review of Economics and Statistics*, vol. 62, no. 1, pp. 7-13.

Claessens, S., Demirgüç-Kunt, A., Huizinga, H. 2001, "How does foreign entry affect domestic banking markets?", *Journal of Banking & Finance*, vol. 25. no. 5, pp. 891-911.

Clark, J. 1988, "Economies of Scale and Scope at Depository Institutions: A Review of the Literature", Federal *Reserve Bank of Kansas City Economic Review*, September/October.

Cohen, J. 1960, "A coefficient of agreement for nominal scales", *Educational and Psychological Measurement*, vol. 20, pp. 37-46.

Cornett, M.M., De, S. 1991, "Common stock returns in corporate takeover bids: Evidence from interstate bank mergers", *Journal of Banking and Finance*, vol. 15, no. 2, pp. 273-295.

Cornett, M.M., Hovakimian, G., Palia, D., Tehranian, H. 2003, "The impact of the manager -shareholder conflict on acquiring bank returns", *Journal of Banking & Finance*, vol. 27, no. 1, pp. 103-131.

Cornett, M.M., Tehranian, H. 1992, "Changes in Corporate Performance Associated with Bank Acquisitions", *Journal of Financial Economics*, vol. 31. no. 2, pp. 211-234.

Cosh, A., Hughes, A., Singh, A. 1984, *The causes and effects of takeovers in the UK: an empirical investigation for the late 1960s at the microeconomic level*, University of Cambridge, Department of Applied Economics, Economic reprint, no. 87.

Cosslett, S.R. 1981, "Efficient estimation of discrete choice models", In *Structural analysis of discrete data with econometric applications*, C.F Manski and D. McFadden (eds), MIT Press, Cambridge MA.

Craig, B., Santos, J.C. 1997, "The Risk Effects of Bank Acquisitions", *Federal Reserve Bank of Cleveland Economic Review*, QII, pp. 25-35.

Cristianini, N., Shawe-Taylor, J., 2000, *An introduction to Support Vector Machines*, Cambridge University Press, Cambridge, New York

Cudd, M., Duggal, R. 2000, "Industry Distributional Characteristics of Financial Ratios: An Acquisition Theory Application", *The Financial Review*, vol. 41, pp. 105-120.

Cybo-Ottone, A., Murgia, M., 2000, "Mergers and shareholder wealth in European banking", *Journal of Banking and Finance*, vol. 24, no. 6, pp. 831-859.

Cyree, K.B., DeGennaro, P. 2001, "A Generalized Method for Detecting Abnormal Returns and Changes in Systematic Risk", Federal Reserve Bank of Atlanta Working Paper Series, 2001-8.

Czyz, J., Kittler, J., Vandendorpe, L. 2004, "Multiple classifier combination for face based identity verification", *Pattern Recognition*, vol. 37, pp. 1459-1469.

De Bandt, O., Davis, E. 1999, "A cross-country comparison of market structures in European banking", European Central Bank Working Paper Series 7.

DeLong, G.L. 2001, "Stockholder gains from focusing versus diversifying bank mergers", *Journal of Financial Economics*, vol. 59, no. 2, pp. 221-252.

Demsetz, R.S., Strahan, P.E. 1997, "Diversification, size, and risk at bank holding companies", *Journal of Money, Credit and Banking*, vol. 29, pp. 300-313.

Dermine, J. 2002, "Banking in Europe: Past, Present and Future", in *The transformation of the European financial system*, Gaspar V., Hartmann Ph., Sleijpen O. (eds), Second ECB Central Banking Conference, pp. 32-86.

Dettmer, R. G. 1963, "Reasons for Mergers and Acquisitions", in *American Management Association: Corporate Growth through Merger and Acquisition*, Management Report 75, New York.

DeYoung, R. 1997, "Bank mergers, X-efficiency, and the market for corporate control", *Managerial Finance*, vol. 23, pp. 32-47.

Diaz, B.D., Olalla, M.G., Azofra, S.S. 2004, "Bank acquisitions and performance: evidence from a panel of European credit entities", *Journal of Economics and Business*, vol. 56, no. 5, pp. 377-404.

Dietrich, J.M., Sorensen, E. 1984, "An Application of Logit Analysis to Prediction of Merger Targets", *Journal of Business Research*, vol. 12, pp. 393-402.

Dietrich, J.R. 1984, "Discussion of Methodological Issues Related to the Estimation of Financial Distress Prediction Models", *Journal of Accounting Research*, vol. 22 (Supplement), pp. 83-86.

Dodd, P., Ruback, R. 1977, "Tender offers and stockholder returns: An empirical analysis", *Journal of Financial Economics*, vol. 8, pp. 105-137.

Doumpos, M. 2002, "A Stacked Generalization Framework for Credit Risk Assessment", *Operational Research: An International Journal*, vol. 2, no. 2, pp. 261-278.

Doumpos, M., Kosmidou, K., Baourakis, G., Zopounidis, C. 2002, "Credit risk assessment using a multicriteria hierarchical discrimination approach: A comparative analysis", *European Journal of Operational Research*, vol. 138, no. 2, pp. 392-412.

Doumpos, M., Kosmidou, K., Pasiouras, F. 2004, "Prediction of Acquisition Targets in the UK: A Multicriteria Approach", *Operational Research: An International Journal*, vol. 4, no. 2, pp. (in press).

Doumpos, M., Pasiouras, F. 2004, "Developing and testing models for replicating credit ratings: A multicriteria approach", *Computational Economics*, (forthcoming).

Doumpos, M., Zopounidis, C. 2001, "Assessing financial risk using a multicriteria sorting procedure: the case of country risk assessment", *Omega The International Journal of Management Science*, vol. 29, pp. 97-109.

Doumpos, M., Zopounidis, C. 2002a, "Business Failure Prediction: A Comparison of Classification Methods", *Operational Research. An International Journal*, vol. 2, no. 3, pp. 303-319.

Doumpos, M., Zopounidis, C. 2002b, *Multicriteria Decision Aid Classification Methods*, Kluwer Academic Publishers, Dordrecht.

Doumpos, M., Zopounidis, C. 2004, "Developing sorting models using preference disaggregation analysis: An experimental investigation", *European Journal of Operational Research*, vol. 154, no. 3, pp. 585-598.

Dunis, Ch.L., Klein, T., 2005, "Analysing mergers and acquisitions in European financial services: an application of real options", *The European Journal of Finance* (forthcoming).

Efron, B. 1979, "Bootstrap methods: another look at the jackknife", *Annals of Statistics*, vol. 7, pp. 1-26.

Efron, B. 1981a, "Nonparametric estimates of standard error: the jackknife, the bootstrap and other methods", *Biometrika*, vol. 68, pp. 589-599.

Efron, B. 1981b, "Nonparametric standard errors and confidence intervals (with discussion)", *Canadian Journal of Statistics*, vol. 9, pp. 139-172.

Efron, B. 1982, *The Jackknife, the Bootstrap and Other Resampling Plans*, Philadelphia: SIAM.

Efron, B. 1983, "Estimating the error rate of a prediction rule: improvement on cross-validation", *Journal of the American Statistical Association*, vol. 78, pp. 316-331.

Efron, B. 1985, "Bootstrap confidence intervals for a class of parametric problems", *Biometrika,* Vol. 72, pp. 45-58.

Efron, B. 1987, "Better bootstrap confidence intervals (with discussion)," *Journal of the American Statistical Association*, vol. 82, pp. 171-200.

Efron, B. 1990, "More efficient bootstrap computations", *Journal of the American Statistical Association*, vol. 85, pp. 79-89.

Eisenbeis, R.A. 1977, "Pitfalls in the application of discriminant analysis in business, finance, and economics", *Journal of Finance*, vol. XXXII, no. 3, pp. 875-900.

Eisenbeis, R.A., Gilbert, G.G., Avery, R.A. 1973, "Investigating the Relative Importance of Individual Variables and Variable Subsets in Discriminant Analysis", *Communications in Statistics*, vol. September, pp. 205-219.

Espahbodi, H., Espahbodi, P. 2003, "Binary choice models for corporate takeover", *Journal of Banking and Finance*, vol. 27, no. 4, pp. 549-574.

Estrella, A., Park, S., Peristiani, S. 2000, "Capital Ratios as Predictors of Bank Failure", *Federal Reserve Bank of New York Economic Policy Review*, July.

European Central Bank (ECB). 2000, *Mergers and acquisitions involving the EU banking industry-Facts and implications*, December.

Fairclough, D., Hunter, J. 1998, "The Ex-ante Classification of Takeover Targets Using Neural Networks", in *Technologies for Computational Finance*, Refenes and Moody (eds) Decision, Kluwer Academic Press.

Faraone, S.V., Tsuang, M.T. 1994, "Measuring diagnostic accuracy in the absence of a "gold standard", *American Journal of Psychiatry*, vol. 151, pp. 650-657.

Farell, K.R., Mammone, R.J. 1995, "Data fusion techniques in speaker recognition", in *Modern Methods of Speech Processing*, Ramachandran, R.V, Mammone, R.J (eds), Kluwer Academic Press, Boston, MA, pp. 279-297.

Fischer, R.A. 1936, "The utilization of multiple measurements in taxonomic problems", *Annals of Eugenics*, vol. 7, pp. 179-188.

Focarelli, D., Pozzolo, A.F. 2001, "The patterns of cross-border bank mergers and shareholdings in OECD countries", *Journal of Banking and Finance*, vol. 25, no. 12, pp. 2305-2337.

Franks, J.R., Harris, R.S., Mayer, C. 1988, "Means of Payment in Takeovers: Results for the United Kingdom and the United States", In *Corporate Takeovers: Causes and Consequences*, edited by Auerbach A.J., Chicago: University of Chicago Press, pp. 221-263.

Fraser, D.R., Kolari, J.W. 1987, "Determinants of Small Bank Acquisitions Premiums", *Proceedings of Federal Reserve Bank of Chicago Conference on Bank Structure and Competition*, May 8.

Freund, Y., Schapire, R.E. 1997, "A decision-theoretic generalization of on-line learning and an application to boosting", *Journal of Computer and System Sciences*, vol. 55, no. 1, pp. 119-139.

Frieder, L., Petty, P. 1991, "Determinants of bank acquisition premiums: Issues and evidence", *Contemporary Policy Issues*, vol. 9, no. 2, pp. 13-24.

Froot, K., Stein, J. 1998, "Risk Management, Capital Budgeting, and Capital Structure Policy for Financial Institutions: an Integrated Approach", *Journal of Financial Economics*, vol. 47, no. 1, pp. 55-82.

Fukunaga, K., Flick T. 1984, "An optimal global nearest neighbour metric", IEEE Trans. Pattern Anal.PAMI, vol. 6, no. 3, pp. 314-318.

Galindo, J., Tamayo, P. 2000, "Credit Risk Assessment Using Statistical and Machine Learning: Basic Methodology and Risk Modeling Applications", *Computational Economics*, vol. 15, no. 1, pp. 107-143.

Gammelgaard, J. 1999, "Competence: A Dynamic Extension of the Existing Typology of Acquisition Motives", Department of International Economics and Management, Copenhagen Business School, available at:
www.cbs.dk/departments/int/publications/wp_1999/wp12.pdf

Gart, A., Al-Jafari, M. 1999, "Revisiting the determinants of large bank merger and acquisition premiums", *Journal of Applied Management and Entrepreneurship*, vol. 4, no. 2, pp. 76-86.

Gaughan, P.A. 1996, *Mergers, Acquisitions and Corporate Restructurings*, New York: John Wiley & Sons, Inc.

Geisser, S. 1975, "The predictive sample reuse method with applications", *Journal of the American Statistical Association*, vol. 70, pp. 320-328.

Gilbert, R. 1984, "Bank market structure and competition- a survey", *Journal of Money Credit and Banking*, vol. 16, pp. 617-645.

Goddard, J, Molyneux, Ph., Wilson, J.O.S. 2001, *European banking: Efficiency, Technology and Growth*, John Wiley & Sons Ltd.

Golin, J. 2001, *The Bank Credit Analysis Handbook: A Guide for Analysts, Bankers and Investors*, John Wiley & Sons (Asia) Pre Ltd.

Grossman, S.J., Hart, O.D. 1980, "Takeover bids, the free-rider problem, and the theory of the corporation", *Bell Journal of Economics,* vol. 11, pp. 42–64.

Group of Ten. 2001, *Report on Consolidation in the Financial Sector*, January 25, available at http://www.imf.org/external/np/g10/2001/01/Eng/

Gual, J. 2003, "Deregulation, Integration, and Market Structure in European Banking", *Journal of the Japanese and International Economics*, vol. 13, pp. 372-396.

Gunter, S., Bunke, H. 2004, Feature selection algorithms for the generation of multiple classifier systems and their application to handwritten word recognition, *Pattern Recognition Letters*, vol. 25, pp. 1323-1336.

Gupton, G.M., Stein, R.M. 2002, "LossCalc™: Moody's Model for Predicting Loss Given Default (LGD)", Moody's Investors Service Global Credit Research, Special Comment, February.

Hadlock, Ch., Houston, J., Ryngaert, M. 1999, "The role of managerial incentives in bank acquisitions", *Journal of Banking and Finance*, vol. 23, no. 2-4, pp. 221-249.

Hakes, D., Brown, K., Rappaport, A. 1997, "The impact of state deposit caps on bank merger premiums", *Southern Economic Journal*, vol. 63, pp. 652-662.

Hamer, M.M. 1983, "Failure prediction: Sensitivity of classification accuracy to alternative statistical methods and variable sets", *Journal of Accounting and Public Policy*, vol. 2, pp. 289-307.

Hannan, T., Rhoades, S. 1987, "Acquisition targets and motives: The case of the banking industry", *The Review of Economics and Statistics*, vol. 69, no. 1, pp. 67-74.

Harris, R.S., Risk, J.L. 1983, "Toehold Acquisitions in U.S. Corporations: An Examination of Stock Returns", *Paper presented at the Western Finance Association Meeting*, June.

Harris, R.S., Stewart, J.F., Carleton, W.T., 1982, "Financial Characteristics of Acquired Firms", in *Mergers and Acquisitions: current problems in perspective*, Keeman, M., White, L.J (eds), N.Y University, Lexington Books, pp. 223-241.

Hasbrouck, J. 1985, "The Characteristics of Takeover Targets: q and Other Measures", *Journal of Banking and Finance*, vol. 9, no. 3, pp. 351-362.

Hawawini, G.A., Swary, I. 1990, *Mergers and Acquisitions in the U.S. Banking Industry: Evidence from the Capital Markets*, North-Holland, Amsterdam.

Henley, W.E., Hand, D.J. 1996, "A k-NN classifier for assessing consumer credit risk", *Statistician*, vol. 45, pp. 77-95.

Highleyman, W.H. 1962, "The design and analysis of pattern recognition experiments", *Bell Systems Technical Journal*, vol. 41, pp. 723-744.

Ho, T., Hull, J., Srihari, S. 1994, "Decision combination in multiple classifier systems", *IEEE Transactions on Pattern Analysis and Machine Intelligence*, vol. 16, no. 1, pp. 66-75.

Hoadley, B., Oliver, R.M. 1998, "Business measures of scorecard benefit", *IMI Journal of Mathematics Applied in Business and Industry*, vol. 9, pp. 55-64.

Houston, J.F., James, Ch.M., Ryngaert, M.D. 2001, "Where do merger gains come from? Bank mergers from the perspective of insiders and outsiders?", *Journal of Financial Economics*, vol. 60, no. 2-3, pp. 285-331.

Houston, J.F., Ryngaert, M.D. 1994, "The overall gains from large bank mergers", *Journal of Banking and Finance*, vol. 18, no. 6, pp. 1155-1176.

Houston, J.F., Ryngaert, M. 1997, "Equity issuance and adverse selection: A direct test using conditional stock offers", *Journal of Finance*, vol. 52, pp. 197-219.

Huang, W., Nakamori, Y., Wang, Sh.-Y. 2005, "Forecasting stock market movement direction with support vector machines", *Computers & Operations Research*, (in press).

Huang, Y., Suen, C. 1995, "A method of combining multiple experts for the recognition of unconstrained handwritten numerals", *IEEE Transactions on Pattern Analysis and Machine Intelligence*, vol. 17, no. 1, pp. 90-94.

Huang, Y.S., Suen, C.Y., 1993, "The behavior-knowledge space method for combination of multiple classifiers", *Proceedings of IEEE Conference CVPR*, pp. 347-352.

Huang, Z., Chen, H., Hsu, Ch.-J., Chen, W-H., Wu, S. 2004, "Credit rating analysis with support vector machines and neural networks: a market comparative study", *Decision Support Systems*, vol. 37, no. 4, pp. 543-558.

Huberty, C.J. 1984, *Applied Discriminant Analysis*, John Wiley & Sons Inc.

Hudgins, S.C., Seifert, B. 1996, "Stockholders and international acquisitions of financial firms: an emphasis on banking", *Journal of Financial Services Research*, vol. 10, pp. 163-180.

Hughes, J.P., Mester, L.J., Moon, Ch.-G. 2001, "Are scale economies in banking elusive or illusive?: Evidence obtained by incorporating capital structure and risk-taking into models of bank production", *Journal of Banking & Finance*, vol. 2 , no. 12, pp. 2169-2208.

Huizinga, H.P., Nelissen, J.H.M., Vander Vennet R. 2001, "Efficiency Effects of Bank Mergers and Acquisitions in Europe", Tinbergen Institute Discussion Paper, 2001-088/3.

Humphrey, D.B. 1993, "Cost and technical change: effects from bank deregulation", *Journal of Productivity Analysis*, vol. 4, pp. 9-34.

Hunter, W., Timme, S. 1989, "Does Multiproduct Production in Large Reduce Costs", *Federal Reserve Bank of Atlanta Economic Review*, May/June

Hunter, W., Wall, L. 1989, "Bank Merger Motivations: A Review of the Evidence and an Examination of Key Target Bank Characteristics", *Economic Review of the Federal Reserve Bank of Atlanta*, September/October.

Hunter, W.C., Timme, S.G. 1991, "Technological change in large US banks", *Journal of Business*, vol. 64, pp. 339-362.

Jackson, R., Gart, A. 1999, "Determinants and non-determinants of bank merger premiums", *The Mid-Atlantic Journal of Business*, vol. 35, no. 4, pp. 149-157.

Jacquet-Lagreze, E., Siskos, J. 1982, "Assessing a set of additive utility functions for multicriteria decision making: The UTA method", *European Journal of Operational Research*, vol. 10, no. 2, pp. 151-164.

Jacquet-Lagreze, E., Siskos, J. 1983, *Methodes de Decision Multicritere*, Editions Hommes et Techniques, Paris.

Jacquet-Lagreze, E., Siskos, J. 2001, "Preference disaggregation: Twenty years of MCDA experience", *European Journal of Operational Research*, vol. 130, no. 2, pp. 233-245.

Jensen, M.C., Meckling W.H. 1976, "Theory of the Firm: Managerial Behaviour, Agency Costs and Ownership Structure", *Journal of Financial Economics,* vol. 3, no. 4, pp. 305-360.

Jitpraphai, S. 2000, "Financial variables and merger premiums: Evidence from bank mergers", Doctor Dissertation, Nova Southeastern University

Jo, H., Han, I. 1996, "Integration of case-based forecasting, neural network, and discriminant analysis for bankruptcy prediction", *Expert Systems with Applications*, vol. 11, no. 4, pp. 415-422.

International Federation of Accountants. 2000, *The Audit of International Commercial Banks: Proposed International Auditing Practice Statement*, International Auditing Practices Committee, September.

Kachigan, S.K. 1991, *Multivariate statistical analysis: A Conceptual Introduction*, second edition, Radius Press, New York.

Kane, E.J. 2000, "Incentives for banking megamergers: What motives might central-bank economics infer from event-study evidence?", *Journal of Money, Credit and Banking*, vol. 32, no. 3, pp. 671-699.

Kanji, G.K. 1993, *100 Statistical Tests*, SAGE Publications Ltd, London.

Karceski, J., Ongena, S., Smith, D.C. 2004, "The impact of Bank Consolidation on Commercial Borrower Welfare", *Journal of Finance*, (forthcoming).

Karson, M.J., Martell, T.F. 1980, "On the Interpretation of Individual Variables in Multiple Discriminant Analysis", *Journal of Financial and Quantitative Analysis*, March, pp. 211-217.

Kim, E., Kim, W., Lee, Y. 2002, "Combination of multiple classifiers for the customer's purchase behavior prediction", *Decision Support Systems*, vol. 34, pp. 167-175.

Kim, K-j., 2003, "Financial time series forecasting using support vector machines", *Neurocomputing*, vol. 55, no. 1-2, pp. 307-319.

Kim, W.G., Arbel, A. 1998, "Predicting merger targets of hospitality firms (a Logit model)", *International Journal of Hospitality Management*, vol. 17, no. 3, pp. 303-318.

King, R.G., Levine R. 1993, "Finance and growth: Schumpeter might be right", *Quarterly Journal of Economics*, vol. 108, pp. 717-737.

Kinnear, P.R., Gray, C.D. 2000), *SPSS for Windows Made Simple Release 10*, Psychology Press Ltd, UK.

Kira, D., Morin, D. 1993, "Prediction of takeover targets of Canadian Firms", in *Applied Stochastic Models and Data Analysis*, Janssen, J., Skiadas, C.H. (eds), World Scientific Publ. Co., pp. 507-518.

Kocagil, A.E., Reyngold, A., Stein, R.M., Ibarra, E. 2002, "Moody's RiskCalc™ Model For Privately-Held U.S. Banks", Moody's Investors Service, Global Credit Research, July.

Kwan, S.H., Eisenbeis, R. 1999, "Mergers of publicly traded banking organizations revisited", *Federal Reserve Bank of Atlanta Economic Review*, vol. 84, pp. 26-37.

Lachenbruch, P.A. 1967, "An Almost Unbiased Method of Obtaining Confidence Intervals for the Probability of Misclassification in Discriminant Analysis", *Biometrics*, pp. 639-645.

Lachenbruch, P.A. 1975, *Discriminant Analysis*, Hafner Press.

Lachenbruch, P.A., Mickey, M.R. 1968, "Estimation of error rates in discriminant analysis", *Technometrics*, vol. 10, pp. 1-11.

Laderman, E.S. 2000, "The potential diversification and failure reduction benefits of bank expansion into nonbanking activities", Federal Reserve Bank of San Francisco in its series Working Papers in Applied Economic Theory, 2000-01.

Laitinen, E.K. 1992, "Prediction of failure of a newly founded firm", *Journal of Business Venturing*, vol. 7, pp. 323-340.

Lam, K.F., Moy, J.W. 2002, "Combining discriminant methods in solving classification problems in two-group discriminant analysis", European *Journal of Operational Research*, vol. 138, no. 2, pp. 294-301.

Lam, L., Suen, C.Y. 1997, "Applications of majority voting to pattern recognition: a analysis of its behaviour and performance", *IEEE Transactions on Systems, Man, and Cybernetics*, vol. 27, no. 5, pp. 553-568.

Lane, S. 1972, "Submarginal credit risk classification", *Journal of Financial and Quantitative Analysis*, vol. 7, pp. 1379-1386.

Lang, G., Welzel, P. 1996, "Efficiency and technical progress in banking: empirical results from a panel of German banks", *Journal of Banking and Finance*, vol. 20, no.6, pp. 1003-1023

Lawrence, M.L. 2001, "The key financial and nonfinancial variables that help explain commercial bank merger and acquisition premiums", DBA Dissertation, Nova Southeastern University.

Lee, G., Sung, T.K, Chang, N. 1999, "Dynamics of modeling in data mining: interpretive approach to bankruptcy prediction", *Journal of Management Information Systems*, vol. 16, pp. 63-85.

Lee, T-S., Chiu, Ch.-Ch., Lu, Ch-J., Chen, I-F. 2002, "Credit scoring using the hybrid neural discriminant technique", *Expert System with Applications*, vol. 23, pp. 245-254.

Leonard, J., Glossman, D., Nasheck, J., Strauss, R. 1992, "European bank mergers: Lessons of experience for the future", Salomon Brothers International Equity Research, May.

Lepetit, L., Patry, S., Rous, Ph. 2004, "Diversification versus specialization: an event study of M&As in the European banking industry", *Applied Financial Economics*, vol. 14, no. 9, pp. 663-669.

Levine, P., Aaronovitch, S. 1981, "The financial characteristics of firms and theories of merger activity", *Journal of Industrial Economics*, vol. XXX, pp. 149–172.

Levine, R. 1997, "Financial development and economic growth: views and agenda", *Journal of Economic Literature*, vol. 35, pp. 688-726.

Levine, R. 1998, "The legal environment, banks, and long-run economic growth", *Journal of Money, Credit and* Banking, vol. 30, pp. 596-613.

Linder, J.C., Crane, D.B. 1993, "Bank Mergers: Integration and Profitability", *Journal of Financial Services Research*, vol. 7 (January), pp. 35-55.

Liu, Y. 2002, "The evaluation of classification models for credit scoring", Institut fur Wirtschaftsinformatik, Georg-August-Universitat Gottingen

Lo, A. W. 1986, "Logit Versus Discriminant Analysis: A Specification Test and Application to Corporate Bankruptcies", *Journal of Econometrics*, vol. 31, pp. 151-178.

Maddala, G.S. 1983, *Limited Dependent and Qualitative Variables in Econometrics*, Econometric Society Monographs, Cambridge University Press, Cambridge.

Madura, J., Wiant, K.J. 1994, "Long-term valuation effects of bank acquisitions", *Journal of Banking and Finance*, vol. 18, no. 6, pp. 1135–1154.

Mahmood, M., Lawrence, E. 1987, "A Performance Analysis of Parametric and Nonparametric Discriminant Approaches to Business Decision Making", *Decision Sciences,* vol. 18, pp. 308-326.

Manne, H.G. 1965, "Mergers and the market for corporate control", *Journal of Political Economy,* vol. LXXIII, no.1, pp. 110–120.

Manski, C.F., Lerman, S.R. 1977, "The estimation of choice probabilities from choice based samples", *Econometrics,* vol. 45, no. 8, pp. 1977-1988.

Manski, C.F., McFadden, D. 1981, "Alternative estimators and sample designs for discrete choice analysis", in *Structural analysis of discrete data with econometric applications,* Manski, C.F., McFadden D. (eds), MIT Press, Cambridge MA.

Maudos, J., Pastor, J.M., Quesada, J. 1996, "Technical progress in Spanish banking : 1985-1994", Instituto Valenciano de Investigaciones Economicas (IVIE) discussion paper 4.

McKee, T.E., Lensberg, T. 2002, "Genetic programming and rough sets: A hybrid approach to bankruptcy classification", *European Journal of Operational Research,* vol. 138, no. 2, pp. 436-451.

McKillop, D.G., Class, C.J., Morikawa, Y. 1996, "The composite cost function and efficiency in giant Japanese banks", *Journal of Banking and Finance,* vol. 20, no. 10, pp. 1651-1671.

McLachlan G.J., (1992), Discriminant Analysis and Statistical Pattern Recognition, John Wiley & Sons, Inc.

Meador, A.L., Church, P.H., Rayburn, L.G. 1996, "Development of prediction models for horizontal and vertical mergers", *Journal of Financial and Strategic Decisions,* vol. 9, no. 1, pp. 11-23.

Meeks, G. 1977, *Disappointing Marriage: a Study of Gains from Merger,* Cambridge University Press, Cambridge.

Menard, S. 1995, *Applied Logistic Regression Analysis,* Thousand Oaks, CA: Sage Publications

Mensah, Y.M. 1984, "An Examination of the Stationarity of Multivariate Bankruptcy Models: A Methodological Study", *Journal of Accounting Research,*vol. 22, pp. 380-395.

Miller, S.M., Noulas, A.G. 1996, "The technical efficiency of large bank production", *Journal of Banking and Finance,* vol. 20, no. 3, pp. 495-509.

Molyneux, P., Thorton, J. 1992, "Determinants of European bank profitability: A Note", *Journal of Banking and Finance,* vol. 16, no. 6, pp. 1173-1178.

Molyneux, P., Altunbas, Y., Gardener, EPM. 1996, *Efficiency in European Banking,* John Willey and Sons, Chichester.

Moore, R.R. 1996, "Banking's Merger Fervor: Survival of the Fittest?", *Federal Reserved Bank of Dallas Financial Industry Studies,* vol. December, pp. 9-15.

Moore, R.R., Siems, T.F. 1998, "Bank mergers: creating value of destroying competition?" *Federal Reserve Bank of Dallas Financial Industry Issues,* Third Quarter.

Morck, R., Shleifer, A., Vishny, R. 1988, "Characteristics of Targets and Hostile and Friendly Takeovers", in *Corporate Takeovers: Causes and Consequences,* Auerbach A.J. (ed), National Bureau of Economic Research, Chicago University Press, Chicago.

Morrison, D.G. 1969, "On the Interpretation of Discriminant Analysis", *Journal of Marketing Research,* vol. May, pp. 156-163.

Mosteller, F., Wallace, D.F. 1963, "Inference and the Authorship Problem", *Journal of the American Statistical Association,* vol. June, pp. 275-309.

Mueller, D.C. 1969, "A Theory of Competitive Mergers", *Quarterly Journal of Economics,* vol. 83, pp. 643-659.

Mueller, D.C. 1989, "Mergers: Causes, Effects and Policies", *International Journal of Industrial Organization,* vol. 7, pp. 1-10.

Murphy, K.J. 1999, "Executive Compensation", in *Handbook of Labor Economics,* Orley Ashenfelter O., Card D. (eds.), vol. 3, North Holland.

Neely, M.C., Wheelock, D. 1997, "Why does bank performance vary across countries?", *Federal Reserve Bank of St. Louis Review,* March, pp. 27-40.

Nelson, R., 1959, *Merger Movements in American Industry: 1895-1956,* Princeton University Press, Princeton.

Nowman, K.B., Saltoglu, B. 2003, "Continuous time and nonparametric modelling of U.S. interest rate models", International *Review of Financial Analysis,* vol. 12, no. 1, pp. 25-34.

Palepu, K.G. 1986, "Predicting Takeover Targets: A Methodological and Empirical Analysis", *Journal of Accounting and Economics,* Vol. 8, pp. 3-35.

Palia, D. 1994, "Recent evidence on bank mergers", *Financial Markets, Institutions and Instruments,* Vol. 3, pp. 36-59.

Pasiouras, F., Gaganis, Ch., Zopounidis, C. 2004a, "Replicating auditors' opinion on UK manufacturing firms: multicriteria approaches", *Paper presented at the 2nd Meeting of the Greek working group on Multicriteria Decision Aid,* October 21-22, Chania, Greece.

Pasiouras, F., Kosmidou, K. 2005, "Factors influencing the profitability of domestic and foreign commercial banks in the European Union", Working Paper, Financial Engineering Laboratory, Department of Production Engineering and Management, Technical University of Crete, Greece.

Pasiouras, F., Zopounidis, C., Doumpos, M. 2004b, "Predicting Financial Distress of UK Firms: A Multicriteria Approach", *Paper presented at the 20th European Conference on Operational Research,* July 4-7, Rhodes, Greece.

Peristiani, S. 1993, "Evaluating the Postmerger X-efficiency and Scale Efficiency of U.S. Banks", *Federal Reserve Bank of New York,* August.

Peristiani, S. 1997, "Do mergers improve the X-efficiency and scale efficiency of US banks? Evidence from the 1980s", *Journal of Money, Credit and Banking,* Vol. 29, pp. 326-337.

Perry, P. 1992, "Do Banks Gain or Lose from Inflation", *Journal of Retail Banking*, Vol. 14, no. 2, pp. 25-40.

Pilloff, S.J. 1996, "Performance changes and shareholder wealth creation associated with mergers of publicly traded banking institutions", *Journal of Money, Credit and Banking*, Vol. 28, no. 3, pp. 294-310.

Pinches, G.E. 1980, "Factors Influencing Classification results from Multiple Discriminant Analysis", *Journal of Business Research*, Vol. December, pp. 429-456.

Platt, H.D., Platt, M.B. 1990, "Development of a Class of Stable Predictive Variables: The Case of Bankruptcy Prediction", *Journal of Business Finance and Accounting*, Vol. 17, pp. 31-51.

Platt, H.D, Platt, M.B. 1991, "A note on the use of industry-relative ratios in bankruptcy prediction", *Journal of Banking and Finance*, Vol. 15, pp. 1183-1194.

Powell, R.G. 1997, "Modelling takeover likelihood", *Journal of Business Finance and Accounting*, Vol. 24, no. 7 & 8, pp. 1009-1030.

Powell, R.G. 2001, "Takeover Prediction and Portfolio Performance: A Note", *Journal of Business Finance & Accounting*, Vol. 28, 7 & 8, pp. 993-1011.

Provost, F., Fawcett, T. 1997, "Analysis and Visualization of Classifier Performance: Comparison Under Imprecise Class and Cost Distributions", *Proceedings Third International Conference on Knowledge Discovery and Data Mining*, Newport Beach, CA, August, pp. 14-17.

Quenouille, M. 1949, "Approximation tests of correlation in time series", *Journal of Royal Statistical Society*, B, 11, pp.18-84

Rajan, R. G., Zingales L. 1998, "Financial dependence and growth", *American Economic Review*, Vol. 88, pp. 559-586.

Ravenscraft, D.J., Scherer, F.M. 1987, *Mergers, Sell-Offs, and Economic Efficiency*, The Brookings Institution, Washington D.C.

Rege, U.P. 1984, "Accounting ratios to locate take-over targets", *Journal of Business Finance and Accounting*, Vol. 11, no. 3, pp. 301-311.

Rhoades, S.A. 1986, "The operating performance of acquired firms in banking before and after acquisition", *Staff Economic Studies 149, Board of Governors of the Federal Reserve System*, Washington DC.

Rhoades, S.A. 1987, "Mergers and Acquisitions by Commercial Banks 1960-83", *Staff Study No. 142, Board of Governors of the Federal Reserve System*, January.

Rhoades, S.A. 1990, "Billion dollar bank acquisitions: A note on the performance effects", *Board of Governors of the Federal Reserve System*, Washington DC.

Rhoades, S.A. 1993, "The efficiency effects of horizontal bank mergers, *Journal of Banking and Finance*, Vol. 17, no. 2-3, pp. 411-422.

Rhoades, S.A. 1994, "A Summary of Merger Performance Studies in Banking, 1980-93, and an Assessment of the "Operating Performance" and "Event study" Methodologies", *Staff member studies series of the Board of Governors of the Federal Reserve System*, summarized in the July Federal Reserve Bulletin.

Rhoades, S.A. 1998, "The efficiency effects of bank mergers: An overview of case studies of nine mergers", *Journal of Banking and Finance*, Vol. 22, no. 3, pp. 273-291.

Rhoades, S.A. 2000, "Bank Mergers and Banking Structure in the United States, 1980-98", *Board of Governors of the Federal Reserve System*, Staff Study 174, August.

Ripley, B.D. 1996, *Pattern Recognition and Neural Networks*, Cambridge University Press, Cambridge.

Roberts, D. 1956, A General Theory of Executive Compensation Based on Statistically Tested Propositions, *Quarterly Journal of Economics*, Vol. 70, no. 2, pp. 270-294.

Rogowski, R.J., Simonson, D.G. 1989, "Bank Merger Pricing Premiums and Interstate Bidding", *in Bank Mergers: Current Issues and Perspectives,* Gup B.E. (ed), , Kluwer Academic Publishers, pp. 87-104.

Roli F. 2002, *Tutorial on Fusion of Multiple Classifiers – Part III*, available at: http://www.diee.unica.it/informatica/en/publications/papers-prag/MCS-Tutorial0 01%28Part3%29.pdf

Roll, R. 1986, "The Hubris Hypothesis of Corporate Takeovers", *Journal of Business*, Vol. 59, no. 2, pp. 197-216.

Rose, R.S. 1987, "Improving Regulator Policy for Mergers: An assessment of Bank Merger Motivations and Performance Effects", *Issues in Bank Regulation*, Winter, pp. 32-39.

Saranli, A., Demirekler, D. 2001, "A statistical unified framework for rank-based multiple classifier decision combination", *Patter Recognition*, Vol. 34, pp. 865-884.

Scarborough, E., 1999, "Valuation determinants used in bank take-overs and mergers", Doctoral Dissertation, Nova Southeastern University.

Schiereck D., Strauss M. 2000, Zum Ankundigungseffekt großer Bankfusionen, M&A Review, 11/2000, pp. 421-425.

Seidel, G.R. 1995, "Kritische Erfolgsfaktoren bei Unternehmensubernahmen: Eine Analyse der US-Bankenbranche", Wiesbaden, Gabler.

Shao, J., Tu D. 1995, *The jackknife and Bootstrap*, Springer Series in Statistics, Springer – Verlag New York, Inc.

Shawky, H., Klip, T., Stass, C. 1996, "Determinants of bank merger premiums", *Journal of Economics and Finance*, Vol. 20, no. 1, pp. 117-131.

Shin, K., Lee, T.S., Kim, H. 2004, "An application of support vector machines in bankruptcy prediction model", *Expert Systems with Applications*, (in press).

Short, B.K. 1979, "The relation between commercial bank profit rate and banking concentration in Canada, Western Europe and Japan", *Journal of Banking and Finance*, Vol. 3, no. 3, pp. 209-219.

Short, R., Fukunaga K. 1980, "A new nearest neighbor distance measure", Pr*oceedings of the fifth IEEE Computer Society Conference on Pattern Recognition*, IEEE Computer Society Press, pp. 81-86.

Siems, T.F. 1996, "Bank mergers and shareholder wealth: Evidence from 1995s megamerger deals", *Federal Reserve Bank of Dallas Financial Industry Studies*, pp. 1-12.

Simkowitz, M., Monroe, R.J. 1971, "A discriminant analysis function for conglomerate mergers", *Southern Journal of Business*, Vol. 38, pp. 1-16.

Singh, A. 1971, *Takeovers: Their relevance to the stock market and the theory of the firm*, Cambridge University Press, Great Britain.

Singh, A. 1975, "Takeovers, economic natural selection and the theory of the firm: evidence from the post-war UK experience", *Economic Journal*, Vol. 85, pp. 497-515.

Slowinski, R., Zopounidis, C., Dimitras, A.I. 1997, "Prediction of company acquisition in Greece by means of the rough set approach", *European Journal of Operational Research*, Vol. 100, no. (1), pp. 1-15.

Sobehart, J.R., Keenan, S., Stein, S. 2000, "Benchmarking quantitative default risk models: A validation methodology", Moody's Investors Service Global Credit Research, March.

Sobek, O. 2000, *Bank mergers and acquisitions*, Narodna Banka Slovenska, December.

Spathis, Ch., Doumpos, M., Zopounidis, C. 2003, "Detecting falsified financial statements, a comparative study using multicriteria analysis and multivariate statistical techniques", *European Accounting Review*, Vol. 11, no. 3, pp. 509-535.

Spearman, C. 1904, "General Intelligence Objectively Determined and Measured", *American Journal of Psychology*, Vol. 15, pp. 201-293.

Spindt, P.A., Tarhan, V. 1992, "Are there synergies in bank mergers?", Working paper, Tulane University, New Orleans, LA.

Srinivasan, A. 1992, "Are There Cost Savings from Bank Mergers?", *Federal Reserve Bank of Atlanta Economic Review*, Vol. 77 (March-April), pp. 17-28.

Srinivasan, A., Wall, L.D. 1992, "Cost Savings Associated with Bank Mergers", Working Paper 92-2, Federal Reserve Bank of Atlanta, February.

Staikouras, Ch., Wood, G. 2003, "The Determinants Of Bank Profitability In Europe", Paper *presented at the European Applied Business Research Conference*, Venice, Italy, 9-13 June.

Stein, R.M. 2002, "Benchmarking default prediction models: Pitfalls and Remedies in Model Validation", Moody's KMV Technical Report #030124, June 13.

Stevens, D.L. 1973, "Financial Characteristics of Merged Firms: A Multivariate Analysis", *Journal of Financial and Quantitative Analysis*, Vol. 8 (March), pp. 149-158.

Stone, M. 1974, "Cross-validatory choice and assessment of statistical predictions (with discussion)", *Journal of the Royal Statistical Society*, series B, 36, pp. 11-147.

Subrahmanyam, V., Rangan, N., Rosenstein, S. 1997, "The role of outside directors in bank acquisitions", *Financial Management*, Vol. 26, no. 3, pp. 23-26.

Suen, C.Y., Legault, R., Nadal, C., Cheriet, M., Lam, L. 1993, "Building a new generation of handwriting recognition systems", *Pattern Recognition Letters*, Vol. 14, no. 4, pp. 303-315.

Tabachnick, B.G., Fidell, L.S. 2001, *Using Multivariate Statistics*, 4th edition, Allyn & Bacon, USA.

Taffler, R.J. 1982, "Forecasting Company Failure in the UK using Discriminant Analysis and Financial Ratio Data", *Journal of the Royal Statistical Society*, Vol. 145, pp. 342-358.

Tam, K. Y., Kiang, M.Y. 1992, "Managerial Applications of Neural Networks: The Case of Bank Failure Predictions", *Management Science*, Vol. 38, no. 7, pp. 926-947.

Tartari, E., Doumpos, M., Baourakis, G., Zopounidis, C. 2003, "A stacked generalization framework for the prediction of corporate acquisitions", *Foundations of computing and decision sciences,* Vol. 28, no. 1, pp. 41-61.

Tay, F.E.H., Cao, L. 2001, "Application of support vector machines in financial time series forecasting", *Omega: The International Journal of Management Science*, Vol. 29, no. 4, pp. 309-317.

Tay, F.E.H., Cao, L. 2002, "Modified support vector machines in financial time series forecasting", *Neurocomputing*, Vol. 48, no. 1-4, pp. 847-861.

Thomas, H.M. 1997, "Discussion of modelling takeover likelihood", *Journal of Business Finance and Accounting*, Vol. 24, no. 7 & 8, pp. 1031-1035.

Tourani-Rad, A., Van Beek, L. 1999, "Market Valuation of European Bank Mergers", *European Management Journal*, Vol. 17, no. 5, pp. 532-540.

Toyne, M.F., Tripp, J.D. 1998, "Interstate Bank Mergers and Acquisitions and Their Impact on Shareholder Returns: Evidence from the '90s", *Quarterly Journal of Business and Economics*, Vol. 37, no. 4, pp. 48-56.

Tzoannos J., Samuels J.M., 1972, "Mergers and takeovers: the financial characteristics of companies involved", *Journal of Business Finance*, Vol. 4, no. 3, pp. 5-16.

Vander Vennet, R. 1994a, "Economies of scale and scope in EC credit institutions", Cahiers Ecnomiques de Bruxelles, 1994/4, no. 144, pp. 507-548.

Vander Vennet, R. 1994b, "Concentration, efficiency, and entry barriers as determinants of EC bank profitability", *Journal of International Financial Markets, Institutions and Money*, Vol. 4, no 3-4, pp. 21-46.

Vander Vennet R. 1996, "The effect of mergers and acquisitions on the efficiency and profitability of EC credit institutions", *Journal of Banking and Finance*, Vol. 20, no.9, pp. 1531-1558.

Vander Vennet, R. 1998, "Cost and profit dynamics in financial conglomerates and universal banks in Europe", *Paper presented at the Societe Universitaire Europeenee de Recherchers Financiers/CFS colloquium*, Frankfurt, 15-17 October.

Vander Vennet, R. 2002, "Cost and profit efficiency of financial conglomerates and universal banks in Europe", *Journal of Money, Credit and Banking*, Vol. 34, no. 1, pp. 254-282.

Vapnik, V.N. 1995, *The nature of statistical learning theory*, Springer-Verlag, New York.

Vapnik, V.N. 1998, *Statistical learning theory*, Wiley, New York.

Walter, R.M. 1994, "The Usefulness of Current Cost Information for Identifying Takeover Targets and Earning Above-Average Stock Returns", *Journal of Accounting, Auditing and Finance*, Vol. 9, pp. 349-377.

Wansley, W., Lane, W. 1983, "A Financial Profile of Merged Firms", *Review of Business & Economics Research*, pp. 87-98.

Weiss, S.M., Kulikowski, C.A. 1991, *Computer systems that learn: Classification and prediction methods from statistics, neural nets, machine learning, and Expert Systems*, Morgan Kaufmann Publishers Inc., San Francisco, California.

Went, P. 2003, "A quantitative analysis of qualitative arguments in a bank mergers", *International Review of Financial Analysis*, vol. 12, no. 4, pp. 379-403.

West, D. 2000, "Neural network credit scoring models", *Computers and Operations Research*, vol. 27, no. 11-12, pp. 1131-1152.

Weston, J. F., Chung, K.S., Hoag, S. E. 1990, *Mergers, Restructuring, And Corporate Control*, New Jersey, Prentice-Hall

Wheelock, D.C., Wilson, P.W. 2000, "Why do banks disappear? The determinants of U.S. bank failures and acquisitions", The *Review of Economics and Statistics*, vol. 82, no. 1, pp. 127-138.

Wheelock, D.C, Wilson, P.W. 2004, "Consolidation in US banking: Which banks engage in mergers?", *Review of Financial Economics*, vol. 13, no. 1-2, pp. 7-39.

Wilson, N., Summers, B., Hope, R. 1999, "Predicting Corporate Failure and Payment Behaviour: Addressing Some Pertinent Issues for Practitioners", Working Paper, Credit Management Research Centre, Leeds University Business School, University of Leeds, September.

Winton, A. 1999, "Don't Put All Your Eggs in One Basket? Diversification and Specialization in Lending", Mimeo, pp. 1-39.

Wolpert, D.H. 1992, "Stacked Generalization", *Neural Networks*, Vol. 5, pp. 241-259.

Wood, D., Piesse, J. 1987, "The information Value of MDA Based Financial Indicators", *Journal of Business Finance and Accounting*, vol. 14, 27-38.

Xu, L., Kryzak, A., Suen, C.Y. 1992, "Methods of combining multiple classifiers and their applications to handwriting recognition", *IEEE Trans. System Man. Cybernet*, vol. 23, no. 3, pp. 418-435.

Zanakis, S.H., Walter, G. 1994, "Discriminant Characteristics of U.S. Banks Acquired with or without Federal Assistance", *European Journal of Operational Research*, vol. 77, no. 3, pp. 440- 465

Zanakis, SH., Zopounidis, C. 1997, "Prediction of Greek company takeovers via multivariate analysis of financial ratios", *Journal of the Operational Research Society*, vol. 48, pp. 678-687.

Zhang, H. 1995, "Wealth effects of U.S. bank takeovers", *Applied Financial Economics*, vol. 55, no. 5, pp. 329-336.

Zitouni, I., Kuo, H-K J., Lee, Ch-H. 2003, "Boosting and combination of classifiers for natural language call routing systems", *Speech Communication*, vol. 41, pp. 647-661.

Zmijewski, M.E. 1984, "Methodological Issues Related to the Estimation of Financial Distress Prediction Models", *Journal of Accounting Research*, Vol. 22 (Supplement), pp. 59-86

Zollo, M., Leshchinkskii, D. 2000, "Can Firms Lear to Acquired? Do Markets Notice?" Working Paper, Financial Institutions Center, The Wharton School, Philadelphia, PA.

Zopounidis, C., Doumpos, M. 1999a, "Business failure prediction using the UTADIS multicriteria analysis method", *Journal of Operational Research Society*, vol. 50, pp. 1138-1148.

Zopounidis, C., Doumpos, M. 1999b, "A multicriteria decision aid methodology for sorting decision problems: The case of financial distress", *Computational Economics*, vol. 14, pp. 197-218.

Zopounidis, C., Doumpos, M. 2000, "Building additive utilities for multi-group hierarchical discrimination: the M.H.D.I.S method", *Optimization Methods and Software*, vol. 14, no. 3, pp. 219-240.

Zopounidis, C. Doumpos, M. 2002, "Multi-group discrimination using multi-criteria analysis: Illustrations from the field of finance", *European Journal of Operational Research*, vol. 139, no. 2, pp. 371-389.

Index

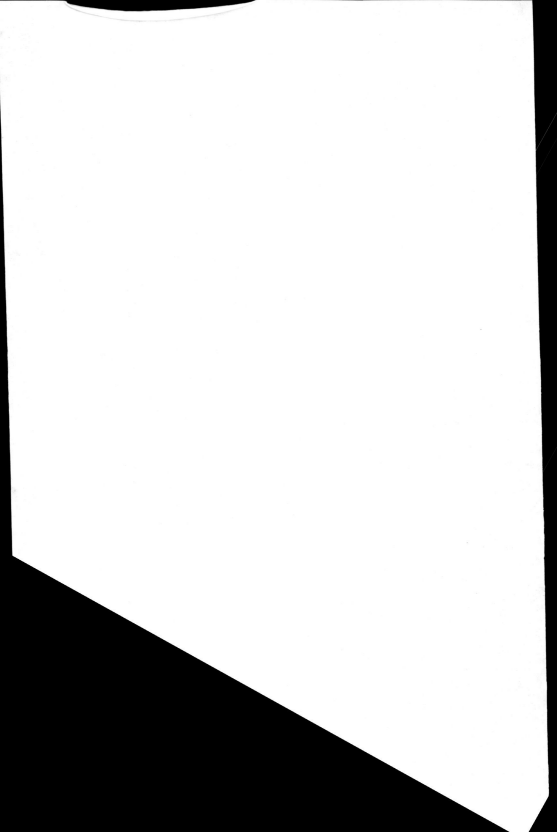